D1085009

Latin American Monographs

Second Series

The Moving Frontier

II

Center for Latin American Studies
University of Florida

The Moving Frontier

Social and Economic Change in a Southern Brazilian Community

Maxine L. Margolis

University of Florida Press
Gainesville - 1973

Library of Congress Cataloging in Publication Data

Margolis, Maxine L. 1942–
The moving frontier.

(Latin American monographs, 2d ser., no. 11)
Bibliography: p.
1. Brazil—Economic conditions—Case studies.
2. Brazil—Social conditions—Case studies.
3. Agriculture—Economic aspects—Brazil—Case studies.
I. Title. II. Series: Florida. University,
Gainesville. Center for Latin American Studies. Latin
American monographs, 2d ser., no. 11
HC187.M2856 330.9′81 73–7730
ISBN 0–8130–0380–6

A University of Florida Press Publication

SPONSORED BY THE
CENTER FOR LATIN AMERICAN STUDIES

PRINTED BY THE STORTER PRINTING COMPANY
GAINESVILLE, FLORIDA

For

Jerry

Acknowledgments

THE RESEARCH for this study was carried out in Paraná, Brazil, on three separate occasions. From June through August 1966, a survey of the coffee-growing region was undertaken with the sponsorship of a Ford Foundation Fellowship for Study of the Brazilian Frontier. The grant was awarded to Professor Charles Wagley who graciously made a portion of the funds available to me for a summer field trip. The bulk of the research was carried out from August 1967 to July 1968 when I resided in the northern Paraná community of Ouro Verde,* the focus of this study. This research was supported by a Fulbright-Hays Graduate Research Fellowship (GHF 7–8). A brief restudy of the community in July–August 1971 was made possible through grants from the Social Science Institute of the University of Florida, the National Science Foundation (GS–28813), and the Wenner-Gren Foundation for Anthropological Research.

Without the cooperative aid of the Companhia Melhoramentos Norte do Paraná, this study would have been made far more difficult, if not impossible. During my first field trip to Paraná, the

*Ouro Verde ("Green Gold") is a pseudonym for an actual community. The names of all persons also have been changed for the purposes of this study.

officials of the company allowed me to reside on one of their plantations while I was doing a survey of the region. In addition, the company's records regarding land sales and deeds were made available to me and maps of Ouro Verde were supplied freely. I would particularly like to thank Dr. Anibal Bianchini da Rocha, an agronomist employed by the company, for sharing with me his immense knowledge of local agriculture.

Thanks also go to the many people in Ouro Verde and the neighboring counties who helped me in my research and made my stay in Brazil a most pleasant one. I owe a special debt of gratitude to Laurenço Bernardes dos Santos, my principal informant and guide in Ouro Verde, who was an invaluable source of information on many aspects of community life. His intimate knowledge of Ouro Verde and its people smoothed the way for my research and helped me avoid many of the pitfalls of field work.

To my very good friends Margot and Frederico Goldschmidt, Lulli and Ricardo Vitelleschi, and Giovanni Bonardelli, I offer my deeply felt thanks for their patient understanding and assistance during my stay in Ouro Verde.

Professor Florestan Feranades of the Faculdade de Filosofia at the Universidade de São Paulo visited me in the field during my first trip to Paraná and made many valuable suggestions regarding my research. His kind hospitality in São Paulo is also very much appreciated.

Thanks are due to Ms. Barbara Coaxum who typed the final draft of this manuscript, and to Mr. Harold Tupper for drawing the maps and figures. I am most grateful to my husband, Dr. Jerald T. Milanich, for painstakingly editing my dissertation upon which this monograph is based, for compiling the index, and for supplying the photographs.

Finally, I would like to thank the members of my doctoral committee at Columbia. Professor Allen Johnson's helpful suggestions concerning this manuscript were most welcome. I owe appreciation to Professor Marvin Harris whose own work in anthropology has had a profound influence on my theoretical approach in this research, as well as on my anthropological outlook in general. To Professor Charles Wagley, the chairman of my doctoral committee, I wish to express deep thanks. His generous assistance throughout my graduate career was invaluable. His immense knowledge of and love for Brazil inspired my interest in that country, the result of which is this monograph.

Preface

I SPENT a total of seventeen months in northern Paraná. During the summer of 1966, I did a survey of the coffee-growing region extending north of Maringá to the Paranapanema River on the border with São Paulo, and west to Cianorte, a county founded in 1952 near the edge of the frontier. My home base during this stay was Fazenda Pitanga, a company-owned plantation in the county of Uniflor just south of Ouro Verde. The aim of the survey was to locate a representative community to serve as a focal point for further study of the socioeconomic changes occurring throughout most of the region. Since the study was to concentrate on the reasons for and effects of the gradual changeover from coffee to cattle through intensive research on the local level, I sought a community that typified these changes.

Ouro Verde, located about fifty kilometers northwest of Maringá, was well suited to the purpose of this study. Its brief history (it was founded in 1952) encompassed the forest-coffee-cattle sequence; yet it was not close enough to a complete substitution of cattle for coffee that one could not study the circumstances under which the changeover was taking place. Ouro Verde seemed about midway along a continuum whose extremes were communities still devoting most of their land to coffee cultivation and those where coffee had almost entirely been replaced by cattle. In addition, the county of Ouro Verde, compared with others in the region, was of average size in area and population. Local landholdings included the entire regional range, from small farms of less than 10 acres to large plantations of more than 600 acres. Work systems ran the gamut from sharecropping, and renting, to piece work, all of which are found in neighboring counties. Finally, the makeup of Ouro Verde's population reflected that of northern Paraná. Its important contingent of native Brazilians, mostly from the Northeast, and a sizeable number of second-generation Brazilians, of Italian, Portuguese, Spanish, and Japanese extraction, reflected the ethnic composition of other counties in the area.

Ouro Verde, then, was chosen as the focal point for further research during my survey of northern Paraná. When I returned to Brazil in August 1967, I settled in Ouro Verde, where I remained, except for brief vacation trips outside the state, until July 1968. Throughout my field work I worked closely with a paid informant and guide who knew the county intimately since he had conducted local censuses for the regional office of the Instituto Brasileiro de Geografia e Estatística (Brazilian Institute of Geography and Statistics), or IBGE. He accompanied me on most visits to the rural area of the county, introducing me as a North American student who was "writing a book" on life in the community. Excepting one or two occasions, I was well received by local residents who willingly agreed to fill out questionnaires and answer my inquiries. Although rumors periodically circulated that I was a "spy" or a "tax collector," I do not think that they were ever taken very seriously, and they certainly did not affect my field work.

Four methods were used to secure information pertaining to the county. First, I had access to written records. Those of the Companhia Melhoramentos Norte do Paraná (Northern Paraná Land Improvement Company), or CMNP, provided data on original land sales and ownership of the holdings in the county, and the prices and contract stipulations involved. In addition, maps supplied by the company were useful in locating farms and plantations during field work, and in orienting myself to the county's layout. Records kept by the IBGE in the neighboring county of Paranacity were used for population figures, land usage, and size of agricultural yields. However, I viewed the IBGE data with scepticism since sometimes their accuracy was questionable and had to be cross-checked with local informants. Finally, the forms submitted by all of Ouro Verde's landowners to the Instituto Brasileiro de Reforma Agrária (Brazilian Land Reform Institute,) or IBRA, were examined during a ten-day trip to Curitiba, the state capital. These were helpful in checking figures supplied by local cultivators concerning the sizes of their holdings, their annual yields, and the types of work systems which they employed. Here again, however, caution was used, since part of the IBRA data clearly were inaccurate because a few landowners had purposely underestimated their production and net worth, fearing higher taxes if they filled out their forms accurately. But these inaccuracies were easily discovered by questioning local informants, and they were few enough in number not to affect seriously the quality of the data.

The formal tape-recorded interview was another method used to gather data on Ouro Verde. I used this rarely, however, and only to collect precise information such as exact crop yields and other figures which would have been difficult to record by simple note-taking.

The unstructured interview was used frequently in field work, usually in conjunction with the completing of questionnaires. That is, informal conversations were held with many of those who agreed to fill out the questionnaires. Information was collected from perhaps one hundred people in this way. The technique was useful in gathering data on local attitudes toward the economic changes taking place, as well as their effects on individual families. Residents' perceptions of class differentials and attitudes toward them were derived also from informal interviews.

Throughout field work, I periodically engaged in what usually is termed "participant observation." I attended church functions, dances, and festivals, and often visited workers at various agricultural tasks. I was able to gather data on class interactions, work patterns, and agricultural techniques by this method.

Perhaps the most important single source of detailed information was acquired by administering a five-page questionnaire to a selected group of families (a copy of the questionnaire appears in the appendix). A total of 125 families, 57 from town and 68 from the rural area, were included in the sample which represents slightly less than 10 per cent of the county's population. The technique used was that of stratified sampling (see Pelto 1970:165). Ouro Verde's population was divided into categories based on ethnic background, occupation, and land ownership. Samples were then taken from all the occupational and ethnic subgroups approximately in accordance with their percentages in the overall population. For example, 50 per cent of all landowners in the county have Italian surnames; half of the landowners chosen to fill out questionnaires were of Italian extraction. This sampling technique was used so that representatives from all ethnic and occupational groups would be included, an unlikely event had a purely random sample been employed.

In general, the questionnaires were submitted to the head of the household, and if he (or she) were not at home I returned another day. In only two or three cases were they filled out by older adolescent sons or daughters. I went through the list of questions, noting the answers in writing, but was frequently sidetracked by discussions which came up during the question period. In all instances, I let these conversations run their course and collected much valuable data in the process.

A brief restudy of Ouro Verde was made in the summer of 1971. It was concerned with continued documentation of the social and economic changes observed during my initial residence in the community. The findings of this restudy appear in the postscript.

Contents

1. Brazilian Economic Cycles / 1
2. The Setting / 24
3. Changing Patterns of Agriculture / 42
4. The Role of the Town in an Agricultural Economy / 86
5. Rural Life / 124
6. Social Class and Social Mobility / 180
7. Coffee's Decline: Causes and Effects / 215
8. Postscript / 234
Appendixes / 251
Glossary / 259
Bibliography / 263
Index / 267

. . . the onlooker remains transfixed before the abominable devastation that in the short period of a half century destroyed forever a marvelous and majestic forest treasure without leaving behind in its place wealth, comfort, activity, flourishing industry, commercial expansion—all signs of the perpetual strength of a flowering civilization.

Stanley Stein
Vassouras: A Brazilian Coffee County

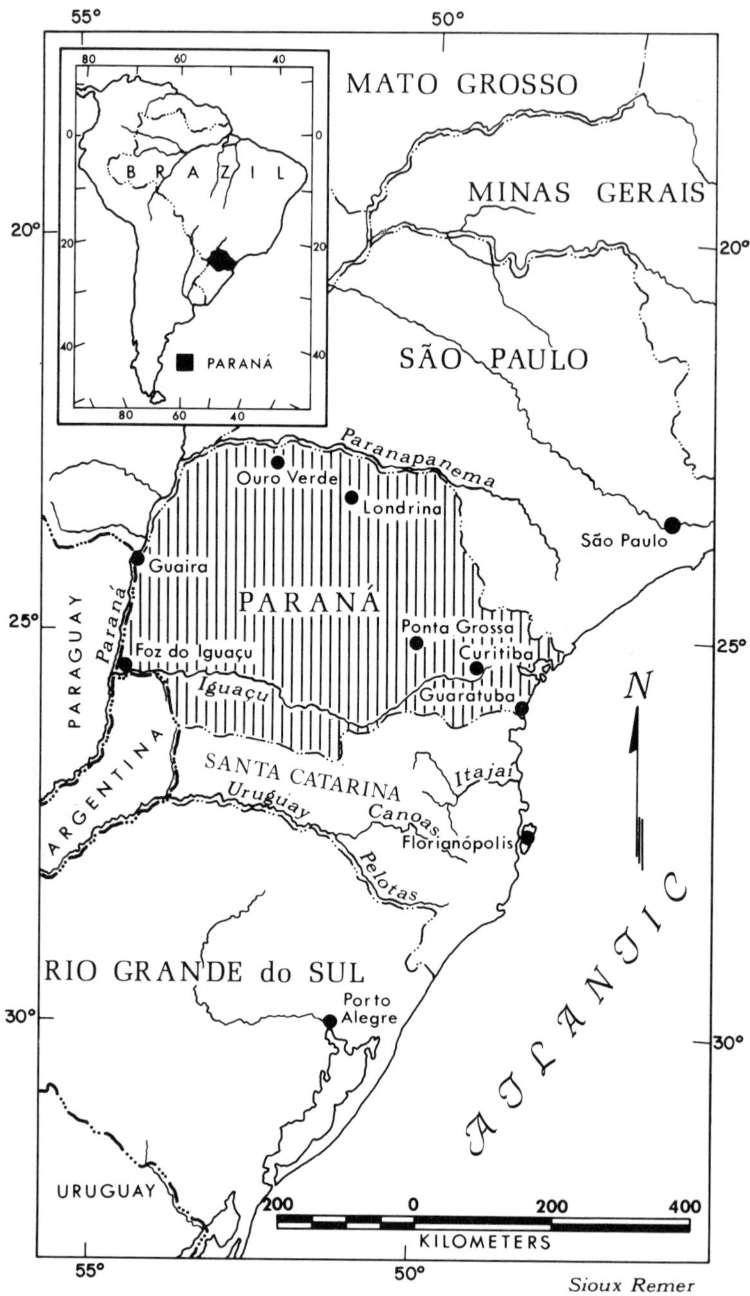

1. Paraná and Ouro Verde

I. Brazilian Economic Cycles

Ouro Verde, a coffee-growing community in northern Paraná, Brazil, is the focus of this study. Although the community was founded only twenty years ago, the changes which it is undergoing are typical of those occurring over much of northern Paraná. Until nine or ten years ago, nearly 100 per cent of Ouro Verde's land was planted in coffee. Today this percentage has been cut almost in half, and cotton and cattle have rapidly gained ascendancy.

Ouro Verde, because of its lack of historical depth and the rapidity with which it is changing from coffee to cattle, presents an excellent opportunity to study the cyclical nature of Brazilian monocrop systems. The fifty- or sixty-year forest-coffee-cattle sequence which occurred in the Paraíba Valley of Rio de Janeiro and the interior of São Paulo state in the late nineteenth and early twentieth centuries has, in effect, been compressed into less than two decades in Ouro Verde and over a wide area of northern Paraná. Effects of the coffee cycle on the community, and reasons for its occurrence, will be the subject of this monograph.

The "boom-bust" nature of Brazil's agricultural past is perhaps the most noticeable characteristic of its economic history, and a vast amount of literature deals with the cyclical nature of its cash crops. This pattern of development has repeated itself from the time the first Portuguese colonists established sugar mills on Brazil's northeast coast in the middle of the sixteenth century to the most recent thrust of coffee into the virgin forests of Paraná state. There are abundant descriptions of this phenomenon:

> Each cycle centered around a particular commodity in which—at the height of the cycle—Brazil occupied the leading position in world production and subsequently declined as the result of competition from other producing areas (Carlson 1951:226).

> The history of the Brazilian economy is a sensational record with amazing fluctuations. It is the history of the appearance and disappearance of entire industries. Its leit-motif is the perpetual change of the "kings." Sugar, cacao, gold, tobacco, cotton, rubber, coffee . . . each of these products was at one time the axis of the national (or state) economy, lending to Brazil a temporary world supremacy (Normano 1935:18–19).

Each agricultural or commodity cycle was limited to a clearly defined geographical region where it passed through a series of stages. The first stage was a rapid expansion of the product coinciding with the period in which Brazil held a monopoly of it. A large migration of population to the areas where natural conditions were favorable to the commodity resulted in a rapid rise in its production. A concomitant development was the partial depopulation of older regions as their inhabitants left to take advantage of the opportunities afforded by the current "boom" product. At the beginning of the second stage, other world areas began to produce the commodity, and Brazil's share of the market remained the same or declined. Then, as a result of high production costs, soil depletion, and inefficient technology, Brazil was no longer able to compete successfully in the world market.

The third stage took place in those regions of Brazil where the product was produced or extracted. Competition from other world areas resulted in greatly reduced profits for the producers of the boom commodity, and they began to view it with disillusionment and pessimism. There would be an attempt to find other crops to partially replace the declining product. This was usually unsuccessful, since the huge profits of the boom product were difficult to match, and the gradual depopulation of the region began. This was the fourth stage of the cycle which started anew as another commodity in a different area took hold and a similar sequence got underway.

These cycles had one serious consequence: the destruction of natural resources which they left in their wake. The boom crop was cultivated with a view to quick profits, and little attention was paid to soil conservation. As the production of the product spread, virgin forests were cut down, and the land was cleared by burning off the underbrush. Soil erosion invariably followed, and huge tracts of land were sapped of their original fertility.

There have been a total of six major commodity cycles in Brazil. The first crop to gain prominence was sugar, Brazil's major export during the seventeenth century. Until 1655, Brazil was the largest producer of sugar in the world, but lower costs and mass production of this crop by the Dutch in the West Indies cut severely into Brazil's best markets (Edel 1969:42). Sugar cultivation continued in Bahia and Pernambuco, the principal regions of the cycle, but on a greatly reduced scale.

The second cycle, the "gold rush" in Minas Gerais, lasted from about 1700 to 1750, and drew off much of the population from the older sugar-producing regions. It is estimated that as many as 500,000 people had migrated to the mining area by 1745 (Carlson 1951:227). Many planters, alarmed at their decreased profits from sugar, abandoned their plantations and took their slaves to the mining regions farther south in hopes of making a "strike." An offshoot of this cycle was the diamond rush in Minas Gerais and Goiás which lasted from 1730 to 1800, a period in which Brazil was the world's largest supplier of these stones.

The third cycle occurred in the northeastern states of Bahia, Pernambuco, Maranhão, and Ceará. From 1750 to 1813, Brazil was Europe's chief supplier of cotton, but was then passed by the United States. Aside from a brief revival of the boom during the American Civil War, Brazilian cotton declined in importance as an export commodity. Today it is produced to meet the needs of the country's growing textile industry.[1]

The rubber boom in the Amazon region covered a briefer span of time, from about 1870 to 1910. During this period thousands of workers from the drought-stricken Northeast migrated to the area. This cycle ended with the entrance of East Indian rubber into the

1. In recent years Brazil has been exporting quantities of cotton to Europe.

world market in 1909, but prior to this time Brazil had held a total monopoly of this product. In 1909, Brazil produced 88 per cent of the world's latex, but by 1917 this had fallen to about 22 per cent (Carlson 1951:228). Brazil was unable to compete with East Indian production because of the sparse settlement of the Amazon region and the resulting difficulty of securing an adequate labor supply. In addition, locating and tapping trees was costly and time-consuming since they rarely averaged more than two trees per acre of land (Carlson 1951:229).

The fifth cycle, cacao cultivation in southern Bahia, is, in effect, still in progress, although the margin of profits has been greatly reduced by soil erosion and the aging of the trees. Cacao became a successful commercial crop when a high-yield variety from Ceylon was introduced into the region in 1907 (Wagley 1963:40). The highly seasonal nature of its labor requirements has led to an unstable population in the areas where it is grown, and one of the major problems in its cultivation is difficulty in securing an adequate work force for harvests. Like cotton and rubber, cacao is more important to the regional economy than to the Brazilian economy.

The final cycle has had the greatest and most long-lasting effect on Brazilian political and economic history, and it is the one dealt with in this study. The coffee cycle began in the Paraíba Valley in the state of Rio de Janeiro in the 1830s, and is still in progress today as coffee moves farther and farther into the westernmost regions of northern Paraná, finally reaching the hinterlands of Paraguay.

A variety of explanations has been offered for the agricultural cycles in Brazil. Anthony Leeds suggests that Brazilian agricultural and commodity cycles are caused by "the class relations of production and . . . the class value systems." He argues that the two-class system, in which a handful of people own the strategic resources and control a vast number of improverished workers, has led the owners to resist change, particularly any arising from technological innovation. He believes that the value system of the resource controllers, which he describes as "immediatist, speculative, and urban-oriented," has led to a "strike-it-rich" mentality in which "long term constructive use of resources is not valued." The value system of the lower class also reinforces the status quo; this group puts its trust in "God, Providence, and Lady Fortune" (Leeds 1957:26–28).

Another idealist explanation for certain aspects of Brazilian economic history is offered by Vianna Moog (1964). He rejects ecological and economic factors, for the most part, in attempting to explain differences in historical developments in Brazil and the United States, preferring to call up the spectres of Catholicism, the "Moorish Tradition," and the "Protestant Ethic." The works of Leeds and Vianna Moog represent a widespread reliance on mentalistic explanations of Brazilian economic cycles, and one purpose of this study is to demonstrate the inadequacy of this approach.

Additional interpretations of the cyclical nature of Brazilian agricultural history have been offered by a number of historians and economists. Carlson believes that technological stagnation and the absence of high-cost mechanization in Brazilian agriculture are related to her long-term dependence on fluctuating commodity prices on the world market. He claims that, without a fairly stable market, "there is little incentive to adopt new techniques" (1951: 243). Spiegel, on the other hand, blames the cycles on the extensive use of labor in Brazil: "The low cost of labor in Brazil encourages its wasteful use relative to what it should accomplish under other conditions, and impedes the introduction of improved methods of production. In the past, inertia in the face of advanced techniques elsewhere has been the principal factor accounting for the loss of important markets" (1949:2). Another explanation is based on the continued existence of vast tracts of virgin land on the internal Brazilian frontier: "The economic frontier is still moving as the territorial reserves of [political] Brazil are far from being exhausted. The ease with which extensive expansion has been carried out has handicapped the intensive one . . . and [has led] to a perpetual change of the leading products" (Normano 1935:viii).

While these explanations, particularly the one which emphasizes the role of the frontier, are useful in explaining the problem at hand, none delves deeply into the ecologic and economic conditions under which these cycles operated. With one notable exception (Stein 1957), there have been no attempts to investigate the functioning of this phenomenon on the community level. Although most of the writers cited deal with all of the principal agricultural cycles in Brazilian history, I will examine closely only the latest phase of the most recent cycle in an attempt to demonstrate that the "boom" phenomenon, if studied on the local level, can be explained in an alternative manner. It will be argued that the rise and decline of coffee cultivation in northern Paraná, based on data from an intensive study of a representative community, is the result of clearly identifiable ecologic and economic conditions. It is not based upon some particular set of values attached to the world view of the Brazilian upper and lower classes, as Leeds believes. In fact, the entire area of northern Paraná is notable for the absence of a clearly defined two-class social structure so common in other regions devoted to monocrop cultivation. Small-scale farmers predominate, and even among landless workers a plethora of occupational groups (renters, sharecroppers, day laborers) may be identified. Thus, the cyclical nature of the crop cannot be simplistically linked to a nationwide, two-class social structure under which it is cultivated.

Carlson's suggestion that Brazilian agricultural cycles are due largely to the caprices of the world market is also not fully justified. The fluctuation of commodity prices on the world market is an important factor in the rise and fall of many of the cash crops mentioned but in the case of coffee, at least for the past few decades, world prices have had a very indirect influence on its development. The federal government through the Brazilian Coffee Institute (Instituto Brasileiro de Café, or IBC), has instituted price supports which guarantee the farmer at least the same amount of money he received per sack of coffee the year before.[2] It also agreed to buy all surplus coffee[3] which is stored in warehouses and sold on the world market when coffee is in short supply. Thus, the individual farmer is spared from having to deal directly with the uncertainties of the world coffee market. This is not to imply, however, that the prices paid by the government have no influence on the farmer's decision to plant additional coffee, replace it with other crops, or abandon the land entirely. Prices vary from year to year, and the reduction in the coffee producers' profit margin over the last decade has had important consequences for that crop.

The reasons for the rapid spread of coffee-growing in northern Paraná will be investigated. While it is true that much poor land, not ideally suited to coffee, has been settled for the purpose of planting this crop, it will be shown that the venture, generally, has proven to be a very profitable one. No other crop could compete with coffee as a sound business enterprise. Coffee production in Brazil has long been based on extensive cultivation with a view to maximum production, and little attention was paid to unit costs. According to Schurz, this system has worked out very profitably for

2. Sugar is the only other crop that has government price supports.

3. Surplus here refers to any coffee which exceeds the annual quota alloted to Brazil in the World Coffee Agreement.

the planter: "The good years have paid off so well on this rule that the bad ones are likely to be written off to the caprices of nature or the perversities of fate" (1961:256).

The so-called anti-technologism of the Brazilian planter can be explained better in terms of the ever present frontier than as a cultural quirk. Brazil still has large areas of unsettled and semisettled frontier land in western Paraná, Mato Grosso, and Goiás. Recently, lands just across the border in Paraguay have been opened for coffee cultivation by Brazilian entrepreneurs who are now being called "the imperialists of South America" (Galeano 1968:20). The farmers know that when their land is sapped of fertility, they can buy new land inexpensively at the edge of the frontier, clear it, and plant coffee, a far less costly process than abundant use of fertilizer, pruning operations, and other methods for improving weak soil and lowered yields. In addition, few farmers have the resources to invest in modern farming techniques. Thus, one need not resort to the "wandering instinct" explanation (Morse 1967) to understand the continued attractiveness of the frontier for the Brazilian planter.

Another solution to the problem of infertile land and decreased yields is to turn the land into pasture. This is the trend in areas of sandier soil northwest of Maringá in northern Paraná to the São Paulo border. The most common pattern is for the farmer to cut down his weakened trees and plant pasture as a replacement. He purchases cattle gradually and continues to eradicate the less productive trees until his land is almost completely in pasture, with only a few thousand of the most viable trees left in production.

This trend will be examined closely. That far larger tracts of land are needed for cattle ranching than for coffee cultivation is an important factor in determining who makes this changeover. Clearly, only the owners of large landholdings or those who can afford to purchase additional land can eradicate all of their coffee and live off the proceeds of ranching. The man who farms on a small scale must either sell out and buy virgin land on the frontier, or try to effect a transitional accommodation by cutting his least productive trees, planting another cash crop in their place (usually cotton or peanuts), and turning his least fertile land to pasture.

The growing importance of cattle ranching in Ouro Verde has had far-reaching effects on its social structure, and on individual chances for upward mobility. The numerically important group of owners of small and medium-sized farms is being depleted as they sell their local holdings and move to the frontier. This group, which perhaps may be termed a rural middle class, was a buffer in the community between the few owners of large amounts of land and the mass of landless sharecroppers, renters, and day laborers. Sharecropping has declined as more and more coffee trees are cut down and the land turned to pasture. This has changed the pattern of upward mobility of many sharecropping families, as measured by ability to purchase small farms. In the recent past, the main avenue of upward mobility was sharecropping highly productive coffee trees. It was not uncommon for a man to be able to purchase a small parcel of frontier land with money from the sale of his share of two or three coffee harvests. Although today, as in the past, success in sharecropping depends largely on the quality of the land which is tilled, the fact that fewer sharecropping positions are available has greatly decreased any family's chances of securing one.

Work systems in Ouro Verde have also been influenced by the changeover. A few years ago large groups of men were hired for such labor-intensive tasks as clearing the forest, planting coffee trees, and harvesting the crop. Today, with fewer trees in production and considerably smaller yields, landowners employ only day laborers to harvest the crop, and the work gang has all but disappeared. In addition, the *colono* system,[4] common in other coffee regions of Brazil, is extinct in northern Paraná, especially in those areas of sandy soil where cattle raising has made the greatest inroads.

As noted, sharecropping is on the decline, but land rentals have become more common in the last few years in those parts of the county where coffee has been replaced by cotton and other annual crops. Coffee, a perennial, is never cultivated on rented land, since rental contracts are rarely for more than one year, and coffee takes four years to produce its first harvest.

The changing agricultural base has resulted in a sizable decrease in the *município*'s (county) population, from 12,500 to 10,500 in the last five years. In those areas of the município where cattle are of prime importance, human population has been reduced by as much as 70 per cent. A common local saying is "Where cattle enter, man exits" (*Onde o boi entra, o homem sai*). Certainly the principal factor in population decline is the greatly reduced labor

4. See chap. 5 for a discussion of the colono system. There is a glossary of Portuguese terms at the back of the book.

requirements of cattle ranching compared to coffee cultivation, resulting in unemployment and a fairly sizable emigration from the county both to frontier regions and to the cities of Curitiba and São Paulo. The rate of emigration, especially among sharecroppers, day laborers, and owners of small farms, rose notably after the severe frosts of 1955 and 1963 had hastened the decline of coffee in the region.

Population movement and decline, directly linked to the shift from coffee to cattle, has caused the small businesses of the town and the rural general stores to suffer a noticeable reduction in volume of sales, and many shopkeepers have been forced to sell out and move elsewhere. One of the three local coffee-processing plants has closed and the only townsmen who appear to prosper are those who buy and sell other cash crops, particularly cotton.

A final effect of the changeover is less easily described and measured than the others. It is what the town residents describe as a lessening of local *movimento*, a particularly Brazilian word meaning liveliness, activity, and animation. With the declining population and the falling off of local business activity, there is an indefinable sense of loss and defeat in the town. Many residents remember "the good old days" (of about ten years ago) when the Saturday market was filled to capacity with dozens of wagons and hundreds of rural inhabitants who had come to town to make their weekly purchases. Others say that in the past there was a far larger variety of goods in the local shops, but that today the shelves are stocked with only basic necessities, since now no one can afford such luxuries as canned goods and fine fabrics. There is a widespread feeling that the county reached its peak of prosperity a decade ago, and that opportunities for success in business and agriculture have all but disappeared. Many express the wish to leave the region entirely. A similar lack of "esprit" is found in the rural areas of the county, where dozens of day laborers fondly recall the time when they could return to the Northeast[5] with a tidy sum of money earned in the harvest, adding that now they earn barely enough to keep themselves alive.

In addition to the consequences of the shift from coffee to cattle, the reasons for this phenomenon also will be investigated. The factors involved in the decline of coffee production in Ouro Verde and throughout Paraná may be divided into two related categories,

5. The Northeast refers to the Brazilian states of Bahia, Pernambuco, Alagoas, Sergipe, Paraíba, Rio Grande do Norte, Piauí, and eastern Maranhão.

economic and ecologic. Although the prices paid for coffee by the government are still higher than those received for any other crop, the rising costs of cultivation have cut seriously into net profits. Weakened soils have necessitated the use of fertilizers for the first time; the cost of these is often prohibitive, and can only be financed through bank loans. Rising labor costs and the purchase of insecticides to combat a coffee pest, *broca* (*Hypothenemus hampei* Ferrari), which recently appeared in the region, have also cut into profits. Severe frosts in 1955 and 1963 temporarily cut yields as much as 90 per cent, and lesser frosts, particularly in the low-lying areas of the county, have affected the size of the harvest almost annually. In addition to higher costs and lower yields, the price currently paid for coffee by the government is relatively lower than it was ten years ago.

The overproduction of coffee in Brazil led the government to institute an eradication program in which the grower was paid a predetermined price for every tree he cut down. Although the program was aimed at eliminating nonprofitable, poorly producing trees, many farmers in financial difficulty took advantage of the opportunity for immediate cash and cut down some of their productive trees. The eradication program is not the *cause* of the decline of coffee in the region, but it has given impetus to a process that was underway before the program was instituted.

A final factor in the decline of coffee in the area, already mentioned, is the continued availability of cheap virgin frontier land. The frontier never has ceased to have a strong attraction for the people of Ouro Verde and northern Paraná. While part of this drawing power appears to lie in the mystique of frontier life and the belief that out there fortunes are to be made, it is true that only in that area are real opportunities for upward mobility to be found.

The effect of the ever present frontier on the decline of coffee in Ouro Verde and as an outlet for the upwardly mobile in the community will form the final section of this study. It is an important factor in the current socioeconomic changes in Ouro Verde and in its past history, for the community itself was a frontier region only fifteen years ago. The availability of inexpensive frontier lands has had a dual effect on the local social structure. It has provided an outlet for successful sharecroppers in Ouro Verde who wish to purchase their own farms but cannot afford the high prices asked for land in the community itself, and it has helped to rigidify class lines in Ouro Verde by drawing off its prosperous sharecroppers and owners of small farms, leaving behind the wealthier landholders and impoverished day laborers in a more clearly defined two-class system.

The frontier has created a pattern of geographical social mobility that has recurred throughout northern Paraná. As a frontier community is settled, a significant portion of its land is purchased by former sharecroppers and renters who have earned money in older, more easterly areas of the state. Their small capital does not permit them to buy land in these former frontier regions, for by the time they have sufficient savings to invest in farms land values have skyrocketed, and they can afford to buy only the inexpensive lands of the frontier. As the frontier moves farther westward, leaving settled communities in its wake, former sharecroppers move along with it, buying small farms at its outer fringes. Upward mobility (as measured by the acquisition of land) does not occur in the same community where the sharecroppers worked to earn the purchase price of land. Invariably, the transition from sharecropper to farmer takes place in two geographically distinct communities.

Although the frontier has served as an outlet for some of the upwardly mobile in Ouro Verde, I will question the frequent claim that the frontier provides unlimited opportunities for even the poorest stratum of society. The data demonstrate that two factors, time of arrival in the community and the amount of capital in hand on arrival, are important determinants of upward mobility. Thus, I seriously question Turner's famous thesis (Turner 1920), that frontier areas afford the lower class opportunities not available elsewhere.

It is apparent that these patterns of upward mobility have been strongly influenced by the decline of coffee in the region, since the process described, with few exceptions, was based on sharecropping this highly lucrative crop. The decreased opportunities for upward social mobility, as well as the rigidifying of class lines in Ouro Verde, are the result of complex relationships among the decline of coffee, the growing importance of cattle, and the continued availability of cheap frontier lands.

The Coffee Frontier in Rio de Janerio and São Paulo

Before a presentation of the history of coffee cultivation in northern Paraná, it would be useful to review briefly the history of the coffee frontier in Brazil and its influence on political and economic life. Coffee was introduced into Brazil around 1723 from French Guiana, and at first was grown in patches along the coast from the port of Santos to the Amazon. Coffee as a commercial crop resulted solely from its increasing popularity in the United States and Europe in the early 1800s. At about this time, coffee cultivation spread from the hillsides around Rio de Janeiro, where it had been grown as a decorative exotic plant, to the Paraíba Valley just north of the city. Its cultivation became heavily concentrated in this region for it had the "virgin soil and well-drained land that are essential to coffee's profitable cultivation" (Stein 1951:64). The effects of this new crop were momentous. Economic power shifted from Bahia and Pernambuco to the south, thus creating a new aristocracy based on plantations and slaves. Coffee rapidly became Brazil's most important export, increasing from 18 per cent of total exports in the 1820s to 44 per cent in the 1830s (Morse 1958: 111).

Settlement of the coffee-growing region was very rapid, with a large portion of its population coming from the mining regions of Minas Gerais. Before the real boom in coffee cultivation, the area had been devoted to small-scale cultivation carried on by a few slaves. It was during this period that "coffee was slowly, hesitatingly adapted to the highlands, when *fazendeiros* [planters or owners of much land] learned the agricultural know-how they were to follow for the rest of the century" (Stein 1957:23). With the expanding demand for coffee in the United States and Europe, there was a related demand for more virgin land and more slaves. This land hunger tended to absorb small and medium-sized holdings, and the few farmers who managed to survive the encroachments of the plantation earned their livelihood by supplying its masters and slaves with food crops.

The decade 1850–60 marked the "Golden Age of Coffee" in the Paraíba Valley, but even then the signs of decline could be seen by a careful observer. The trees were aging and gave indications of producing lower yields even at this early stage. Soil erosion and insect pests plagued many plantations, and heavy rains only sped up the process of decay. Slave labor became increasingly expensive after the slave trade was abolished. Stein (1951:86) notes that the slave labor force was rapidly aging and contained a large number of dependents, that is, young children and old people. Another warning signal was the sharply reduced supply of virgin land for new coffee plantings. After 1850, with the increasing scarcity of virgin land and the shortage of labor, planters concentrated on coffee at the expense of food crops. The plantations lost their self-sufficiency, and, where coffee progressed the most, the cost of foodstuffs was highest.

At the beginning of the economic squeeze, around 1860, some planters began to question their methods of cultivation and processing. Some invested in expensive modern milling machinery to clean and hull the beans, but very few adopted the use of fertilizer or irrigation. Many planters were illiterate and could not benefit from the few available agricultural manuals (Stein 1957:79). Profits were still high, so expensive technological innovations did not seem necessary.

Planters became increasingly indebted to banks whose credit they sought in order to buy additional slaves. They continued to cut down virgin forest to increase coffee production which was, in turn, the key to securing more credit. The high coffee yields of the 1860s and the continued availability of some virgin land held off the impending disaster for a decade. By 1870, however, most planters realized that their once lucrative plantations were doomed. They blamed their hard times on the scarcity of slave labor, the lack of modern coffee-processing equipment, and the increasing inavailability of cheap agricultural credit. Few attributed the decline to sapped soils and weakened trees (Stein 1957:214).

By the 1880s the crisis had worsened. A significant portion of the planters' capital was wiped out with the abolition of slavery in 1888—for the first time they were forced to pay wages to their labor force. Land prices continued to spiral, reaching a peak about 1890. Perhaps the most serious blow was the sharp fall in production: where 1,000 trees had once produced 300 *arrôbas* of coffee, they now only produced 50 arrôbas (Stein 1957:219). Many trees were abandoned or cut down for firewood, and although there were short-term attempts to substitute other cash crops for coffee, mainly cotton and sugar, these were unsuccessful because of poor land.

Another important factor in the decline of Paraíba Valley plantations was the growing competition from São Paulo. In 1883, São Paulo's coffee production for the first time, matched that of Rio de Janeiro's, and by 1886 had surpassed it. After the abolition of slavery, there was an exodus of freedmen from the Paraíba Valley, and planters had trouble securing an adequate labor supply. In addition, Rio de Janeiro's depleted soil and lower yields could not compare with the high productivity of the newly opened lands in central São Paulo, where coffee was produced more economically.

The final blow to the Paraíba Valley planters came in the late 1890s; as coffee prices reached a new low, they were unable to pay off longstanding debts and were forced into bankruptcy. Foreclosures followed and many planters and their families were forced to leave the region. Ranchers from Minas Gerais moved in and set up extensive cattle *fazendas* on the old coffee lands. Unemployment became a problem for those who remained in the area. As hundreds of workers and owners left the region and cattle raising became the dominant economic activity, the entire character of the Paraíba Valley changed. The legacy of coffee was little but destruction and depopulation.

The second phase of the coffee boom took place in the interior of São Paulo state. When the crop first reached the region it followed the existing roads, but once the qualities of soil and surface best fitted to coffee cultivation were identified, settlement tended to be limited to areas of rich *terra roxa*[6] soil. Coffee entered São Paulo in its "northern zone," the area between the cities of Rio de Janeiro and São Paulo, in the 1850s. The Campinas area was settled between 1860 and 1885, and for a long time this was the major coffee-producing region of the state. From there, coffee cropping spread northward through Mogi-Mirim to Uberaba in southern Minas Gerais and northwestward through Limeira to Araraquara. The rich terra roxa lands around modern-day Riberão Preto and São Carlos also were opened to coffee growing in this period.

Coffee production spread past the outer edges of the regions of rich soil and continued westward to regions of less fertile, sandier soils. James notes that these areas did not prove to be unprofitable for coffee cultivation, however, for they gave very high yields when they were first cleared. He also mentions the significant fact that "in spite of the sustained yields no tendency to intensify methods of production on terra roxa had yet appeared. The lure of virgin lands beyond was too strong" (1959:486).

As coffee cultivation continued to spread in São Paulo, some of its older settled regions began to suffer a fate similar to that of the Paraíba Valley. In the northern and central zones, as yields declined, many of the groves were abandoned or turned into pasture, and a partial depopulation of the area followed. The noted Brazilian

6. A dark red, porous soil particularly well suited to coffee cultivation.

economist Celso Furtado offers the following analysis of the situation: "Whenever land showed signs of exhaustion, there was some justification for the entrepreneur to abandon it and transfer his capital to virgin soils of higher yield. The destruction of soils—which from the social standpoint may seem inexcusable—is perfectly justifiable from the viewpoint of the private entrepreneur, whose goal is to obtain the maximum profit from his capital" (1965: 178–79).

By 1935, most of the former "coffee counties" of São Paulo were no longer devoted to monocrop cultivation. Milliet notes that many of the towns in these regions did not suffer economic decline and depopulation, despite coffee's reverses, for they had become important market centers which serviced the countryside and later the sites of small industries (1938:32). In the Mogiana and Paulista zones[7] the network of railroads and roads which followed the entrance of coffee cropping afforded necessary access for marketing other crops that replaced coffee. The facility of communication in this area compensated for the extra expenses of fertilizer necessitated by coffee's degenerative effects on local soils (Milliet 1938: 55–56).

The high prices paid for coffee before the 1929 crisis spurred the settlement of other areas of São Paulo: Araraquara, Alta Sorocabana, and Noreste. Many settlers in these regions had migrated from the older coffee counties of the state, seeking to recapture the fabulous profits that can be made when coffee is cultivated on virgin soil. By 1935, when coffee production reached its peak in these zones, they were nearly monocrop regions, with little cotton grown and only small areas for subsistence cultivation.

Today there is little coffee in these regions of São Paulo; cattle and cotton have become the principal products. A gradual reduction in coffee yields and great fluctuations in price prompted the changeover (Monbeig 1952:chap. 3). A large number of residents in Ouro Verde come from these zones, particularly Araraquara and Noreste.

Perhaps the most important result of the constant expansion of coffee westward across São Paulo into northern Paraná is the great overproduction that occurred. After 1899, production rose rapidly, and its decline in certain years was only because of frosts and intermittent government controls on new plantings. In 1899, Brazil

7. These zones are commonly called by the names of the railroads which service them.

TABLE 1. COFFEE PRODUCTION AND POPULATION IN THE STATE OF SÃO PAULO

	1866		1920		1935	
	Population	Coffee production (in arrôbas)	Population	Coffee production (in arrôbas)	Population	Coffee production (in arrôbas)
Araraquara	43,358	420,000	579,653	4,152,438	890,095	14,126,113
A. Sorocabana	54,004	151,000	326,994	1,676,228	576,812	6,524,410
Noreste			136,454	722,119	608,627	12,544,045

SOURCE: Milliet 1938:60–63.

produced 9 million bags of coffee,[8] in 1900, 11 million, and in 1901, 16 million. In 1906, 20 million bags were produced in a year when world consumption was only 12 million (James 1959:488). In that same year a series of "valorization programs" was instituted. Coffee was bought by state and federal governments and stored until the world market could absorb it without lowering its price. This was thought to be a solution for the overproduction of coffee, since its demand is fairly inelastic and it can be stored for a number of years without affecting the quality of the beans. The first four valorization programs (1906, 1917, 1921, and 1924) involved the storage of surplus coffee. These worked fairly well; the government unloaded

TABLE 2. Average Coffee Prices on the New York Exchange—Santos 4[a]

Year	Price per pound (in cents)
1910	10
1924	22
1930–40	7
1950	51
1953	88
1958	48
1961	36
1963	34
1964	41
1965	45

Source: Schurz 1961:254.
a. Constant dollars.

most of the coffee after the disastrous frost of 1918 which greatly reduced yields for two or three years. In 1924, the valorization of coffee became a permanent policy of the Brazilian government, but because it failed to enforce its prohibition on new plantings, production continued to rise. In 1924, 26 million bags of coffee were produced and by 1928, 28 million (James 1959:489).

During the depression, the federal government could no longer afford to buy up the surplus; a fifth valorization plan was set up which placed a heavy tax on all new plantings. At the same time, prices on the world market fell drastically. In March 1929, coffee sold for 24.8 cents a pound, but by October 1931, the price had fallen to 7.6 cents a pound.[9] The 1930 revolution in which Vargas came to power was a direct result of the collapse of Brazil's

8. One bag contains 60 kilograms of coffee.
9. These are 1930–31 unadjusted dollars.

economic base, so largely dependent upon coffee. The fifth and sixth valorization programs were the government's last attempts to stabilize world coffee prices through unilateral action. In 1940, Brazil entered the Inter-American Coffee Agreement in which export quotas were given to fourteen Latin American countries (Carlson 1951:288).[10]

TABLE 3. BRAZIL'S PERCENTAGE OF WORLD COFFEE PRODUCTION

Year	Per cent
1890s	75
1939–40	64
1944–45	38
1956–57	40
1958–59	50[a]
1963–64	36
1968–69	37

SOURCE: Pan-American Coffee Bureau 1964:15.
a. Result of a bumper crop of 31 million bags.

The Coffee Frontier in Northern Paraná

The third coffee cycle, based in northern Paraná, is the one that is the primary concern of this study. Throughout most of its history, Paraná was an unexplored territory with a population of around 150,000 Guaraní Indians. The first large-scale settlement of the northern portion of the state began only about forty years ago, but some areas had been explored earlier. Until the early seventeenth century, most of the territory which forms the present-day state of Paraná, then known as Guayra, was under Spanish rule. In 1608, the province was entrusted to the Jesuits who established thirteen missions (*reducciones*). From the beginning they were attacked by *bandeirantes*[11] from São Paulo who sought to enslave their Indian charges. The province officially became Brazilian territory in 1750 after the Portuguese successfully routed the Spanish from Vila Rica, their principal settlement in the region (Dozier 1954:40–41).

With the demise of the Jesuit missions, the Guaraní succumbed to slave raids, disease, and migration, and northern Paraná remained

10. The government's most recent attempt to control overproduction through an eradication program is discussed in chap. 3.

11. Bandeirantes were groups of adventurers who penetrated the Brazilian interior in the seventeenth and eighteenth centuries in search of gold and slaves. See Morse 1967.

virtually uninhabited for the next 150 years. The area was traversed only by bandeirantes in search of slaves, but no attempt at settlement was made; Paraná lacked the gold that had spurred the populating of Minas Gerais and Goiás. The mule drives from Rio Grande do Sul to Sorocaba, São Paulo, passed close to the northern Paraná frontier, but never crossed it. The northern portion of the state also was by-passed when parts of western Paraná were opened up for cattle ranching in the eighteenth century, and again during the westward trek of European immigrants in São Paulo in the nineteenth century (Dozier 1954:34).

During the nineteenth century, expeditions were sent to explore the area between the Paranapanema and Iguacú rivers, but there were no attempts at settlement. Paulista and Mineiro[12] farmers settled the São Paulo side of the Paranapanema River, but few ventured across into northern Paraná, for Indians[13] were still a threat to settlers. The first permanent settlements on the eastern fringe of the region, Boa Vista, Colônia Mineira, and Siqueira Campos, were founded by Paulista fazendeiros between 1860 and 1870. They grew coffee as a supplementary cash crop, but its importance was not realized until the end of the century. The later Paulista-Mineiro settlements of Jacarézinho, Riberaõ Preto, and Santo Antonio de Platina, founded between 1856 and 1894, were clearly based on a coffee economy, but they were isolated until the railroad between Ourinhos and Jaguariaiva was installed (Bernardes 1953:358).

The impetus for the settlement of northern Paraná did not come from within the state, but from across the border in São Paulo; its settlers continued to push westward in search of virgin soils for coffee cultivation. By 1900, coffee cropping and the railroad simultaneously penetrated the western plateau region of northern Paraná. At the same time government-subsidized immigration was at its peak and coffee prices were rising. The railroads continued west, and in 1908, when Ourinhos was reached, northern Paraná was linked for the first time to the city of São Paulo and the port of Santos. From Ourinhos, the *boca de sertaõ* (mouth of the backlands) settlers moved west, and the towns of Cambará (1904), Bandeirantes (1921), and Cornélio Procopio (1924) were founded by Paulista fazendeiros (Müller 1956).

After World War I, coffee prices continued to rise, stimulating

12. Inhabitants of São Paulo and Minas Gerais.

13. Botucatú Indians, who had been pushed south from Mato Grosso, had for the most part replaced the Guaraní by this time.

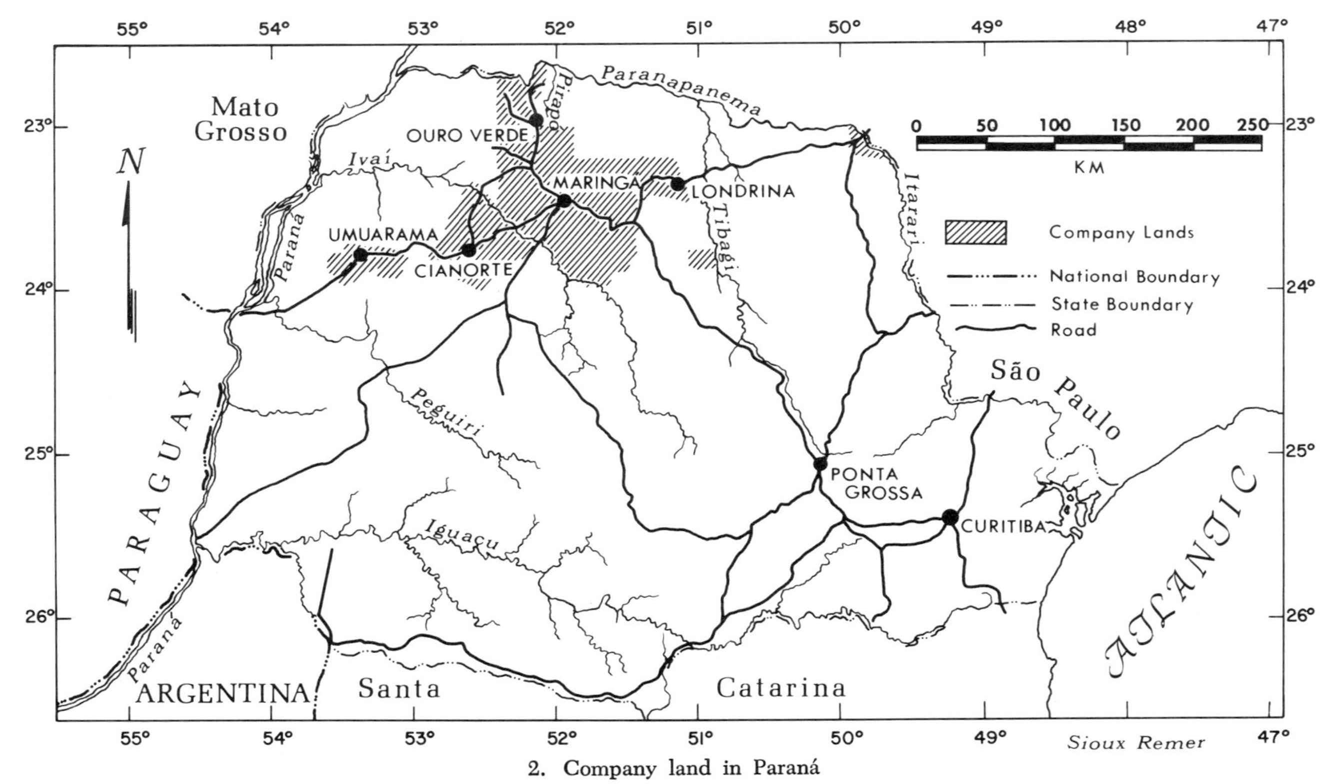

2. Company land in Paraná

new plantings. In this period a group of São Paulo planters financed a railroad extending west from Ourinhos to the edge of frontier settlement. The depression of 1929 and falling coffee prices did not halt the movement west, but it did change the character of the region's settlers. The earlier towns had been founded by fazendeiros with large plantations in São Paulo, where land was losing its fertility; the later pioneers were largely European immigrants who had worked previously as colonos on coffee fazendas in São Paulo. Small holdings tooks precedence over large ones as the immigrants bought *sítios* (small farms) with the money they had earned as colonos in São Paulo in the 1920s (James 1933:232).

Aware of the dangers of falling coffee prices, a number of fazendeiros put their capital into large tracts of virgin land which they subdivided and sold to immigrant settlers as small farms. Many of the buyers had owned small tracts of land in contiguous areas of São Paulo and had been prohibited from planting new trees by the government's efforts at limiting production in that state. The ban did not extend to Paraná, however, and its untouched soil was excellent for coffee cultivation.

In 1924, Paraná Plantations Limited was founded, an important event in the subsequent development of northern Paraná. An English company, it was headed by Lord Lovat, a pioneer in the problems of land use and planned colonization, who had worked for the British government in the Anglo-Egyptian Sudan. He came to Brazil as part of a commission to study the Brazilian economy, and was invited to northern Paraná where he was impressed by its possiblities for colonization. Dozier terms the program of the company which Lovat founded "the most successful experiment to date in coordinated regional planning and colonization" (1956: 318), and James calls the area which the company colonized "the largest and most prosperous pioneer zone of small, independent farmers in all Latin America" (1959:494).

Paraná Plantations Limited operated two Brazilian subsidiaries: one was for colonization, the Companhia de Terras Norte do Paraná (Northern Paraná Land Company), and one was for transport, Estrada de Ferro São Paulo–Paraná (São Paulo–Paraná Railroad), which built a westward continuation of the Ourinhos-Cambará line. The integration of planned colonization and transportation facilities contributed to the subsequent success of the venture. The colonizing agency bought from the state government 12,463 square kilometers (about 2.7 million acres) of virgin land in northern Paraná. This area extended westward from the Tibagí River and included a major part of the northern portion of Paraná. It constituted about one-ninth of all the land in the state. For two years old claims were adjusted so that future ownership would not be disputed. One of the hallmarks of the company was guaranteed security of tenure on all plots it sold.

In 1929, groups of surveyors began a detailed survey of the company's land, paying special attention to its water resources. Land was to be subdivided in a standard pattern, with the construction of roads at the heights of divides and plots stretching lengthwise from them to the valley bottoms. This insured all settlers outside access and a secure water supply. The company encouraged small landholdings which were thought the only means for insuring integrated regional development. By avoiding monocrop cultivation and creating a demand for the services of its planned towns and cities, the company sought to protect the area from the economic uncertainties of dependence on a single crop. It did not prohibit the sale of fazenda-sized tracts, but limited them to a circumscribed orbit outside the towns. Adjacent to the fazendas, sítios averaging 41 hectares were mapped out. Surrounding the towns were even smaller plots, *chácaras,* averaging about 12.5 hectares; these were intended as land to produce food crops for the adjacent towns, but this plan was not followed. Towns were to be built at intervals of 15 kilometers and urban centers every 100 kilometers. Londrina, Maringá, Cianorte, and Umuarama, in order of size and age, are the four principal cities of northern Paraná, all of them founded by the company.

The company's land was divided into sections of 200,000 hectares, to be settled in the future. Each area was a unit with roads, towns, and property divisions mapped out and constructed at the same time. The fazendas, sítios, and chácaras in a given sector were then put up for sale. During the 1930s, only the eastern portion of the company's land, centering around Londrina, was colonized, and development was slowed by the depressed economy. By 1943, however, when the railroad reached the town of Apucarana, large-scale settlement got underway. High coffee prices after World War II spurred colonization and the demand for company land grew.[14] Prospective buyers came mainly from São Paulo, but also from

14. Between 1940 and 1950 population density in the Maringá zone of the company's land went from 14.5 to 99.8 people per square mile (Nicholls 1969:49).

Minas Gerais and a few from the northeastern states. In addition, earlier settlers around Londrina bought virgin tracts of company land in the newly opened sectors farther west. Many of the *sitiantes* (owners of sítios) in Ouro Verde followed this pattern; natives of São Paulo, they bought land in the Londrina area in the 1930s, sold it in the late 1940s and early 1950s, and moved to their present farms in the county.

During the war, the British government required its citizens to sell their foreign holdings in order to acquire additional funds for the war effort. At the same time the Brazilian government wanted Brazilian control of all railroads near her international borders (in this case, the border with Paraguay). These pressures led to the sale of the company's property in 1944 to a consortium of São Paulo bankers and businessmen. The name was changed to Companhia Melhoramentos Norte do Paraná (Northern Paraná Land Improvement Company). The new owners followed the plans and policies instituted by Lord Lovat, and continued to colonize the undeveloped sections of their lands.

Railroad construction reached Maringá in 1953 and Cianorte, the third of the company's four regional centers, in 1967. By 1953, the company had begun colonization of its last remaining sector, the lands to the south of the left bank of the Ivaí River. Up to that time, it had made over 25,500 individual sales of land, totaling 1,101,100 hectares out of the original 1,245,300 hectares (CMNP:8). Today, virtually all of its land has been sold except for a few scattered parcels on the western edge of its holdings. The company, however, still owns a great deal of urban real estate whose value has soared as population increased in its towns and cities. In addition, the company runs thirteen cattle and coffee fazendas on which it attempts to demonstrate modern agricultural techniques to local farmers.

As a result of the company's colonization of northern Paraná, coffee cultivation there has grown tremendously, and has served to aggravate the constant problems of overproduction. In the 1959–60 harvest, Paraná for the first time produced more coffee than São Paulo.[15] This lead has continued, making Paraná the largest coffee-producing region in Brazil, thus in the world.

15. Paraná produced 20,410,000 sacks of 60 kilos to São Paulo's 15,601,000 sacks (IBC:Produção Exportável do Brasil 1934–64).

2. The Setting

THE BOUNDARIES of northern Paraná are coterminous with the regions of the state in which coffee can be cultivated successfully. This zone extends from the Paranapanema River on the north to the Tropic of Capricorn on the south, and runs the full width of the state from its border with São Paulo to the Paraná River. It comprises only 25 per cent of the state's total area, but accounts for 75 per cent of its total agricultural output (IBC 1964:2).

Geologically, all of northern Paraná lies within the Guarapuava Plateau which is characterized by diabase rocks and lava flows (Dozier 1954:4). The soils are derived largely from basaltic lava, the outcroppings of which, in the area from the São Paulo border to Maringá, produce rich terra roxa soils. North and west of Maringá in the subregion in which Ouro Verde is situated, terra roxa gives way to *terra mista,* a mixture of terra roxa and sandier soils, and *terra arenosa,* a poor soil derived from sandstone. Of the 50,000 square kilometers planted mainly in coffee in northern Paraná, 20,000 are made up of terra roxa, 16,000 of terra mista, and 14,000 of terra arenosa (IBC 1964:42). Thus, less than half the territory planted in coffee has soils that are best suited to this crop. Climate, rather than soil, has had a more limiting effect on the extension of coffee cultivation.

Northern Paraná is a transitional zone between the subtropical region to the south, which has rich soils but is subject to annual frosts, and the tropical climate which characterizes western São Paulo. The latter lacks sufficiently rich soils for coffee cultivation. Northern Paraná has a moderately hot, rainy climate. The summer months (December to February) are humid, with a mean temperature of 70.5° F. The winter (June through August) is fairly temperate and dry with a mean temperature of 63° F. However, there may be great fluctuations over a period of a few hours (Dozier 1954: 10–11). Because of the fairly high elevation and subjection to cold winds from the south, the danger of frost is enhanced. For this reason, the elevated divides, which are less subject to frost, are planted in coffee and other tropical crops, and the low-lying valleys are in pasture and frost-resistant crops. Severe frosts occurred in 1935, 1942, 1948, 1953, 1955, 1964, and 1969 with less damaging frosts in some of the intervening years.

Since there is at least some rain during all months of the year, there are no clearly defined rainy and dry seasons, although in winter, particularly August, rainfall may be sparse. The average yearly rainfall in the region is 1,250 millimeters.

Northern Paraná has a "youthful topography" characterized by broad flat divides between major streams. Its principal drainage points are the Paranapanema and Ivaí rivers. The average elevation of the area is 600 meters, with river valleys descending to 300 to 450 meters. The topography descends gradually from east to west, and gently rolling slopes combined with the absence of concentrated rainfall make the soils relatively resistant to erosion (Dozier 1954:7–8).

The original vegetation of northern Paraná has all but disappeared, except in those areas in the extreme western part of the state near the Mato Grosso and Paraguay borders that are just now being opened to settlement. With the advance of coffee, the forests were cut down indiscriminately, and today one can travel for miles without seeing a patch of virgin green. Before colonization, northern Paraná was covered by luxuriant tropical and subtropical vegetation, the result of well-distributed rainfall and good drainage and soils. The tropical vegetation in valleys and plateaus of up to 500 meters was characterized by epiphytes, lianas, and palms. The higher areas had subtropical vegetation, mainly arboreal ferns (IBC 1964:1).

Town and Country

The county of Ouro Verde, about 50 kilometers northwest of Maringá, occupies an area of 220 square kilometers, or about 63,000 acres. It is the northernmost extension of the lands which belonged to the CMNP.[1] The counties to the north and east of it were settled by smaller colonization companies or the land was sold by the state. The main river in the region is the Pirapó, which divides Ouro Verde from the neighboring município of Lobato. Another river on the west and innumerable small rivulets and streams insure the county of sufficient water. All landholdings have immediate access to rivers or streams, a result of the company's planning.

Ouro Verde lies within the zone of Botucatú and Baurú type soils, although there are a few scattered patches of terra roxa near the streams. Botucatú soil (terra mista) predominates, but its quality varies greatly in different parts of the county, depending on the proportion of sand which it contains. Approaching the county seat (*sede do município*) from the south along the main road, one might believe that the majority of the farms are planted entirely in coffee, because coffee is always cultivated on the highest land, that which is visible from the road. Still, as one continues toward town, there are also fairly large areas of pasture and patches of corn and cotton. At first, it appears as though the county is made up of large fazendas, for land divisions are not apparent along the road, the houses are in the valleys below, and the entrances to the smaller farms are on the narrow subsidiary roads which interlace the county.

The town of Ouro Verde, at an elevation of 450 meters, is in the northern part of the county, two kilometers from its border with Paranacity.[2] The town has a population of 1,229 and the rural area about 9,300 (IBGE 1967). Nearly half the town's residents are involved in agriculture. Many are local landowners who live in town; others are sharecroppers, renters, and day laborers who are employed on the surrounding farms. A number of shopkeepers also own sítios in the county. Of the other town inhabitants, the majority are salaried employees in local stores, banks, schools, and the "town hall" (*prefeitura*). There are also a number of self-employed

1. The Northern Paraná Land Improvement Company, hereafter referred to as the CMNP.

2. Since the region was colonized by a British company, many of the place names are in English. The county's main road is called the "English Road."

carpenters, bricklayers, construction workers, general handymen, and chauffeurs (*motoristas*). There is one local lay dentist who never studied formally, as well as a doctor who divides his time between patients in Ouro Verde and a lucrative practice in São Paulo.

The town has very little industry. There are two coffee processing plants, one of which is owned by a large exporting company based in Santos, and three smaller enterprises which process rice and peanuts, but a large part of the county's crops are processed in the neighboring município of Nova Esperança. The other small businesses include a sawmill, twelve general stores, five bars, three butcher shops, two pensions, one gas station, one tailor shop, one vegetable stall, one beauty parlor, and one movie theater whose projector has not worked within recorded memory. The town is also the site of the county's one bank, the Banco Commercial Norte do Paraná (Commercial Bank of Northern Paraná), which is privately owned.

Electricity reached Ouro Verde in June 1966, but the expense of installing it in houses has meant that only wealthier residents have benefited from it. In 1968, the mayor used municipal taxes to pay for the building of a large artesian well, which has his name conspicuously painted in large red letters at the top of the water tower, but few townspeople can afford installation of water pipes and meters in their homes so that only a handful of people receive water from the well. A loudspeaker (*alto-falante*) owned by a former mayor blares popular and martial music most of the day and well into the night. Some of the local shopkeepers advertise over it, and it creates a constant din which gives the town a deceptive feeling of liveliness and activity.

As one approaches the town from the south, the first sight is a few general stores, usually with two or three horse-drawn wagons (*carroças*) and perhaps a Volkswagen parked in front. A small dilapidated bus station farther down the street houses a ticket office and two tiny refreshment stands. To one side of it is being built a large new brick station, financed by municipal taxes. The main street bisects the town which is laid out on a grid system (see map 3). In the heart of town, a thin haze of reddish dust lightly tints all of the wooden houses and shops, giving them a uniform color. None of the streets in Ouro Verde is paved and there are no sidewalks, so that a few days without rain makes them sandy and difficult to walk on. After a heavy downpour, they become muddy

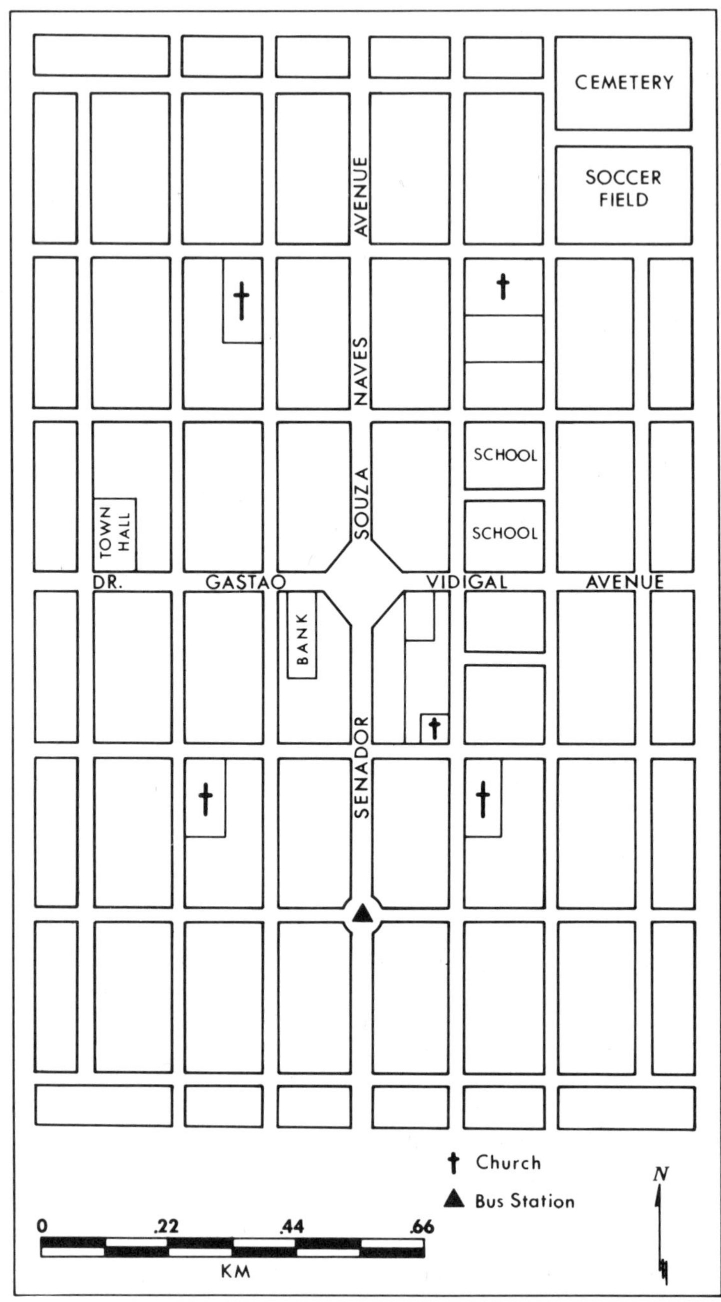

Sioux Remer

3. Town plan of Ouro Verde

streams which make the passage of wagons and cars very difficult.

Farther along the main street is a large open square (*praça*), with flowers and palm trees. Its stone benches are often occupied by sleeping men and it is the site of much social activity when families congregate there after Sunday mass to chat and pass the time before returning home for dinner. The square is surrounded by three bars, the drugstores, and some of the better houses. The new town hall is located on one of the streets leading off the square. The single story, white cement building houses the mayor's office, post office, and county records. Directly across the street from it is the agricultural post (*pôsto de agricultura*), a state-financed store where farmers purchase seeds, insecticides, fertilizers, and farm tools at a slight discount. Farther along the road is a large shedlike building which houses the town's biggest coffee-processing plant. An adjoining two-story house contains the company's local office and an apartment in which the owner resides when he comes to Ouro Verde in June and July for the coffee harvest.

On another street leading off the main square, there is a large wooden Catholic church, and beside it a partially completed brick church, unfinished due to lack of funds. The primary school, also of wood, is nearby, with a small playing field next to it. All of the other churches in Ouro Verde (Adventist, *Cristão do Brasil,* Baptist, and Presbyterian) are housed in small, plain, wooden buildings scattered throughout the residential areas of town.

Although there are a few houses on the main street, most of the dwellings are on smaller side streets. About 95 per cent of the houses are made of *peroba,* a hard, durable wood native to the region. Cement block construction is prized, but, with the exception of eight houses built by the coffee processor for his employees and a few along the main street, it is not common. Wooden houses vary according to the inhabitants' economic situation. The better homes are large, with as many as six or seven rooms, wooden floors, well-kept gardens, and walls painted both inside and out. The poorer houses have fewer rooms, with wooden partitions that do not reach to the roof, and open kitchens in the back yard. In all houses, there is a living room at the entrance with small bedrooms leading off of it. Only the largest houses have separate dining rooms; most families eat at a table in the front room.

Most of the furnishings, typically a table, a few chairs, beds with straw mattresses, and a sideboard for dishes, are made of un-

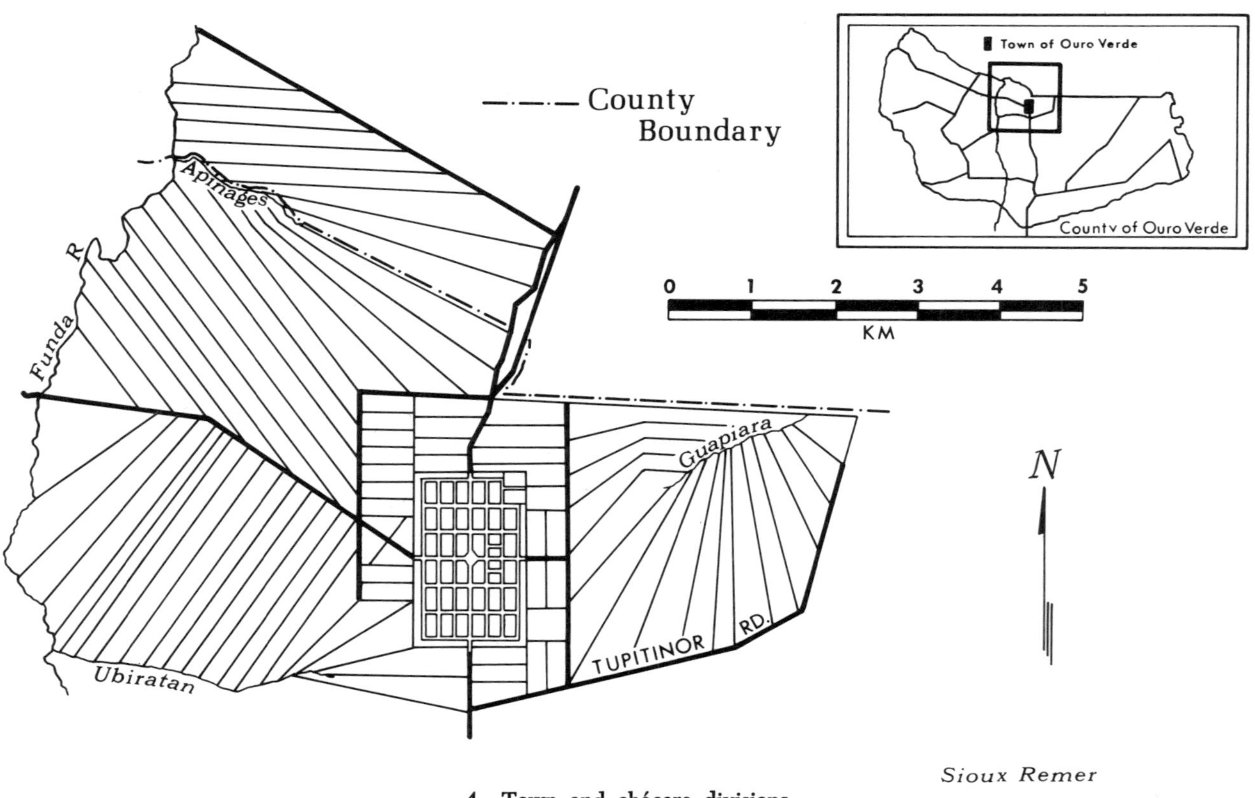

4. Town and chácara divisions

painted wood. Many wealthier residents have brightly colored plastic sofas and chairs and large collections of dishes and bric-à-brac. The most modest houses have dirt floors, and the only furniture is one or two rough-hewn benches, a wooden chair, and mattresses placed directly on the floor. Photographs of family members, colorful calendars, and pictures of saints decorate the walls of many homes. There are no rich or poor "neighborhoods" in town, although the better houses tend to be along the main street.

The rural area of the county is in two sections. The first is termed a "suburban zone" by the census, and consists of chácaras adjacent to the town (see map 4). The sítios and fazendas at a greater distance from town constitute the heart of the rural area. The population of both regions is approximately 9,300, but it fluctuates greatly throughout the year, reaching a peak in June and July during the coffee harvest. Residents divide the rural zone into two principal subregions, Vagalume ("firefly") and Ipiranga, following the CMNP's original names for these areas. Vagalume lies to the southeast of town. It has the lowest elevation in the county, thus has been most subject to frosts. It is here that cattle have made the largest inroads on coffee, and consolidation of sítios into large fazendas has reached its greatest extent. Ipiranga, comprising the entire western half of the county, is still the principal coffee producer, although the area northwest of town has large cattle farms and some cotton and rice.

The one hamlet (*povoado*) in the county, Vila Franki, lies in the Ipiranga zone. It consists of three general stores and a bar; it is surrounded by small farms, primarily planted in coffee, and a number of large cattle fazendas. Just to the east of it along the São Francisco River are low-lying, well-watered fields (*varzeões*) where wet rice is cultivated. Most of the Japanese-owned farms are along the main road about five kilometers southwest of town. These are medium-sized holdings with coffee, cotton, rice, fruit orchards, and vegetable gardens, and they are the only ones in the county on which coffee trees have been planted recently. In this area also are two large chicken farms, owned by Japanese. On the road just south of the region, there is a heavy concentration of small sítios owned by farmers of European descent, principally Italians and Spaniards.

Those who live at the outer edges of the county do not patronize the shops in the town of Ouro Verde, but rather those in neighboring counties, which actually are closer to their homes. Thus,

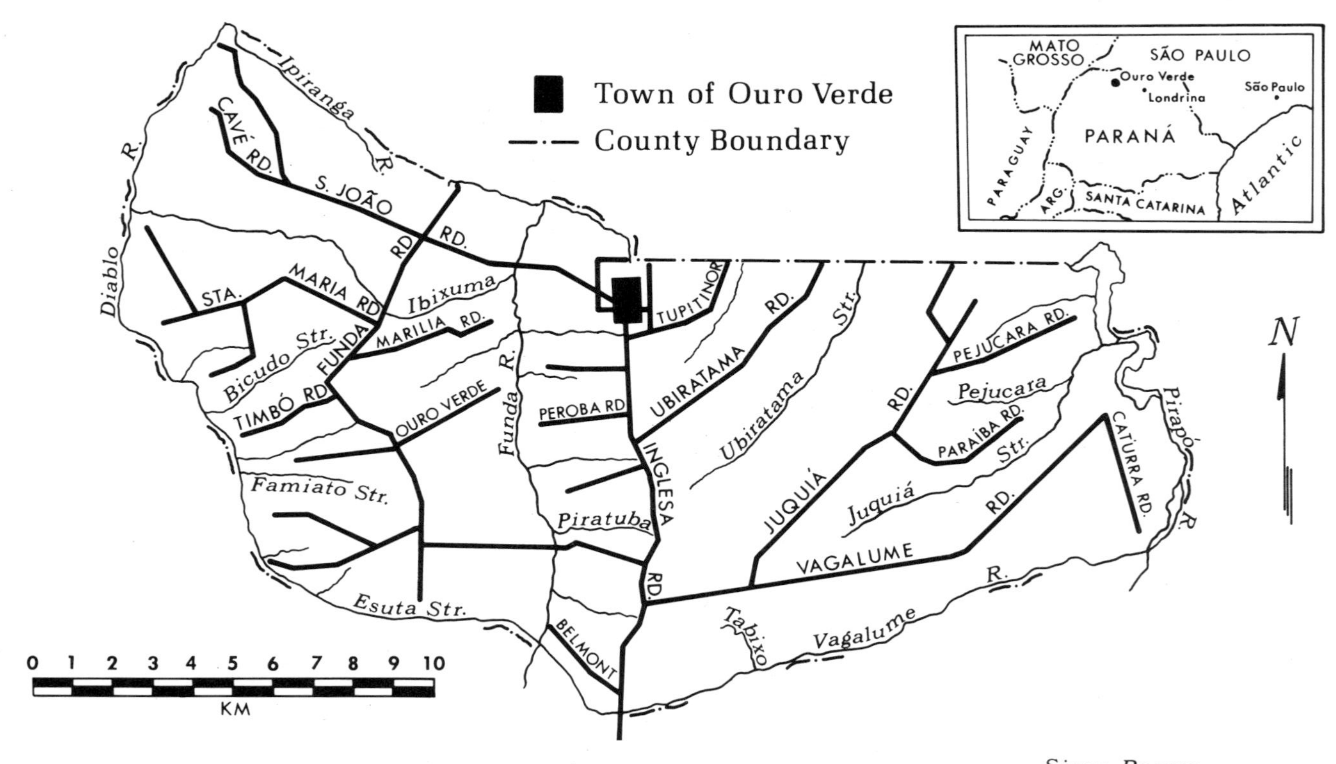

5. County road and river systems

those who live in the southern Vagalume region are more likely to shop and have postal boxes in Nova Esperança, a town of 15,000 about 20 kilometers away, than in Ouro Verde. Prices in Nova Esperança are somewhat lower and the variety of goods far larger than in any of the neighboring towns. Similarly, those who live near the eastern border of the county are apt to view the county of Lobato as their center of social activities, church-going, and shopping.

Ouro Verde's principal link with the other towns of northern Paraná is the English Road, which begins at the Paranapanema River on the border with São Paulo, passes through Ouro Verde, and continues south to Nova Esperança. There it links up with the newly paved "Coffee Road" (*Estrada do Café*) which leads to Maringá, the largest city in the region with a population of 80,000. The road then continues west through the towns and cities of northern Paraná up to the São Paulo border, where it meets the road which leads to the capital of that state. The English Road is unpaved to Nova Esperança, but it is continually leveled so that it is passable throughout the year.

There are 146 kilometers of subsidiary roads which reach virtually every part of Ouro Verde (see map 5). All farms have immediate access to one of the tiny dirt roads which crisscross the county, although after heavy rains these often become impassable. In addition, there are a number of wider roads which link Ouro Verde to the counties east and west of it.

There are twenty-six buses a day which pass through Ouro Verde. Thirteen originate to the north in Presidente Prudente, a large city just across the border in São Paulo, and pass through a number of counties north and northwest of Ouro Verde, continuing on to Nova Esperança and Maringá. There daily buses connect these towns to Londrina, Curitiba, and São Paulo. The other thirteen come from the south and southeast, originating in Nova Esperança, Maringá, Mandaquaçú, and Paranavaí. Since the bus fare to Nova Esperança is fairly inexpensive (CrN$,90 or about U.S. $.20), it is not uncommon for the townspeople to make frequent trips there to pass the time and shop.

History and Colonization

In 1951 the CMNP began opening the 20-kilometer expanse of forest between Nova Esperança and Ouro Verde. It appointed a local *gato*[3] and the nearly four hundred men who worked under

3. Slang term, literally meaning "cat," for men who head labor gangs.

Main Street, Ouro Verde

The town square

him to start clearing the zone by felling trees and laying out the route for a road. Many of the workers were northeasterners who had come south without their families to work in the coffee harvest and who had stayed on to earn additional money by opening up frontier areas. Most of them came to Maringá from the northeast on *pau-de-araras,*[4] and that city became the distribution point of manpower for the regions north and west of it that were just being opened for settlement. The gato was contracted by the company which agreed to pay him a set price to open up a predetermined area of virgin forest. He, in turn, subcontracted *peões* (members of a work gang) who were paid a set amount for every meter of forest which they cut down. After the work was completed, most of these men returned to their homes in the Northeast, while others moved westward with the frontier.

As soon as the forest was partially cleared and the road completed as far as Ouro Verde, the company started selling plots of land in the county. At this point, many of the new landowners living in the older, more easterly regions of northern Paraná contracted *formadores de café* to go to Ouro Verde, clear their land, and plant it in coffee. Contracts were usually for four- to six-year periods, after which the land was turned over to its owners. The formadores were permitted to plant subsistence crops between the rows of coffee trees, and they were entitled to the first two coffee harvests, that is, the harvests of the fourth and fifth years after the trees were planted. Many formadores bought sítios on the frontier farther west, using the money they had earned from the sale of their coffee harvested in Ouro Verde. Others remained on the same farm sharecropping coffee, often working side by side with the landowner and his family.

The entire county of Ouro Verde was cleared just two years after work had begun, but even before this, in early 1951, the first permanent settlers arrived. A group of Japanese from São Paulo bought neighboring farms in the Ipiranga region of the county, moved their families there, and began planting coffee seedlings and cultivating subsistence crops. Later that same year the town received its first four residents. All of them were shopkeepers in Mandaquarí, the município to which Ouro Verde pertained until 1952. Many of the early settlers came from Mandaquarí, for the company had set up an office there to sell land in Ouro Verde and

4. Literally "parrots' perches," the term used for the crowded open-air trucks used to transport laborers from the northeast to the south.

A small forest preserve in the county

Bringing coffee to town

other counties farther west which were just then being opened for colonization.

During these first years the county was sparsely populated and largely isolated, for the road which led to Maringá was often washed out by heavy rains. Life lacked even the most rudimentary conveniences. Small, make-shift wooden houses were built quickly by both landowners and formadores, and in the rural area the land was soon covered with rows of tiny coffee seedlings, flanked by corn, rice, and beans. Since coffee does not produce its first harvest until the fourth year after planting, money was scarce and the town's few general stores and bars barely survived. Most of the settlers sold the lumber from their land to the newly opened sawmill in town, and, for many, the money received from these sales represented their only cash income during their first years in Ouro Verde. There was little activity in town. The rural inhabitants rarely made trips there, of necessity spending all their waking hours at the difficult task of carving farms out of the virgin forest.

The company's sales policies made it possible for settlers without a great deal of capital to buy small farms. Forty per cent of the total purchase price was given as a down payment on sítios, the balance to be paid over a four-year period. A down payment of 50 per cent was required on chácaras, the remainder to be paid within two years. The company charged an annual interest rate of 8 per cent on the outstanding debt. If payments were late due to crop failures and frosts, the sitiante was given more time to pay the balance. If he was still unable to meet his obligation, the company reclaimed the unpaid portion of land and resold it.

Land prices were reasonable when Ouro Verde first opened for settlement. The price for sítios ranged from Cr$ 2.200,00 to Cr$ 3.000,00[5] per *alqueire* (about six acres), depending on its location. During the same period, chácaras sold for Cr$ 5.000,00 to Cr$ 15.000,00 per alqueire, the price higher because of their proximity to town. Urban lots were also sold, and their prices depended on the closeness to the center of town.

The sales contracts contained the provision that an area of at least 10 per cent of the total land purchased would be left in virgin forest, thus insuring that all of the region's forests would not disappear and create soil erosion. At first, most settlers adhered to this stricture, for there was no lack of virgin soil for planting. As the years passed, however, there was an overwhelming temptation to

5. In 1951, Cr$ 1.000,00 was approximately U.S. $15.00.

cut down these patches of forest as the farmers realized that by planting on these lands, they could attain once again the large yields that their other land originally had produced. Today, nearly all of the county's forest reserves have been felled and planted.

The company has sold all of its rural properties in Ouro Verde, and prospective buyers today must purchase their farms *segunda mão* (second hand), that is, from other owners. Arrangements for payment are not nearly as liberal as those of the company were, and high interest rates are charged on installments. In addition, land prices have skyrocketed, ranging from CrN$ 800 to CrN$ 1.500 per alqueire, depending on the location and condition of the land, equivalent to between U.S. $333[6] and $400 per alqueire or $55 to $66 an acre. These prices are for unplanted land. Land sown

TABLE 4. LAND PRICES IN OURO VERDE

Year	Price range in cruzeiros	Average value in cruzeiros	Wholesale price index[a]	Real value of land—1950 prices
Chácaras per alqueire				
1950	5.000– 8.000[b]	6.500	66	6.500
1951	8.000–12.000[b]	10.000	79	8.316
1952	12.000–15.000[b]	13.500	87	10.230
1953–56	no sales			
1957	54.000–64.000[c]	59.000	197	19.734
1958	100.000[c]	100.000	221	29.832
1959	200.000[c]	200.000	305	43.230
1961	300.000[c]	300.000	552	35.838
Sítios and fazendas per alqueire				
1950	2.200– 3.000[b]	2.600	66	2.600
1951	2.800– 4.000[b]	3.400	79	2.638
1952	no sales			
1953	6.000– 7.000[b]	6.500	100	4.290
1954	6.000– 7.000[b]	6.500	130	3.300
1955	10.000–20.000[b]	15.000	147	6.732
1956	10.000–20.000[b]	15.000	175	5.728
1957–59	no sales			
1960	25.000[b]	25.000	399	4.296
1962	80.000[b]	80.000	846	6.237
1964	150.000[b]	150.000	2813	3.517
1967	800.000–1.500.000[c]	1.150.000	6444	11.774

a. Wholesale price index from the Conjuntura Econômica International.
b. Sold by CMNP.
c. Sold second hand.

6. The official 1967 rate of exchange was CrN$ 2,70 for U.S. $1.00.

with producing coffee trees may cost as much as CrN$ 2.500 per alqueire, or about $133 an acre. A fairly small farm of 8 to 10 alqueires (48 to 60 acres) planted in coffee sells for CrN$ 25.000 to CrN$ 30.000, about U.S. $10,000 in today's market. The same farm, if uncultivated, would cost about U.S. $7,000. Urban lots are selling for CrN$ 80,00 (about U.S. $66) on the outskirts of town, and CrN$ 1.000 (about U.S. $270) in the heart of the shopping district.

About 200 *datas* (urban lots) which are up for sale are still owned by the company, but none is in the central commercial district. Fifteen per cent of these lots are used for subsistence cultivation by the most impoverished citizens in town, with the understanding that when the lots are sold, these people will vacate. In addition, the company still owns two centrally located lots which it has reserved for industry. In the event that someone is interested in building a small factory, the company has promised to donate the land in order to promote the town's development. It also has donated land for the county's schools, city hall, public square, and soccer field.

Differences exist between the policies of the CMNP and those of the smaller colonization companies. As mentioned, one of the most important policies of the CMNP was security of tenure on all of the land which it sold. Many of the smaller companies "bought" land whose title was in question, then sold it to as many as five or six different settlers. Among the problems that ensued, hired gunmen (*capangas*) were often employed to remove the squatters (*grileiros*) from the land, and, as recently as 1950, bloodshed was not uncommon in the counties north and northwest of Ouro Verde, outside the territory colonized by the CMNP. The experience of one sitiante who bought land from a settlement company owned by the Branco Brasileiro de Descontos is not unique. He purchased a ten-alqueire farm with money he had earned over a ten- or twelve-year period as a sharecropper and fazenda administrator. He cleared the land and, with the aid of his sons, planted coffee. After paying for 90 per cent of the property, he encountered difficulty in making the final payment on time. The company wanted to reclaim *all* of his land immediately, but the sitiante was able to trade the farm for ten alqueires in Ouro Verde with another settler who agreed to make the last payment on it. As far as can be ascertained, the CMNP never engaged in such practices. It generally has earned the respect of the local population for its fairness, and it is often said that "there is no other colonization company that can equal it."

The population of Ouro Verde is heterogeneous, as is that of northern Paraná in general. A little over 68 per cent of the town's inhabitants are of Brazilian origin: 37 per cent are from São Paulo, Paraná, and Minas Gerais, 30 per cent from the Northeast, and less than 1 per cent from other regions of Brazil. Sixteen per cent are of Italian descent, 5 per cent of Spanish, 5 per cent of Japanese, 3 per cent of Portuguese, and a little over 1 per cent of Slavic, German, and Russian descent. The figures for the rural area are about the same, with a slightly larger number of people of Italian origin. With the exception of the Japanese, very few of Ouro Verde's inhabitants were born abroad. Those of European descent are predominantly second-generation Brazilians, their children being the third generation. The majority of them were born and raised in the state of São Paulo and migrated to Paraná within the last twenty years.

The company's records on Ouro Verde show that the vast majority of its land buyers in the early 1950s came from São Paulo and the older, more easterly regions of northern Paraná. Of those from São Paulo, over 60 per cent came from the Araraquarense and Noroeste regions, the newest coffee zones of the state. About 14 per cent were from Sorocabana, and far fewer from the Paulista, Mogiana, and Central areas. Nearly 13 per cent of the buyers were from the city of São Paulo, but most of them bought the land for investment purposes and never lived in Ouro Verde. The records do not note the birthplace of the early settlers, only their place of residence at the time of the purchase; thus, it is difficult to determine if they were native Paulistas, or if they came from other regions of Brazil. It is clear from their surnames that there were many of Italian and Japanese descent.

Its inhabitants give diverse reasons for coming to Ouro Verde, but the one common denominator is the idea of "bettering one's life" (*melhorar a vida*). One of the earliest settlers said that he came to Ouro Verde because its land was cheap, it was then the hinterland (*sertão*) and full of "adventure," and opportunities were ripe. A woman remarked that she had come because there were more "comforts and conveniences" in Paraná than in her native Minas Gerais. Others, however, said that they came to Ouro Verde "filled with illusions," and that they would return "home" if they could afford the trip. Most of these readily admit that they have not had great success in Paraná. A bar owner in town, who bought a small sítio and then sold it, said, "I lived far better in Alagoas [a state in the Northeast]. I came south on a pau-de-arara with Cr$ 5,000,000 in cash and I had all sorts of dreams about São Paulo and Paraná. In the Northeast people never stop talking about the opportunities and wealth here. If I can sell my bar, I will return to Alagoas for there you only need CrN$ 200,00 [about U.S. $80] to start a small business and you can always earn a living by selling in the *feira* [market]. Here today in Paraná you need a lot of money to earn money.

3. Changing Patterns of Agriculture

PERHAPS the very first indication of coffee's precarious future in Ouro Verde and the surrounding counties occurred in the winter of 1955. From July 29 to August 2, the region's first major frost since its settlement brought temperatures down to –5° C. The frost was severe enough to kill many of the young trees that had just begun to produce their first harvest. From that time on, a series of frosts, falling prices, soil depletion, and other problems all but sealed the fate of coffee in Ouro Verde. Tables 5 and 6 show the decline in the size of coffee harvests and the decrease in the number of producing trees.

It is difficult to be precise about the effects of various factors on the decline of coffee, but it is clear that some are more important than others. Undoubtedly, soil depletion, frosts, and lowered prices have been the most significant factors in the downward trend. Other, somewhat less important reasons are the increasing frequency of coffee pests, competition with other coffee-producing regions, and the federally financed eradication program. Finally, there is the continued availability of inexpensive frontier land on which large crops can be produced, at least for the first few years.

Every farmer in Ouro Verde knows that coffee yields have diminished continuously since the time of the first harvest in 1954–55.

TABLE 5. COFFEE PRODUCTION IN OURO VERDE

Year	Arrôbas[a]
1951–54	young trees, no harvests
1955–58	no data available[b]
1958–59	2,340,000
1959–60	1,800,000
1960–61	1,530,000
1961–62	1,850,000
1962–63	370,000[c]
1963–64	500,000
1964–65	500,000
1965–66	1,000,000
1966–67	950,000
1967–68	700,000
1968–69	530,000

a. One arrôba equals 15 kilos or 33 pounds.

b. At that time Ouro Verde was part of the município of Nova Esperança and separate records of its production were not kept.

c. Low yield due to 1963 frost.

Despite the fact that, until 1961, more and more trees came into production, the county's total yields have declined. At least part of the explanation lies in the quality of Ouro Verde's soils and those of the region in general. Terra mista, an admixture of terra roxa and sandy soil, predominates, with some patches of terra arenosa

TABLE 6. PRODUCING COFFEE TREES IN OURO VERDE

Year	Number
1951–54	only young trees
1955–58	no data available[a]
1958–59	17,000,000
1959–60	15,000,000
1960–61	17,000,000 (plus 3,000,000 new trees)
1961–62	18,500,000
1962–63	10,000,000[b]
1963–64	10,000,000
1964–65	10,000,000
1965–66	8,000,000 (plus 2,000,000 new trees)
1966–67	10,000,000
1967–68	5,700,000[c]

a. At that time Ouro Verde was part of the município of Nova Esperança and separate records of its production were not kept.

b. Reduction due to 1963 frost and first government eradication program.

c. Reduction due to second government eradication program.

throughout the county. There is no terra roxa, the most fertile and durable coffee soil, in the immediate vicinity. An agronomist employed by the CMNP stressed the great difference in the yields from each soil type. On terra roxa, harvests of up to 500 or 600 sacks of coffee per 1,000 trees[1] are not uncommon in good years, with average yields of 350 to 400 sacks per 1,000 trees. Yields on terra mista vary according to the percentage of terra roxa it contains. Because of this difference in quality, variation is great, with averages of 150 to 250 sacks per 1,000 trees. Terra arenosa, the least fertile type, may produce 100 sacks under optimal climatic conditions, and less than 40 sacks in times of slight drought.[2]

Another difference in the suitability of these soil types for coffee cultivation is the rapidity with which they lose their organic and chemical elements. On terra roxa, well-cared-for coffee trees sometimes bear fruit for up to fifty years. On terra mista, trees produce for an average of fifteen to twenty years, though yields continuously decline, and on sandy soil the life of a coffee tree may be as little as eight years. All of these figures are for unfertilized soils.

Frosts are the second ingredient in the decline of coffee in the region, and within Ouro Verde itself, Vagalume, the lowest-lying area of the county, has been most affected by them. In July 1963, temperatures fell below 0° C. for a few hours and the entire coffee harvest was nearly lost. One sitiante who had planted his trees five years earlier harvested a total of 216 sacks on his 30-alqueire farm.[3] One fazendeiro whose 100,000 coffee trees were destroyed cut them down and planted pasture. Most of the Vagalume's small-scale landowners whose first crop was ruined did not have enough capital to carry them to the next year and were forced to sell their farms for low prices. A German fazendeiro took advantage of the situation and bought seven sítios of varying sizes which he consolidated into one large cattle ranch. Similarly, a man who owned a 30-alqueire sítio, which was only slightly damaged by the frost, gradually bought up a number of neighboring five- and ten-alqueire farms, raising his holdings to 125 alqueires.

The frosts of 1955 and 1963 were the most severe that the county

1. Coffee yields are always measured by the average number of sacks of uncleaned coffee produced by 1,000 trees.

2. In chapter 5 the actual yields on individual sítios and fazendas in Ouro Verde are discussed.

3. He had 25 alqueires (one alqueire equals approximately six acres) of the farm planted in coffee, and since each alqueire has an average of 2,000 coffee trees, his yield averaged 4.2 sacks per 1,000 trees!

has witnessed, but in many of the intervening years there have been milder frosts which only "burn" the topmost branches, but have little effect on the size of the harvest.[4] Even when a severe frost occurs, it does permanent damage only if it comes shortly after a rainy period, when the leaves and trunks are still wet. When this happens, the water freezes and splits the trunk, its cells broken by the expansion caused by the ice. The only remedy is to cut the tree to within one or two feet of the ground, in the hope that it will sprout new branches. Severe frosts following droughts can eliminate as many as two or three harvests, but will not actually kill the trees. It is difficult to predict where a frost will occur, although lower regions are almost invariably more affected than higher ones. In some years, only a small section of the county freezes, leaving neighboring areas untouched.

The first frost to affect the coffee crop in Ouro Verde was in 1953, and, although fairly mild, it did considerable damage to the seedlings, most of which were only one or two years old. The 1953 frost affected approximately 95 per cent of the coffee trees in the county and involved 98 per cent of its farms. Over half of the trees were permanently destroyed and had to be uprooted and replaced. Only three farmers of the fifty questioned about frost damage said that they were unaffected by the 1963 frost. Many reported that they lost harvests in 1962, 1966, and 1967 because of frosts, but these lived only in the low-lying areas of the county.

Frosts are a constant topic of conversation in Ouro Verde, and most of the people who have lived in coffee regions for twenty-five or thirty years can list the precise dates, times, and extent of damage done by the major frosts during this time. The man who runs the local agricultural post noted the changing frequency of frosts in recent years: "In São Paulo there were frosts once every ten or twelve years. They did a lot of damage but there were enough good harvests in between to make coffee worthwhile. But in Paraná it freezes a little bit every year, and although these frosts don't destroy the trees or take out the entire harvest, as the big frosts of 1942, 1955, and 1963 did, they still reduce its size, and the farmer suffers losses [*tem prejuízo*] every year." Many blame the frosts for the decline in agricultural production: "It isn't the people, but the frosts that have ruined agriculture"; "The major sickness in Paraná is the frosts. If it weren't for them Paraná would be the richest state

4. Severe frosts are called *geadas negras,* or black frosts; milder frosts are *geadas sapecar* or *geadas brancas,* singeing or white frosts.

in Brazil"; "This is the misery of monoculture. We are sitting on a bomb. What if it explodes? For us the bomb is the frost." It was often said that one frost can affect a man's livelihood for a long period of time: "If it freezes there are three years of disaster, and one good harvest does not compensate for these three years. Before it froze my trees were like jewels, the most beautiful thing in the world. But afterwards, I didn't even have enough coffee to drink."

There is a tendency for people to compare current weather conditions with those of past years when frosts occurred. In 1968, it was unseasonably cold in May, but it warmed up a great deal in June, which some said was the exact sequence of changes which took place before the frost of 1963. Others demurred and claimed that there is a "frost scare" every year, particularly when the following harvest is expected to be very large. The phrase "if it doesn't freeze" (*se não gear*) is said with about the same frequency as "if God wills it" (*se Deus quiser*) after optimistic statements such as "This year's harvest will be the biggest ever, if it doesn't freeze, if God wills it."

At the end of July 1966, there was a frost scare while I was living on a farm in the vicinity of Ouro Verde. As the sky darkened toward evening and a cold chill fell, a night-long vigil began. A group of farmers had gathered to drink *cachaça,* (a strong alcoholic drink made from sugarcane) and discuss the possible losses they would incur if it froze. Every five or ten minutes one would go out to look at the thermometer and report. As the temperature inched downward, an air of anxiety began to fill the room; when it finally fell below zero for about ten minutes, all of those present silently crossed themselves. It turned out that the frost was a moderate one, and those who were most affected lost about half of their coffee crop.

The majority of the farmers in Ouro Verde attribute their present financial difficulties to the constantly lower prices which the government pays for their coffee, at a time when the costs of production are rising. The prices the planter receives from the Brazilian Coffee Institute vary according to the quality of the coffee produced. Each 40-kilo sack of unprocessed coffee (*café em côco*) gives an average of 20 kilos of "clean coffee" (*café limpo,* hulled coffee with the outer parchment removed). If the coffee is of superior quality and the beans are large, one sack of café em côco may give up to 23 kilos of clean coffee. If, on the other hand, coffee has been attacked by broca, thus reducing its weight, one sack may produce only 12 to 15 kilos of salable coffee after processing. The farmer with quality coffee will be paid CrN$ 17,60 to CrN$ 19,20[5] (U.S. $5.50 to $6.00) per sack of café em côco. For inferior coffee (producing 12 to 15 kilos of clean coffee), he receives from CrN$ 9,60 to CrN$ 12,80 (U.S. $3 to $4) per sack.

The average annual expenses for the care and harvesting of 1,000 coffee trees is about equal to the money received from the sale of 40 to 50 sacks of average quality, unprocessed coffee, or CrN$ 640,000 to CrN$ 800,000 (U.S. $200–$250). If a farmer's yield is 100 sacks per 1,000 trees, his net return after expenses (including interest on bank financing) equals the value of 50 to 60 bags of uncleaned coffee, or U.S. $250 to $300 per 1,000 trees, $500 to $600 per alquiere. Since the vast majority of farmers in Ouro Verde produce considerably less than 100 sacks per 1,000 trees, their returns are very much lower. One fazendeiro who has a 35-alqueire farm on terra arenosa averages only 35 sacks per 1,000 trees. He claims that he loses money every year and must be continually financed by the bank to pay the expenses of his next crop.

Since 1956, the prices paid to planters for their coffee crops have decreased considerably. During the 1954–55 harvest, they received an average of U.S. $15 per bag for café em côco; in 1967 they received about $5 per bag. Until 1956, the farmer was free to sell his crop directly to a coffee exporter, but the following year a law was passed making it mandatory that all coffee be sold to the federal government through its agency, the Brazilian Coffee Institute. The institute would guarantee the planter a minimum price for his crop, and he would no longer be subject to the uncertainties of the world market price. The drawback of this plan was that the price paid to the farmer was lower than it had been in the past.

Of the U.S. $46 (CrN$ 144,00) that the Brazilian government receives per sack of coffee on the world market, $20 (CrN$ 65,00) goes to the farmer;[6] the remaining $26 (CrN$ 79,00) is used to administer the institute, build warehouses for storing coffee,[7] and

5. May 1968 price.

6. This is the price received if the farmer pays for the processing himself and then sells his coffee to IBC. If he sells it to a coffee processor who in turn sells it to IBC, then the farmer receives about CrN$ 20,00 per sack of café em côco.

7. The government often stores coffee to wait for the world market price to rise before selling it.

finance various federal programs. It is said that Brasilia was built with government funds received in this way.

The U.S. $20 which the farmer is paid for one bag of processed coffee is not all profit. Out of it he must pay a 15 per cent tax for Imposto Commercial de Mercadoría or ICM (Commercial Commodities Tax) which is charged on all goods sold outside of the county, and 1 per cent to the Instituto Nacional de Proteção Social or INPS (National Institute of Social Protection). Thus, he pays 16 per cent of his coffee's value, or $3.20, in taxes, leaving him with $16.80. In addition, the farmer pays an average of $1.65 (CrN$ 5,76) to clean and transport his coffee. After these deductions, he is left with $15 per sack, but this figure is not net profit since it does not include the expenses of cultivating and harvesting the crop.

Even though the government guarantees the farmer a minimum price for his crop, and the price never has actually fallen below that of the previous harvest, frequently the increase from one year to the next is so slight that it covers only a fraction of Brazil's annual inflation; thus, the planter's profit margin is reduced substantially. In 1968, inflation was about 35 per cent according to the Instituto Getulio Vargas in Rio de Janeiro, while the price of coffee was only raised by CrN$ 3,00, from CrN$ 17,00 in 1967 to CrN$ 20,00 in 1969, an increase of less than 17 per cent. For this reason many farmers are reluctant to invest money in nonessential cultivating operations and fertilizer, for they can never be certain that the slightly higher price received for their coffee the following year will cover these additional expenses. It is not surprising that, during the years of bumper crops, there is a great hue and cry among planters for the government to raise the price it pays per sack, and a token increase usually is granted. When the crop is small, there is much less pressure on the government, for the farmer would gain little if he has few sacks of coffee to sell.

A large number of planters name as the principal cause of coffee's decline the government's present policy in regard to prices: "The main problem of coffee is the price. The government is not interested in coffee. If things go on as they are, coffee is not going to last. On both good and bad land people are disheartened [*desanimado*]. They only talk about higher prices, but nothing ever happens." One Italian fazendeiro disagreed with his friend who argued that coffee's decline was the result of soil depletion, lack of modern agricultural practices, and overproduction. Rather, he claimed, lowered prices were the main factor, and, if coffee's price suddenly shot up to pre–1955 levels, it would be cultivated again on every available piece of land. The company's agronomist blamed soil depletion rather than falling prices for the downward trend, for, he said, even in times of low prices the large yields produced on terra roxa still allow for sizable profits. On terra mista soils, however, like those in Ouro Verde, lowered prices greatly reduce the profit margin, for harvests on this type of land are far smaller.

Broca (*H. hampei* Ferrari), a tiny parasite which burrows into the coffee beans and hollows them out, affects the quality and weight of the crop. The pest was virtually unknown in Ouro Verde until 1964, but since then it has become an important factor in declining yields. Only 17 landowners out of the 66 interviewed said that their crops had never been affected by the disease. Of the remainder, the majority claimed that between 40 and 100 per cent of their trees had been infected, and that the resulting yields declined by as much as 50 per cent in weight. Since 1967, an inexpensive insecticide has been used to combat broca; it is less of a problem now than in the past.

The potential competition from other regions is another factor which may influence coffee's decline in Ouro Verde and the surrounding counties.[8] One farmer of Italian origin stated the problem well: "In this area the land is worn out and we must use expensive fertilizers if we want the soil to produce good crops. In the new regions the farmer has little to do to encourage growth for the lands are virgin and rich. So the sitiantes in the older areas cannot compete with those in the newer ones for our expenses are much higher, and we both receive the same price for our coffee. This situation is unlike that of my native Italy where all of the land has been cultivated for 1,000 years. You ask how it is still being used without wearing out? The reason is that in Italy *everyone* has to contend with the same lack of fertility for no one's land is very good. Everyone has the same high expenses in trying to make the land produce so one farmer has no great advantage over the rest. But in a country like Brazil where there are still large areas of unexploited virgin land, competition is not equal, and will not be so long as these undeveloped regions continue to exist."

In addition to these frontier zones, competition with areas of terra roxa from Londrina to Maringá, where yields of 250 to 300

8. Thus far, there is only *potential* competition since the government still pays the same price to farmers with high and low yields.

TABLE 7. Coffee Eradication and Crop Diversification in Counties North and West of Maringá

County	Number of contracts	Contracted trees erad.	Actual no. eradicated	Liberated area (hect.)	Rice[a]	Beans	Corn
Ouro Verde	104	1,375,798	1,382,916	1,835,913	178,160	50,921	700,615
Alto Paraná	135	1,142,920	1,245,149	1,565,428	225,047	52,085	487,421
Atalaia	37	422,165	423,813	579,330	155,470	66,148	249,610
Inajá	88	1,269,498	1,418,783	1,768,620	9,280	63,102	808,066
Nova Esperança	144	1,465,412	1,474,084	1,986,860	255,659	68,749	828,897
Paranacity	147	1,256,871	1,481,705	1,777,510	64,882	94,518	856,185
Paranavaí	108	2,710,980	2,834,517	3,696,820	30,105	612,070	1,744,079
São Antonio do Caiuá	47	578,103	636,871	777,170	61,931	53,683	257,033
São João do Caiuá	163	2,168,548	2,364,282	2,991,650	60,120	209,650	1,456,170
Uniflor	8	61,496	61,496	87,790	8,720	10,120	42,060
Totals	981	12,451,791	13,323,616	17,067,091	1,049,374	1,281,046	7,430,136

County	Soybeans	Sun-flowers	Castor beans	Peanuts	Cotton	Manioc	Reforesta-tion	Other crops
Ouro Verde	256,504		20,405	472,163	136,490	2,465		7,860
Alto Paraná	318,969	15,400	22,850	324,257	106,476	12,923		
Atalaia	79,710		5,525	22,867				
Inajá	60,500		1,000	510,177	316,495			
Nova Esperança	403,350		9,515	281,570	99,800	4,740	14,080	19,050
Paranacity	176,132	4,840	46,985	346,780	183,858	1,330		
Paranavaí	621,325	9,220	87,345	207,481	354,020	30,175		1,000
São Antonio do Caiuá	35,640			218,648	150,235			
São João do Caiuá	198,680	32,120	23,200	552,470	448,850	9,897		
Uniflor	230			22,100	4,240			320
Totals	2,151,040	61,580	216,825	2,958,513	1,800,464	61,530	14,080	28,230

a. The figures for the areas freed from coffee and planted in alternative crops are in hectares.

sacks per 1,000 trees are not uncommon, presents an additional threat to farmers in Ouro Verde and the other counties in the vicinity, where yields of 70 sacks per 1,000 trees are considered "good" (few farmers ever produce more than 25 to 30 sacks per 1,000 trees). The state of São Paulo will probably also come into competition with northern Paraná since its coffee is being replanted scientifically with selected seeds, and fertilizer and contour planting are being used. Only frost-free regions with rich soils will be cultivated, and production, once under way, is expected to be high. Some banks are financing this project with the aim of producing large yields in a limited area ideally suited to coffee. Still, São Paulo planters may encounter difficulty in securing an inexpensive work force, for the state's minimum wage is higher than that of Paraná and its labor laws are more strictly enforced.

The federally financed eradication program is not the cause of coffee's decline over a large portion of northern Paraná, but it has given great impetus to a process that was already underway. The government instituted two eradication programs, in 1964 and 1967. In addition, many farmers took out coffee trees on their own without government compensation. Between 1962 and 1965, 3 million of Ouro Verde's 12 million coffee trees were cut down, and since that time an additional 3.5 million have been displaced by pasture, cotton, peanuts, and other crops. Thus, today's 5.5 million trees represent less than half the total in production six or seven years ago.

Brazilian Coffee Institute figures for the 1967 eradication program show that 104 landowners in Ouro Verde contracted to cut down 1,375,798 coffee trees, and that an additional 7,118 trees were cut independent of the program (see Table 7). The latter figure is an extremely low estimate since, according to my data, less than half of the county's coffee trees were cut down with compensation from the eradication program. There does not seem to be any notable correlation between size of landholding and participation in the eradication program. Chácara owners (those with under 5 alqueires) and fazendeiros (those with over 50 alqueires) participated with about the same frequency. There was a difference, however, in method: in general, the *chacrista* with low-yield coffee trees cut them all down, while the fazendeiro chose only his weakest trees for eradication, leaving the rest in production. On small holdings the quality of the coffee varied little because it was usually cultivated on a fairly uniform type of soil, all parts of which were subject to more or less similar weather conditions. On large fazendas, however, especially those over 100 alqueires, soil and weather conditions varied, resulting in considerable differences in the size of the yields.

A little over one-third of those coffee growers interviewed had never cut down any of their trees either on their own or as part of an eradication program. The key factors in participation seem to have been the location of the land, the quality of its soils, and its subjection to frosts. By far the largest number of farmers who eradicated all or part of their coffee have holdings in the Vagalume region, the lowest portion of the county and the one touched by frosts almost annually. In this part of Ouro Verde, those with large and small holdings were involved in the program, most of them reasoning that "coffee has no future here in the Vagalume" (*o café não tem futuro aqui*) because of frequent frosts.

The 1967 eradication program was administered by the Bank of Brazil. A farmer was paid CrN$,50 (about 14 cents) for every tree he agreed to cut down, with the exception of trees which produced no yields; farmers received no compensation for eradicating these. Payments were made in three parts, one-third when the trees were cut down, one-third when the land was cleared and other crops were planted on it, and the final third after the crops were harvested. The eradication contract strictly specified which crops could replace coffee: rice, beans, corn, cotton, manioc, sunflowers, soybeans, castor beans, peanuts, ramie (a type of fiber), and fruit trees. If the farmer preferred, he could replant land in forest. The government agreed to buy all of these crops, although it ordinarily has no dealings with any agricultural products except sugar and coffee. There was a clear stricture that no one participating in the eradication program could plant pasture until at least two harvests of the substitute crops (about two years) had been completed. Although the contracts did not officially expire until December 1968, the government did permit farmers to start planting pasture in April of that year; if they had had to wait until the end of 1968, pasture could not have been sown until April or May of 1969.

Why the government included the clause restricting pasture as part of its eradication program is a debatable point. The local head of the Brazilian Coffee Institute claimed that this was done to create an intermediate stage between an economy based on coffee and one reliant on cattle. If pasture had been planted immediately after coffee was taken out, thousands of people would have been thrown out of work since cattle ranching requires a far smaller labor force than coffee cultivation. If other crops were planted in the interim, the former coffee workers would still have employment, and this period was thought to be long enough for them to adjust to the changeover and find other work. The agronomist for the Associação de Crédito e Assistencia Rural do Paraná, or ACARPA (Rural Paraná Credit and Assistance Association),[9] took issue with this view: he said that the prohibition on pasture was included because the government realized that small landholdings predominated in the eradication area, and that they would be unsuitable for cattle which requires larger tracts of land than coffee. The provision, in other words, sought to insure the continuance of the small farm and avoid the consolidation of land into large cattle ranches.

According to the terms of the eradication contract, the landowner had to either hire *volantes* (day laborers) to plant the new crops or do the work himself. He was not allowed to employ sharecroppers or renters for the interim period; if he were to do this, they would be assuming the expenses of cultivation, and the money paid to the landowner would be used for purposes other than the intended crop diversification. Some farmers have not adhered to this provision and have given out land on a rental or sharecropping basis until they are allowed to plant pasture. They hope that local bank and IBC officials will not discover this, and bribes have made the latter "unaware" of what is going on.

Many farmers readily admitted that they participated in the eradication program because of the money involved. One fazendeiro who cut down 65,000 coffee trees, about 90 per cent of his total, said, "I like the money they [IBC] were paying. My coffee didn't produce very well anyway and now I can plant pasture and have fewer worries." The temptation to eradicate coffee was particularly strong among those with small sítios who were heavily in debt to the banks and *intermediários* (middlemen). In one part of Ouro Verde, a large number of farmers cut down trees which produced fairly adequate yields, and later regretted having done so. In no known case did anyone eradicate trees with very high yields.

One effect of the program was not given prior consideration by its formulators at IBC. Land on which poorly producing coffee

9. A state-financed organization which gives technical assistance to farmers and eventually hopes to supply agricultural credit. See chap. 5.

trees had been cultivated for a number of years clearly had lost much of its fertility, causing the various alternative crops grown on it to give low yields also. A number of farmers were seriously hurt by this; not only did they receive relatively lower prices for these substitute crops than they had for coffee, but the new crops produced poorly, affording them still lower returns.

The final factor in the decline of coffee in Ouro Verde and the surrounding area is one whose importance is most difficult to assess: the continued availability of inexpensive, virgin land on the Paraná frontier. Quite a few of the Ouro Verde farmers also have holdings in the frontier regions, and they often send their grown sons there to cut down the forest and plant the land in coffee. Not infrequently these tracts are given to the sons when they marry; buying land for them in Ouro Verde is out of the question because of its high cost. This practice is particularly common when the holding in Ouro Verde is too small to accommodate more than one family, and married sons must find outside work or purchase land of their own. Successful sharecroppers and renters who manage to save money from the sale of their share of the cotton harvest often use it as down payment on small farms on the frontier.

The largest group in Ouro Verde to move to the frontier are owners of small farms who eradicated all or part of their coffee and planted substitute crops, usually cotton, peanuts, corn, and beans, only to find that the income from them was insufficient to support their families. Those who cut down all of their coffee trees had the greatest difficulties, for it is virtually impossible to live securely for any time solely on the profits from cereal crops grown on small acreages, except in years of unusually large harvests.[10] Since the government guarantees no minimum price for these crops as it does for coffee, these farmers found themselves at the mercy of current supply and demand. In addition, the prices received for these crops, particularly corn, beans, and rice, are infinitely lower than that paid for coffee. Thus, after the end of the required two-year planting period of the IBC contract, many of these farmers sold their holdings to fazendeiros who sought additional land for their growing herds of cattle. The money from the sales was used to purchase small farms on the frontier, and many farmers sold their land for less than the going price because they were anxious to leave Ouro Verde before their situations worsened.

10. Cotton is the exception; the 1967 bumper crop will be discussed in chap. 5.

It is principally through the actions of this group that the decline of coffee in the region can be linked with the availability of frontier land. What would these farmers have done if there were no frontier to which they could migrate and buy land cheaply? Would they have kept their farms in Ouro Verde and continued to eke out a meager existence with mixed cultivation based on coffee, cotton, and subsistence crops, or would they have sold their farms and moved to the cities to find work? One option that many farmers have chosen is to sell their land, buy a truck or jeep with the money they receive, move to town, and work as independent drivers transporting passengers and produce. Presumably if there were no frontier lands within easy access, more farmers would have taken this alternative.

But how has the frontier affected the lowered quality and size of coffee yields? Would farmers have made an additional effort to increase coffee production on their holdings if there were no inexpensive land 100 kilometers away? Would they have employed more modern agricultural techniques from the start in order to preserve their land and make it produce for a longer time? These questions are not wholly answerable; the fact is that the frontier does exist within easy reach of Ouro Verde and has a strong drawing power for many of its inhabitants. The presence of the frontier, combined with the high cost of fertilizers and the difficulty of making frost-damaged crops produce, are better explanations for the decline of coffee in the area than seeking an answer in the so-called anti-technological streak in the Brazilian ethos.

The Emergence of Other Crops

Subsistence crops, particularly corn, beans, and rice, have been intertilled (*intercalado*) between rows of coffee trees since the first settlers arrived in Ouro Verde in 1951. These crops were usually only for family consumption, but occasionally, when yields surpassed family needs, the surplus was sold to the general stores in town and in the rural area of the county. Buyers of *lavoura branca*[11] rarely came from outside the county, for all surplus crops were bought by the nonfood producers in the community. Despite continual cultivation of these crops from the beginning of settlement, Ouro Verde and the surrounding counties never have produced enough of them to meet fully their own requirements, and they

11. The term lavoura branca refers to all crops with the exception of coffee, that is corn, rice, cotton, beans, peanuts, and so on.

have had to import additional quantities from other regions of Paraná. This is especially true of manioc, for only one-fifth of the amount needed is produced within the county.

Lack of sufficient food crops has two principal causes. Unlike owners of small farms, fazendeiros usually do not intertill subsistence crops because of the belief that this practice is detrimental to the coffee trees, so they and their workers must purchase most of their food. Because of the small acreages planted in subsistence

TABLE 8. Lavoura Branca Production in Ouro Verde

Year[a]	Cotton (arrôbas)[b]	Peanuts (kilos)	Castor beans (kilos)	Corn (sacks)[c]	Rice (sacks)	Beans (sacks)
1958–59	17,800	8,000	160,000	88,000	93,500	16,570
1959–60	19,450	8,000	144,000	82,800	79,500	4,320
1960–61	19,780	14,200	383,000	63,300	79,620	8,800
1961–62	18,400	16,400	386,000	63,600	82,000	9,000
1962–63	18,400	24,000	102,000	31,500	24,000	3,000
1963–64	24,000	30,000	128,500	32,100	30,000	3,650
1964–65	26,000	no data	128,000	32,100	30,000	3,750
1965–66	51,000	170,000	90,000	32,000	18,750	12,000
1966–67	100,000	1,560,000	525,000	43,500	13,000	3,450
1967–68	440,000	2,400,000	295,000	51,000	21,600	11,000

Source: IBGE data.

a. There is no separate data for Ouro Verde before 1957 for it was a part of the municípios of Mandaquarí and Nova Esperança. Informants said that during these years only coffee and subsistence crops were grown.

b. One arrôba equals 15 kilos.

c. One sack contains 60 kilos.

crops and the fluctuations in the sizes of their harvests, farmers rarely produce enough to meet the needs of their families throughout the year, to say nothing of the requirements of the nonfood producers.

Although there were always some cash crops aside from coffee cultivated in Ouro Verde, they have increased greatly since 1960 both in total production and in the percentage of land used for them. Peanuts and cotton were grown prior to 1960, but, like corn, beans, and rice, they were almost invariably found between rows of coffee trees, not on separate plots of land (*terra solta*). By 1968, however, about 80 per cent of the county's cotton was planted in tracts apart from coffee and other crops. In the same year, less than half of the county's corn was intertilled with coffee, 35 per cent was cultivated along with other crops, and 20 per cent was on terra solta.

The risks of planting lavoura branca exclusively are at least as great as those of planting coffee. Since the government guarantees price supports, coffee values fluctuate far less than prices of peanuts, cotton, rice, and other free-market crops. Even though coffee prices are now lower than in the past, they rise at least slightly every year, and the farmer can be certain that if he receives CrN$ 18,00 per sack this year, he will be paid two or three *cruzeiros* more for his next harvest. Lavoura branca prices, on the other hand,

TABLE 9. Area Planted in Lavoura Branca in Ouro Verde (in hectares)

Year	Cotton	Peanuts	Castor beans	Corn	Rice	Beans
1957–58	390	4	100	2,400[a]	3,350	1,670
1958–59	220	4	90	1,980	2,850	950
1959–60	223	7	97	1,890	2,853	955
1960–61	220	8	98	2,000	2,953	950
1961–62	280	15	64	1,250	600	300
1962–63	300	30	58	2,100	1,000	800
1963–64	380	50	44	740	375	120
1964–65	380	170	350	1,600	375	170
1965–66	1,500	1,200	350	2,700	500	400
1966–67	1,500	1,300	350	3,000	500	510
1967–68	2,200	2,000	350	3,400	600	550

a. The large areas of rice, corn, and beans planted in 1957–61 were almost entirely intertilled with coffee.

vary greatly from one year to the next, depending on the size of the harvest. Not infrequently, prices fall at the same time that expenses for seed and fertilizer increase. In 1968, Ouro Verde's cotton harvest was the largest in history. Prices were high at the start, but fell sharply a few months later when picking was completed and the large size of the yields was fully realized. This overproduction severely hurt buyers who held their cotton hoping for further price increases.

Aside from price fluctuations, the cash value of lavoura branca, particularly rice, beans, and corn, is far lower than that of coffee. One local farmer said, "Coffee gives us more security than lavoura branca for it almost always produces a little (*O café dá nos mas segurança do que lavoura branca porque sempre dá um pouco*)."

Even though the coffee harvest may be reduced by frosts, it is entirely destroyed only when they are very severe as in 1955 and

1963. With rice and cotton, however, if there is too much sun, half of the harvest may be lost, or if it rains heavily there may be no harvest at all. In 1968, a large part of the rice crop was destroyed because of a drought during a critical period in plant development. Additional rice had to be imported to fulfill the county's consumption requirements. The bean crop also failed that year after a drought, and this crop too had to be purchased outside of Ouro Verde. One sitiante lost nearly his entire crop and had to buy beans in town to meet family needs, but the following year, with the same amount of land planted in beans, his yield was sufficiently large so that he could sell a number of sacks after satisfying the subsistence requirements of his family. Coffee, unlike lavoura branca, is far less sensitive to variations in rainfall and sunlight, and is affected only by real extremes in the weather.

There is disagreement among local residents about the minimum land requirements on which a farmer can support his family if the land is planted solely in lavoura branca. One sitiante said that 5 alqueires cultivated in lavoura branca can support only a small family with at most two children, and then only if weather conditions are favorable. In contrast, he estimates that two average-sized families[12] can live from the proceeds of 5 alqueires planted in fairly high yield coffee trees. Another farmer agreed, adding that 1968 was an exception because of the extremely large cotton harvest which made profitable even small acreages planted in cotton. A third sitiante said he could not concur with these opinions, saying that if he had cut down all his coffee trees and planted lavoura branca instead,"I would have already left here" (*Já tinha saído d'aqui*). The head of the local agricultural post said that a 5-alqueire sítio planted entirely in lavoura branca can support (*dá para vivir*) up to six people, assuming that a large portion of it is planted in cash crops, particularly cotton and peanuts, with beans, rice, and corn grown in small quantities for subsistence purposes. But, he added, the success of this scheme "depends upon the year": "This year cotton produced good results [*deu bom resultado*] but next year even more people will plant it so that its price is sure to fall since the government won't support it."

Farmers with different sized landholdings have adapted in a number of ways to eradication of their coffee. One sitiante grows only cotton on his 8-alqueire farm; he says this crop has been very profitable this year and he plans to continue it. A number of farm-

12. Average-sized nuclear families in Ouro Verde have four or five children.

ers with larger holdings (15 to 20 alqueires) have planted differing proportions of cotton and pasture after their coffee was eradicated. Many sitiantes with less than 10 alqueires cut up to 50 per cent of their coffee trees and replanted with cotton. One of them explained the advantages of this system: "My sítio has 3½ alqueires in lavoura branca and 1½ in pasture and coffee. A farm this small only produces [*só dá*] if it is cultivated in this way. If I had only lavoura branca which 'gives' only in good years and then only just covers expenses, I would be in trouble. So having coffee too gives me more security for it always produces a little."

Every small farm has some subsistence crops, either between rows of coffee trees or interspersed with cotton and other cash crops. The most commonly planted are beans, corn, and rice; some farmers grow manioc and vegetables as well. A few sítios have sugarcane in small quantities, to be used as cattle feed but never sold. Mango, papaya, avocado, and guava trees are found on about 90 per cent of the county's holdings, and until two years ago orange trees were equally common. At that time the state government found citric cancer in a number of trees throughout northern Paraná, and initiated a program to eradicate all citrus trees to combat this highly infectious disease.

Both corn and beans are sold in small quantities when yields are unusually large, but there is ordinarily little profit from them. Beans sold for about CrN$ 6,00 (U.S. $1.88) per 60-kilo sack in 1968, and corn for CrN$ 5,00 (U.S. $1.50) per sack. The price of corn usually increases between harvests, and those who store it for a while can earn higher profits when they sell it. This is impractical for the sitiante and sharecropper, for they usually need the money immediately and cannot wait five or six months until the prices go up.

Rice is the only crop grown on a regular basis for both subsistence and sale. The current price of rice is CrN$ 25,00 (U.S. $7.81) per 40-kilo sack, but this is unusually high due to scarcity caused by a massive crop failure during the last harvest. Rice usually brings about CrN$ 10,00 (U.S. $3.12) per sack. One advantage of rice over coffee is that the crop processors in town will clean and dehull it without charge in return for its waste materials (*palha*) which they keep and resell as mulch.

Second to coffee, cotton is the most widespread and lucrative crop grown in Ouro Verde, and in 1968 the county's yields were among the highest in northern Paraná. Extremely favorable weather conditions were responsible for the success, but such optimal amounts of rainfall and sunlight occur about once every five years and it is unlikely that these high yields will be produced annually. One sitiante claimed that this is why the crop is called *algodão* (cotton in Portuguese), really meaning *algum dão,* that is, "some give or produce." Cotton was cultivated on more land in the county than ever before and the yields per alqueire were extremely high. In an average harvest a farmer takes out about 200 arrôbas per alqueire; in 1968 yields averaged 300 to 350 arrôbas and sometimes reached 400. The average price was CrN$ 6,60 (U.S. $1.94) per arrôba.

During the first year or two that cotton is cultivated on land that has recently been planted in coffee, it does not require fertilizer, so that the farmer's only expenses are for seed and insecticide. By the third year, yields start to decrease unless natural or chemical fertilizer is applied. The head of the agricultural post said,"If we don't get government support for agriculture [price supports for cotton and other crops] we are not going to make enough to live on when we have to start paying for fertilizer for cotton along with seeds and insecticides. The land in this region is very acidic and sooner or later we are going to have to use fertilizers for all our crops." When I inquired why it pays to use fertilizer on coffee but not on cotton or peanuts, he replied that coffee yields increase 30 to 40 per cent after the trees are fertilized, and bring in a far greater income which compensates for the extra expenditure. Although lavoura branca yields increase with the application of fertilizer, prices fluctuate greatly, and it is never certain that the additional expenses will be recouped.

Peanuts have been cultivated in Ouro Verde with increasing frequency since 1961. In the years 1966 and 1967, yields were very large, due to favorable weather conditions. In 1966 prices were high since little land was planted in this crop. In 1968, however, nearly every farmer in the county planted at least a small area in peanuts, resulting in overproduction and a sharp decrease in price. The current price of CrN$ 3,50 (U.S. $1.08) per sack barely covers the costs of cultivation. Like cotton, peanuts may be adversely affected by too much rain, which causes premature flowering with a loss of the entire crop.

The third cash crop cultivated widely throughout Ouro Verde is *mamona* (castor beans) which, like cotton and peanuts, took on great popularity after the eradication of coffee. Although about 50 per cent of the small sítios in the county have a few mamona trees, only two families live solely on the income which these provide. Castor beans are a "strong" crop which tends to draw soil nutriments away from coffee, cotton, and peanuts, so they are never intertilled with coffee trees or planted immediately adjacent to other crops. They are rarely grown on fazendas because of detrimental effects on other cultigens. In addition, since the expenses of planting mamona are small, sharecroppers would not need to be financed by their *patrões* (patrons)[13] and the latter are adverse to losing the interest which they earn from lending money to their workers. Mamona requires neither fertilizer nor insecticide. The yield on an alqueire of land averages about 3,000 kilos of castor beans, and the current price is CrN$,35 (about 10 cents) per kilo.

The Rise of Cattle

Cattle have been found throughout Ouro Verde since settlement began in 1951. Nearly every farmer had one or two cows to supply his family with milk; he kept a small portion of land, usually the lowest part of his holding, planted in pasture. Until 1956 there was only one fazenda in the county which raised cattle for sale. This was an enormous property of over 600 alqueires belonging to an absentee landowner living in the state of São Paulo. The great influx of cattle began in 1956, after the frost of the preceding year, and it has continued up to the present.

There appear to have been three upturns in the number of cattle in the county, each followed by a leveling off. There are no data prior to 1958, but I was told that from 1951 to 1955 the number varied between 1,000 and 1,500, with a notable increase in 1956. From 1959 to 1960 the number of cattle in Ouro Verde more than doubled, from 1963 to 1964 more than tripled, and from 1967 to 1968 increased again by more than one-fourth (see Table 10). The reason for the increase from 1959 to 1960 is not completely clear, but on some of the large fazendas the least productive coffee trees were being replaced with pasture, and many landowners were investing in cattle for the first time. The large increase in cattle in 1964 followed the frost of the preceding year and the subsequent coffee eradication program, and much the same thing occurred in 1967 and 1968. The additional cattle brought into the county in 1967 were found only on those holdings whose owners

13. Fazendeiros frequently have patron-client relationships with their workers (see chap. 6).

The agricultural basis of the county: coffee, corn, and pasture

Corn intertilled with coffee trees

did not participate in the IBC program but cut down their trees independent of it—those taking part in the program could begin to plant pasture only after the prohibiting clause lapsed in April 1968. A large number of farmers told me of their plans to start buying cattle at that time, and presumably the number of head in the county has continued to increase.

The reason for a leveling off or decrease in the number of cattle in the county in some years is that most cattle in Ouro Verde are fattened there and then sold to slaughterhouses (*frigoríficos*) outside the county. Few farmers are involved in cattle breeding and none raises milk cows for profit. For this reason the number of cattle in the county may vary greatly from one week to another, depending on how many are sold to the slaughterhouses. Still, the great increases in number during the periods mentioned clearly point to the importation of cattle into Ouro Verde, and not only to the natural increase of the existing herds.

A look at particular areas in the county makes clearer the continual inroads that cattle have made and the concomitant spread of pasture (see Table 11 and map 6). In 1952–53 when the Vagalume region was first settled, 80 per cent of its land was in coffee, the remaining 20 per cent in virgin forest. The enormous growth of pasture began about six years ago, and, at the same time, lavoura branca, particularly cotton and peanuts, made its first appearance. When an Italian fazendeiro was the first to eradicate all of his coffee under the 1962 program, his neighbors laughed at him and told him he would regret this move. He now boasts of his foresight and notes that his was one of the few holdings in the area that

TABLE 10. Cattle in Ouro Verde

Year	Number
1958	1,600
1959	1,900
1960	4,500
1961	4,300
1962	3,000
1963	4,000
1964	14,800
1965	13,800
1966	14,900
1967	14,650
1968	20,000

Source: Based on data from the local census files of the IBGE.

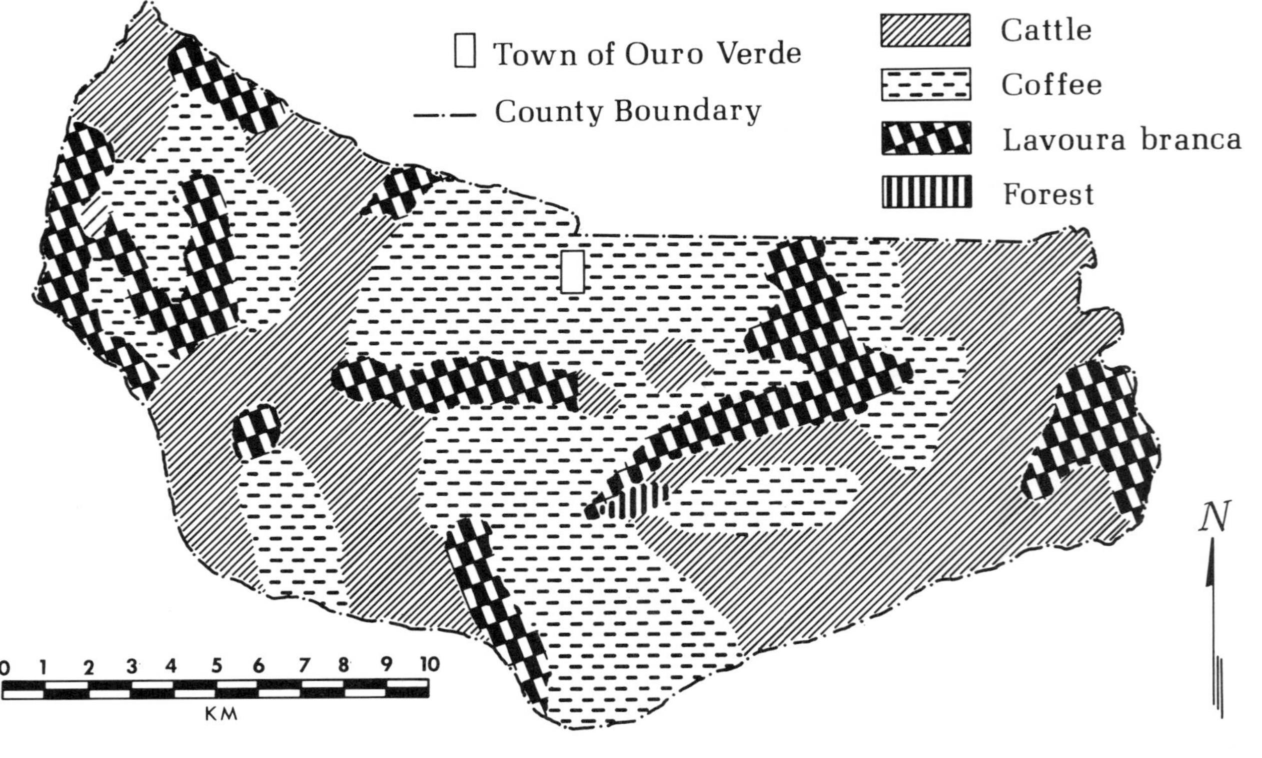

6. Crop regions of Ouro Verde

was little affected by severe frost the following year. Today, approximately 80 per cent of the region is planted in pasture, 15 per cent in cotton, and 5 per cent in coffee. Along the main road through the Vagalume there are now only three sítios that have any coffee trees at all.

The situation in the Vagalume is only an extreme example of a process going on throughout Ouro Verde. In the Santa Maria region a similar change is taking place, although its economic base has not been altered to the same degree since the area is higher and therefore somewhat less affected by frosts. Until 1960, nearly 100

TABLE 11. Land Use in Ouro Verde in 1967

Use on 518 properties[a]	Hectares (alqueires in parentheses)	Percentage of total area under cultivation
Perennial crops (coffee)	8,377 (3,490)	38.5
Temporary crops[b]	3,522 (1,467)	16.0
Pasture	9,775 (4,073)	45.0
Horticulture	103 (43)	.5
Total area under cultivation	21,777 (9,073)	
Forest[c]	1,708 (711)	
Land not utilized[d]	1,753 (730)	

Source: Based on data from the IBGE.

a. Forty properties in Ouro Verde are not included in these data.

b. Includes cotton, peanuts, rice, beans, corn, manioc, and so forth. One estimate I received is that at least half of the land now in lavoura branca will be turned into pasture by 1969 when the IBC contract expires. This would mean another 1,230 alqueires, giving the county a total of 5,303 alqueires of pasture, or nearly 59 per cent of the total land under cultivation.

c. Includes a 200-alqueire reserve belonging to the CMNP.

d. Areas of houses, barns, roads, and so forth.

per cent of Santa Maria's lands were planted in coffee, with only a few scattered patches of pasture and virtually no lavoura branca. By 1967, nearly one-third of the coffee trees had been cut down and replaced with cotton and pasture. At least three local sitiantes with holdings of 6, 8, and 16 alqueires eradicated all of their coffee trees; about 80 per cent eradicated part of them and less than 15 per cent left all of their trees in production. Many of the larger farms now have more than 50 per cent of the land planted in pasture, with the remaining area divided between coffee and lavoura branca. Here also many landowners expressed their intention to plant pasture as soon as the IBC prohibition expired.

The upsurge of cattle ranching in Ouro Verde has occurred in an area highly amenable to this enterprise. The soil in the county and the surrounding region is ideal for it. Unlike coffee, cotton, and other crops, pasture protects the sandy topsoil in terra arenosa and terra mista and does not sap them of their fragile fertility as quickly. Pasture on these soils needs replanting only once every fifteen years or so. The area's climate is as favorable for cattle raising as its soil. Since northern Paraná receives at least some rainfall all year round, pasture lands rarely become as desiccated as farther north and west in the cattle region of Mato Grosso.

The land requirements of cattle depend upon the type of enterprise. If cattle are being *criado*, that is, raised to increase their numbers, an average of eight to ten head can be supported on an alqueire of land of the quality found in Ouro Verde. If they are being fattened (*engordado*) for the slaughterhouse, an alqueire of pasture can support an average of five adult cattle. Both estimates assume that modern techniques of fodder storage are lacking, as, in fact, they are, in the region.

It is difficult to estimate how much land is needed to support an average-sized family whose income is derived solely from the sale of cattle. The minimum requirement appears to be between 30 and 40 alqueires (with 5 head per alqueire) for a family of five or six that wishes to enjoy a moderate standard of living. Since the profit from each head of cattle is approximately CrN$ 40,00 (about U.S. $13) per year, a rancher would need 150 to 200 head to insure himself an annual income of CrN$ 6,000,00 to CrN$ 8,000,00 (U.S. $1,875–$2,200).[14]

Since the majority of farms in Ouro Verde are less than 30 alqueires, there are few that can rely on a livelihood based only on the sale of cattle. Buying additional land is very expensive, an alqueire costing between CrN$ 800,00 and CrN$ 1,200,00, making other alternatives necessary. The most widespread solution to the lack of sufficient grazing land is an annual rental of pasture. Fazendeiros who lack sufficient cattle to fill their large holdings often earn extra income by renting a few alqueires to neighboring sitiantes whose farms are too small to support their herds. There is, for example, a farmer with 10 alqueires of land, 3½ of which are in pasture. He rents another 4½ alqueires on which he grazes some of his 40 head of cattle. The rest of his holding is planted in

14. This income is moderate considering the family has to buy all of its food except meat and milk.

coffee and lavoura branca, and he prefers to rent pasture rather than to eradicate these fairly lucrative crops.

Cattle raising has definite advantages for farmers with regard to the cost of labor. Cattle need only a small fraction of the work force used in coffee and cotton cultivation, and fattening cattle requires fewer workers than cattle breeding. For breeding, a *materneiro* is employed to care for cows during pregnancy and delivery, and an assistant who looks after the other cattle. These two men can care for approximately five hundred head without any difficulty. For fattening cattle, only one man is needed for every five hundred head, as there are not the extra tasks of caring for cows in foal and for newborn calves. Although two men together at all times make work easier, particularly during round-ups, only one is essential. Most *campeiros* (cowhands) have prior experience with cattle branding, vaccinating, and castration, for which two men are always necessary. Aside from these workers, most cattle fazendas employ an administrator (*capataz*) who keeps accounts, directs work, and receives orders from the landowner. This is the total work force needed on even fairly large ranches. For example, a 350-alqueire holding runs smoothly with only six campeiros and an administrator.

Still another advantage of cattle ranching over crop cultivation is that frost and other adverse weather conditions have less serious and less prolonged consequences for cattle than for coffee and lavoura branca. Pasture "burns" when there is a frost, but it regrows quickly and within three months returns to normal. If there is a very severe frost or drought which desiccates pasture land, the cattle will lose an average of 30 kilos per head, but they can easily regain this weight over a six-month period, assuming no further damage to the pasture.

In order to get a clearer picture of the costs and profits involved in coffee, lavoura branca, and cattle enterprises, see Table 12.

There are differences in labor requirements for coffee and lavoura branca and for cattle. One man can care for a maximum of 2 alqueires of coffee with 4,000 trees and perform all the tasks necessary for their upkeep, including weeding, applying insecticide and fertilizer, and cleaning a space under the trees before the harvest. Harvesting requires three men always working together: two strip the beans from the branches and gather them from the ground, while the third separates the beans from the dirt and debris with a round mesh sieve (*peneira*). If picking is uninterrupted by rain,

TABLE 12. AVERAGE ANNUAL RETURNS AND EXPENSES FOR COFFEE, COTTON, CORN, AND CATTLE[a]

Annual yields	Annual expenses	
COFFEE (2,000 trees per alqueire):		
Good harvest, 70 sacks/1,000 trees	Fertilizer (CrN$,125/tree)	CrN$ 250,00
Weak harvest, 30 sacks/1,000 trees	Insecticide (CrN$ 25,00–30,00/1,000 trees)	60,00
Average yield over 2 years, 50 sacks/ 1,000 trees (100/alqueire)	Weeding (5 times, CrN$ 10,00 each)	50,00
	Cleaning and leveling ground before harvest	30,00
Average price per 60-kilo sack (1968), CrN$ 16,00 (CrN$ 1600,00/alqueire)	*Arruação*[b]	40,00
	Repasso[c]	30,00
	Harvesting (CrN$ 2,00/sack)	200,00
Gross intake from 100 sacks, CrN$ 1600,00	Drying, sacking, and transport (CrN$ 1,00/sack)	100,00
	Total expenses for 100 sacks	CrN$ 760,00
Annual net profit from 1 alqueire, CrN$ 840,00 (U.S. $260)		
COTTON (per alqueire):		
Average yield, 200 arrôbas	Clearing land and planting (tractor rental)	CrN$ 120,00
Average price, CrN$ 5,50/arrôba (CrN$ 1320,00/200 arrôbas)	Seed (4 sacks, CrN$ 10,00 each)	40,00
	Insecticide	200,00
	Weeding (4 times, CrN$ 30,00 each)	120,00
Gross intake from 200 arrôbas, CrN$ 1320,00	Harvesting (CrN$ 1,00/arrôba)	200,00
	Total expenses for 200 arrôbas	CrN$ 680,00
Annual net profit from 1 alqueire, CrN$ 520,00 (U.S. $160)		

Intake	Expenses	
CORN (per alqueire):		
Average yield, 8-10 *carros* (100 sacks)	Planting (including tractor rental)	CrN$ 120,00
Average price, CrN$ 5,00/sack (CrN$ 500,00/100 sacks)	Seed	20,00
	Weeding (3 times, CrN$ 30,00 each)	90,00
Gross intake from 100 sacks, CrN$ 500,00	Harvesting	80,00
	Total expenses for 100 sacks	CrN$ 310,00
Annual net profit from 1 alqueire, CrN$ 190,00 (U.S. $46)		
CATTLE (per alqueire; 1 alqueire of pasture supports an average of 5 head)		
Each cow gives an average of 3 liters of milk/day; 15 liters/5 cows, 1,350 liters per 3-month period; average price, CrN$,100/liter (CrN$ 135,00 for 3 months)	Cleaning pasture	CrN$ 50,00
	Milking	200,00
	Salt for cattle	10,00
Each cow averages 1 calf a year; about 20 per cent die, leaving 4 calves/alqueire; each calf is sold for an average of CrN$ 120,00 (CrN$ 480,00 for the 4)	Vaccine for cattle	10,00
	Medicine for cattle	10,00
	Total expenses for 5 head[d]	CrN$ 280,00
Gross intake per year:		
From milk, CrN$ 540,00		
From calves, CrN$ 480,00		
Total gross intake, CrN$ 1020,00		
Annual net profit on 1 alqueire of pasture with 5 head, CrN$ 140,00 (U.S. $231)		

a. The estimates in this table are derived from information supplied by a number of informants and by cross-checking their prices and figures with the local agronomist and with the agricultural supply stores.

b. Building mounds of excess dirt and debris along rows of coffee trees.

c. Culling coffee beans after the harvest as a prophylactic measure against broca.

d. This does not include the purchase price of cattle, which averages CrN$ 300,00–500,00 per head.

three men working in this way can pick 100 sacks of coffee, the average yield per alqueire, in a month. One man can average about 30 sacks for the same period of time, but this is rarely done, for the work is easier with a team. Since one man can care for 2 alqueires of coffee throughout most of the year, but three men are needed for an alqueire during the harvest, labor requirements for the latter period, June through August, increase sixfold.

Cotton requires more manpower than coffee does. One man can plant and care for up to 1½ alqueires of cotton. About four workers per alqueire are necessary during the harvest which must be completed within eight days after the plant matures. If a longer time elapses and it rains in the interim, the cotton turns yellow and decreases in value. Like cotton, 2 alqueires of peanuts require the services of one man, but again additional workers are needed for the harvest. Here, too, the harvest must be completed in a short time (15 days) after the crop ripens to avoid rain damage.

Castor beans, another important cash crop in Ouro Verde, require little labor except during harvest. One man can easily care for up to 4 alqueires planted in castor beans, but during the harvest more workers per alqueire are needed than for any other crop. Picking the beans is a simple task, but afterwards they are transferred to a drying terrace (*terreiro*) where they must be moved about continually until their outer shells fall off.

Corn, beans, and rice do not have heavy labor requirements either during the year or for the harvest. One person can plant and care for up to 3 alqueires of any one of these crops, and can harvest them alone. For beans and rice, however, another worker normally has the task of separating them from the plant proper soon after they are harvested.

As noted, the manpower needs in cattle raising are low, with a maximum of two men necessary to work with up to 500 head of cattle, a labor force averaging out to only two men for every 50 alqueires of pasture. Milking similarly necessitates few hands. One man working approximately four hours a day can milk 40 cows giving 150 to 200 liters of milk.

The Effects of the Changeover

The consequences of the changeover from coffee to cattle are numerous and interrelated. Although the process gained momentum only five or six years ago, clear-cut patterns of change are already apparent. For example, in those parts of Ouro Verde most subject to frosts, coffee has been almost eliminated. The consolidation of small farms into large cattle fazendas is most extensive in those same areas, and has caused unemployment and population decline. Some work systems, particularly those associated with coffee, have been nearly abandoned, to be replaced by those more in keeping with an economic regime based on cattle raising. The rural general stores in those areas have been hard hit by these changes; unemployment and population decline have inevitably cut into volume of sales. This alteration in economic base is taking place throughout the county to a greater or lesser degree, and it has directly affected the townspeople in a number of ways which will be discussed in the next chapter.

The most immediate result of the growing importance of cattle has been the purchase of small sítios by fazendeiros seeking sufficient pasture to accommodate their growing herds of cattle. As noted, there are minimum land requirements for securing an adequate income solely from cattle ranching; for this reason most sitiantes are unable to participate in this enterprise. It involves far more capital than coffee cultivation does, for the purchase of both breeding stock and additional land.

An example of the most extreme case of the trend toward larger holdings is Fazenda São João in the Vagalume, a tract of over 600 alqueires owned by a businessman living in the state of São Paulo. He bought three 100-alqueire fazendas from the CMNP in the early 1950s when land prices were still low. Between 1956 and 1966, he purchased more than 25 sítios, ranging in size from 5 to 25 alqueires. The bulk of these were bought in 1955 and 1963, immediately after the frosts of those years when farmers were anxious to sell out and move to the frontier. The jagged boundaries of the huge tract which resulted attest to the piecemeal manner in which it was acquired. In the same region a 300-alqueire fazenda was formed by similar means, with the absentee landowner buying a total of fifteen sítios and consolidating them with his original 100-alqueire tract. These two large holdings still employ a considerable number of workers since they have not completely eradicated their coffee trees, but a third fazenda, which covers 450 alqueires, is entirely planted in pasture and employs seven campeiros and an administrator. This fazenda displays clearly the headlong rush to plant pasture. Dead, leafless coffee trees stand in rows partially hidden by tall clumps of grass, and cattle can be seen grazing among these relics of the past. The owner did not participate in the eradication program but simply abandoned his coffee trees while pasture was planted around them.

Until six or seven years, ago the Vagalume region was one of mixed sítios and fazendas, but today fazenda-sized holdings of over 50 alqueires predominate. In addition to these cases, there are a large number of landowners who increased their acreages by purchasing small farms. Most of them originally owned large tracts, usually over 50 alqueires, although there are two sitiantes who started out with only 5 alqueires each and now own holdings of 25 and 30 alqueires, made up of small holdings purchased over a period of years. At present, the few small sítios that are left are sandwiched between vast expanses of pasture.

The second region in Ouro Verde that has had much land consolidation is the Estrada Funda, the road in the south of the county which leads to Nova Esperança. Over the last five years about 20 per cent of the area's sítios have been sold to fazendeiros who are forming large cattle ranches. Again, there are few cases in which one sitiante bought out another. Holdings of 5 and 10 alqueires are the ones most frequently sold. One landowner with 20 alqueires bought a neighboring fazenda of 50 alqueires and three or four other properties for a total of about 200 alqueires. A merchant living in Nova Esperança bought five sítios totaling 70 alqueires, and is still seeking additional land. All of these newly formed fazendas are planted in pasture, but this soon after the changeover, they have few cattle. One resident said that when he arrived in Ouro Verde six years ago, the Estrada Funda region was entirely planted in coffee. He listed twenty holdings which at that time were completely planted in coffee, but today are covered with pasture: "When I came here there wasn't one head of cattle and it was difficult to buy milk, but a few people kept a cow or two for this purpose. Now my sítio is completely surrounded by pasture. The cattle ate my neighbor's whole corn crop for the fence which the fazendeiro built isn't very strong and the cattle easily break it if they are hungry enough. What is the poor man [*o coitado*] with 5 alqueires to do in the middle of all these fazendas? He is obliged to sell out."

North from the Estrada Funda is the Estrada Ouro Verde, where most of the county's Japanese population lives. Here too land consolidation is extensive, although it has taken place more slowly than in the two regions cited. One farmer estimated that as much as 60 per cent of the coffee trees in this part of the county have been eradicated. Five years ago when he settled in the area, sítios of 5 and 10 alqueires predominated, and although there are still a few of the latter, all of the 5-alqueire farms have been sold and are now part of large fazendas. The few remaining sitiantes are anxious to sell out, and there is no lack of buyers. Of the original settlers along the Estrada Ouro Verde who bought land from the CMNP in the early 1950s, only two remain. A few have gone to São Paulo; the majority have either moved to town or bought farms on the Paraná frontier.

Even in the neighborhood of Santa Maria, where land consolidation has just begun, there are already a number of sitiantes planting their farms in pasture which the intention of selling them to fazendeiros who are forming cattle ranches. In 1968 alone, six sítios of 5 to 10 alqueires were sold because *"êles não dão para a família comer"* (they don't even produce enough to feed a family). Unlike the other areas discussed, most of the holdings up for sale in Santa Maria are being purchased by sitiantes with small farms in other parts of the município. The difference is that in Santa Maria coffee cultivation can still be a profitable enterprise because the area is less subject to frosts than the rest of the county. Still, only time and the weather will tell how long small holdings will continue to be viable there.

A former mayor of Ouro Verde noted the increasing rate with which large holdings are being formed: "The *minífundia* is going to disappear in our region. The absentee landowners with fazendas in Ouro Verde always want to buy up more land. The *tubarão* [shark or big-time operator] always swallows up the small fish."

One recent law which has sped up the process of land consolidation makes the purchase of a holding of 10 alqueires or less illegal unless it is made by the owner of an adjacent sítio or fazenda. The law was passed to cut down on the vast amount of paper work and legal expenses involved in transferring land titles from one owner to another. With sales of tracts of 10 alqueires or less, the state and municipal governments are unwilling to handle all the paper work, since the taxes collected from them hardly compensate for the time and bother.

Another result of the growing importance of cattle in Ouro Verde and the concomitant consolidation of land has been increasing unemployment. Its extent is difficult to ascertain. Many of the unemployed do not remain in the county long but move to other areas of Paraná in search of work. In addition, there are peak periods of unemployment, such as the end of August after the coffee harvest has been completed and there is little work to be had. The mayor of Ouro Verde estimated that as much as 30 per cent of the county's labor force is unemployed in September, but there are no precise data available on this. Perhaps the time of highest unemployment is November through January. This is the "dead season" when the harvests are completed, the crops have been processed, and the municipal government receives little money from the state for construction projects for which it could hire some of the unemployed. It is at this time of year that many families leave Ouro Verde in search of work.

The unemployed fall into three categories: the independent carpenters, masons, bricklayers, and builders in town; the resident day laborers and piece workers in town and in the rural area; and the migrant workers who come to Ouro Verde for the harvest. The first group may be more accurately termed underemployed since they usually have some work but not enough. They are very indirectly affected by the agricultural changes taking place in the county, so will be dealt with in the chapter on town life.

Many of the resident unemployed live in town. They sometimes remain there for months, not traveling to a neighboring county, in search of work since the same situation exists there. For some, even the expenses of moving to the frontier are too high, and, in any event, there is more security in Ouro Verde where friends and relatives can help out in times of great need. When asked why there was such a high rate of unemployment in town, one resident replied, "It's because of the lack of money in agriculture. The town depends upon the *lavoura* [farming]. It is our only wellspring [*fonte*]. People rent houses in town hoping that the mayor will find work for them, but most of them are still waiting. The mayor sometimes arranges a job requiring ten men, and 40 or 50 show up. The best of them are chosen." The resident unemployed wait for the harvests to begin, trying to find temporary work until then. From the end of January until late August they are occupied with harvesting peanuts (January), cotton (February to April), and coffee (June through August). When the harvests are completed, many return to town in search of work. Some are employed in road construction and repair, in cleaning the city hall and jail, and, recently, in building the new bus station. Still, there is not sufficient work for everyone. Some go door to door and find temporary jobs weeding, clearing land, and building fences, but then they may be unable to secure work for a month. Their wives take in washing to earn extra money. Commonly the entire family is involved in *catando café* for one of the coffee processors. This is the tedious task of separating the beans by hand according to their quality. A family can earn CrN$ 2,00 (about U.S. 70¢) per 60-kilo sack for doing this work, which takes five people an average of two days to complete. This is a particularly popular way of earning extra cash since small children as well as adults can take part. Many of the unemployed are given the use of small unoccupied urban plots (datas) on which they are allowed to cultivate subsistence crops. These plots still belong to the CMNP, but, until the land is sold, municipal officials allow them to be used for this purpose. Only short-term crops can be grown since they may have to be abandoned on short notice.

Housing presents a problem for the unemployed, and sometimes three or four families share accommodations. The municipal government owns four ramshackle houses, in various stages of disrepair, which are loaned rent free to indigent families in town, and the Catholic church also provides free housing for a few of the very poor. Still, many remain homeless, particularly the migrant workers who come to Ouro Verde for the harvests and have nowhere to go after they are completed. At peak periods of unemployment, whole families can be seen taking temporary shelter among the coffee groves in the rural area. During the harvest, housing is not a problem since workers generally live in small wooden shacks on the property where they are employed. Workers with families may have more difficulty, for many landowners only have dormitory accomodations for unmarried men, and will not hire men with wives and children.

In addition to the more or less permanent residents of Ouro Verde who are unemployed at various times of the year, dozens of families arrive at the bus station seeking work during the harvest. Most of them come from Maringá, which is still the central distribution point for labor in the region. Immediately before the coffee harvest begins in June, up to 300 or 400 people a day arrive in Maringá, many of them recent emigrés from the Northeast, but the majority coming from São Paulo and Minas Gerais. As soon as they get to Ouro Verde the mayor advises the local sitiantes and fazendeiros that there are people in town looking for work, and those who need additional hands for the harvest choose the number required from the available labor pool. Those workers who are unable to find jobs in Ouro Verde move on to neighboring counties.

Most of the migrant laborers either are unmarried or have left their families at home. They come to Paraná specifically for the harvest and usually return to their communities soon after it is completed. Those with wives and children with them tend to stay longer, especially if they have relatives in the county. They may even become semipermanent residents, swelling the existing ranks of unemployed.

Since 1963, the number of unemployed in Ouro Verde and the surrounding counties has steadily increased. Not long ago some of the local radio stations advertised job openings in the region, but today the station in Maringá asks prospective employers to come to the city and hire workers from among the recent arrivals there. Undoubtedly, one factor in the growing scarcity of jobs is the mechanization of some of the larger landholdings. The use of plows and tractors is more widespread than in the past, although the latter are still limited to a few of the largest fazendas. With increased mechanization fewer men are needed to do a set amount of work. But by far the most important factor in growing unemployment is the changeover from coffee to cattle. One of my informants said, "The coffee lands once tilled by men are now occupied by cattle. Fazendas that had 200 families now have five. This was our ruin. The unemployed have no future. They don't know where to go next."

With few exceptions, all those I spoke to in Ouro Verde noted the growing number of unemployed. A man who owns a small bar at the bus station said that not a day goes by when people do not arrive by bus or on foot looking for work. One sitiante claims that in one week's time fifteen families asked him if he had any job for them. Sometimes as many as three families a day came to his farm seeking work, and he believes that this is because word got around that he recently purchased his 7-alqueire holding. Another farmer estimated that 90 per cent of the volantes in his part of the county were without steady work: "They come and go, spending at most a few days in one place." Most of them find short-term employment on the sítios, planting, weeding, and harvesting, but fazendeiros are more reluctant to hire them, preferring instead to rely on permanent resident workers who are paid by the month (*mensalistas*). In the Vagalume only about 5 per cent of the men who came to harvest cotton in February were still there in May. Most of them left the area as soon as the harvest was over, and went to look for work in regions where coffee is still grown. The few that remained secured jobs on cattle fazendas, so that in this particular part of the county unemployment does not seem to be a problem. This is probably because the area long ago converted from coffee to cattle and the hundreds of families without work have moved away.

Attitudes toward the unemployed ranged from sympathy to disdain. One of the few people who denied that the problem existed at all was the current mayor of Ouro Verde: "The unemployed? They are only those who never work. They prefer to wander. Jobs exist for all those who want them." One sitiante remarked that "as soon as cattle increase in number, the hunger of the people also increases" (*quando aumenta o gado, também aumenta a fome do povo*). He said that many who come to his farm seeking work are badly in need of medical attention, and they are often "dropping from hunger" (*caindo de fome*), so much so that they are too weak to work. It is common for these migrant laborers to walk 8 to 10 kilometers a day along the county's roads, stopping at every farm to inquire about jobs.

Both volantes and sitiantes expressed anger at the fact that, as soon as pasture is planted, landowners dismantle the dwellings which housed their workers. On one of the largest holdings in the county, over a hundred houses were burned down when the shift from coffee to cattle had been completed. On smaller fazendas sometimes ten, twenty, or thirty houses were dismantled, or simply locked so that workers could not gain access to them. Some landowners will not formally dismiss their volantes; instead they are not given any work so that they will be forced to leave of their own free will. This practice avoids any potential difficulties with the *promotor público* (labor investigator) in Nova Esperança should the workers make a complaint to him about their dismissal. One migrant worker summed up the feelings of many: "There is so much land here and the people have nothing. There are many rich men with wasted lands who won't allow us to plant even a bit of rice. But things are going to get worse once there is more pasture, and many people are going to die of hunger."

If we note the situation on individual sítios and fazendas in Ouro Verde, it will be easier to understand why unemployment has become such a problem. On Fazenda Santa Clara, a 100-alqueire tract in the Vagalume, there are now three families where there once were twelve. Fazenda Primavera which is entirely in pasture employed forty families five years ago and now has eight. Fazenda

Jequiá in the same region has one campeiro to oversee its herds, whereas twenty families worked there when the holding was planted in coffee. Fazenda São José, the largest in the county, employed up to two hundred families eight years ago, but since its changeover to cattle only eight workers care for this huge holding. In the Estrada Funda area one landowner with 65 alqueires has contracts with five sharecroppers and a mensalista, but plans to dismiss all of the sharecropping families this year when the conversion to pasture has been completed.

The situation has not yet reached the extreme which may result if the process of change continues. Volantes are still being hired to plant pasture and build fences, but these too will disappear once the changeover is completed. There are still a number of renters and sharecroppers cultivating peanuts and cotton, but many of them will be unemployed as soon as all of the eradication contracts expire and pasture is planted. Clearly, it is not just migrant and resident day laborers who find themselves without work, but sharecroppers as well. Some sharecroppers have found other positions in Ouro Verde, but the majority have moved to the frontier, hoping to sharecrop coffee there.

Largely as a result of unemployment, the population of the county has declined. According to the most recent data available, there were 10,500 inhabitants in Ouro Verde in November 1967, with 1,200 in town and 9,300 in the rural area. In 1965 the county's population totaled 11,000 with 800 in town, and in 1962–63 Ouro Verde's population reached 12,500, the largest it has ever been. These statistics are incomplete, for migrant laborers are not included in the census since they are not permanent residents. If they were counted, the population would have shown an even greater decline, for every year fewer come to the county seeking work during the harvests.

The unemployment and subsequent migration of volantes and sharecroppers do not account for the total decrease; many sitiantes left the county after selling their properties. On one back road, six sítios were sold in 1968. Their owners had participated in the eradication program, but found that they could not live on the income from lavoura branca alone. The rise in the town's population is entirely due to the fact that some of these farmers moved there after they sold their land. They bought jeeps and trucks and became motoristas in hope of making a better living than they had on their farms. In one area of the county, Santa Maria, about half

of the sitiantes who sold their farms took up residence in town, while the other half purchased land on the frontier. This migration to town largely explains why nearly a hundred additional houses have been built there over the last three years.

The actual extent of population decline has varied throughout the county depending on the degree to which coffee land has been planted in pasture. As expected, Vagalume has shown the greatest population loss, decreasing by 50 to 60 per cent in the last six years. In the first phase of depopulation, sitiantes sold out after their coffee froze in 1963. The second phase, which accounts for a far greater loss, was the exodus of coffee colonos and sharecroppers as pasture land made greater inroads on coffee. Finally, volantes who had cultivated coffee on the large fazendas found themselves with fewer tasks as their patrões bought more cattle, and they too began to leave the region. Before 1963, there were six rural schools in the Vagalume, some filled with workers' children from a single large fazenda. Today there are two schools, the others closed by the county for lack of pupils. The few children living on cattle ranches far from town now have to travel up to eight kilometers to school, since there are no longer any in the immediate vicinity.

Modifications in labor arrangements are another result of the shift from coffee to cattle in Ouro Verde. Those systems most frequently associated with coffee cultivation, colono labor and sharecropping, have been decreasing, while those linked with lavoura branca cultivation and cattle raising have become more common.

There were never very many colonos in Ouro Verde, that is, workers who are paid a fixed monthly salary for taking care of a given number of coffee trees. Today, with a single exception, the colono system has disappeared from the county. Until about 1960, some of the larger coffee fazendas employed colonos, but they gradually were replaced by volantes who are paid by the day or by the task. The colono system fell into disfavor because the labor laws protecting workers with colono contracts are far stricter and more comprehensive than those covering day laborers. Until 1961, the owner of Fazenda Timbó, a large holding on the Estrada Funda, employed twenty families of colonos to care for his coffee trees. When the property was sold, the new owner didn't want "to be bothered" with transferring the colonos' contracts into his name, so he simply replaced them with volantes. As pasture became more prevalent in the county, the few remaining colonos lost their positions, and either turned to sharecropping lavoura branca or left.

Sharecroppers have always been more common in Ouro Verde than colonos, and they still are today. But their numbers have continually decreased over the last five years as cattle ranching became widespread. Although few fazendeiros employed sharecroppers, many sitiantes who lacked sufficient family labor contracted one or two to help care for their coffee trees. As yields declined and trees were cut down, less outside assistance was needed, and many farmers failed to renew their sharecroppers' contracts. On a few fazendas which still have small areas planted in coffee, one or two sharecroppers may be employed. Fazenda São Luis, a 120-alqueire tract, has two sharecropping families who care for its few remaining alqueires of coffee and two campeiros who oversee its herds. When there were more coffee trees, the owner hired volantes, but he now prefers permanent resident workers who require less "supervision" and simply hand over half of the coffee crop to him after it has been harvested.

As sharecropping has declined in importance, land rental has increased. Coffee land is never rented out since rental contracts are usually for one year, and coffee, a perennial, takes four years to produce its first harvest. Therefore, when the county was entirely planted in coffee trees, the renting of land was virtually nonexistent. As plantings of lavoura branca, particularly cotton and peanuts, became more extensive, renting became more common since these crops are annuals and can be sewn and harvested within the span of a one-year contract. Lavoura branca is also sharecropped, but most agricultural workers prefer to cultivate it on a rental basis; compared to coffee its value is low, and they are loath to give the landowner 20 to 30 per cent of the harvest. If land is rented, they know in advance that a specific amount per alqueire will be paid no matter what the size of the harvest. In addition, sharecropping contracts are usually for two-year periods, rentals for one year. Those fazendeiros and sitiantes delegating land to fulfill the eradication contract's requirements of planting lavoura branca prefer to rent it out than to have it sharecropped, for when the contract terminates they intend to plant pasture right away, and do not want to be entangled in long-term sharecropping agreements. A new condition recently added to many rental contracts is that renters plant pasture as soon as their crops have been harvested, thus preparing the land for the immediate entrance of cattle.

Sharecropping is still common in those areas of the county where coffee has been retained, particularly on the small farms adjacent to town. Rentals prevail on larger holdings which are in the interim phase set out in the eradication contracts; coffee trees have been cut down, but cattle have not yet been introduced. About 95 per cent of the Vagalume's inhabitants who do not own land are renters cultivating peanuts and cotton; the rest sharecrop these and coffee.

The number of day laborers has also declined, although they are still employed during harvests. Volantes are still hired to perform such labor-intensive tasks as planting and weeding pasture and building fences on cattle fazendas. In the past, jobs requiring many men were often done by work gangs (peões) under a labor contractor (*empreiteiro* or, colloquially, "gato"). They were employed to harvest the coffee crop when yields were substantial and many hands were needed for a short time. Now, with declining yields and fewer trees, peões are not necessary, since harvests can be handled by a few day laborers. Today there is only one empreiteiro in Ouro Verde, and he is frequently away from the county for weeks at a time, under contract to oversee work in the frontier region of northern Paraná.

The other form of labor more frequently used since the changeover is that which is paid for on a monthly basis. Virtually all of the cattle hands and fazenda administrators in the county earn fixed monthly salaries. Before cattle ranching gained prominence, only coffee colonos were paid by the month, all other workers receiving compensation in kind (sharecroppers), or by the day, hour, or task (volantes). One fazendeiro said that he expected many landowners to start paying their campeiros by the day or the task; this form of labor is not covered by comprehensive labor laws, as is that paid for by the month.

Of all the nonagriculturalists in Ouro Verde, those owning rural general stores (*armazens*) have been most affected by the changeover from coffee to cattle. A store's location in the county has been important in determining to what degree its sales declined as cattle and pasture became more common. In Vila Franki, a hamlet six kilometers northwest of town, there were ten general stores in 1963, but today only four. One store owner said that his sales decreased considerably after the 1963 frost when the first coffee eradication program got underway, and they have continued to fall every year since. He estimated that, from 1963 to the present, his volume of business declined by at least 50 per cent, while the costs of stocking and running the store increased. He noted that people are not buying less, but that there are fewer customers because of the exodus of a large part of the local population. Another armazem owner in the same region said that his sales are down about 30 per cent from five years ago, but he believes that part of the reason is that sitiantes and sharecroppers are purchasing less simply because they have less money.

Both owners with whom I spoke in January 1968 expected business to pick up the following month when the peanut harvest began; farmers and sharcroppers would have more spending money from the sale of the crop, and day laborers from wages. One added, however, that the increase would last only three months; sales would fall off in May, remaining low until the coffee harvest started in June. The slowest months for these shopkeepers are October through January when all the crops have been harvested and there is little work. One said that his sales were about 40 per cent higher in March than in October. Since neither man will extend credit to day laborers ("It is easier to give them things free for they can never pay up"), the loss of business during the "dead season" is a major factor in the decline of sales. Both said they prefer to extend credit to sharecroppers and farmers who cultivate coffee rather than lavoura branca, for the possibility of total crop failure is greater among the latter, making them poorer credit risks.

A store owner whose armazem is located at a crossroads in the Santa Maria region of the county has also been affected by the decline of coffee. Since 1963, sales have decreased even though much of the area is still planted in lavoura branca: "With coffee you can make money, but cereal crops usually just cover expenses. They don't produce 'movimento' in my store." Since there is a great deal of cotton in Santa Maria and yields in 1968 were particularly large, business increased greatly during the harvest in April and May, surpassing even the increase produced by the coffee harvest the following month. During the slack season, from November through February, this man closes his store in the mornings and works on his farm. He fondly recalls the movimento in his store in 1960 and 1966 when the coffee harvests were unusually large, but adds that he almost had to close in 1964–65 after the trees froze and business came to a near standstill.

A shopkeeper in the Vagalume, who has lived there since the region first opened in 1952, said that, for the first decade, his sales remained fairly steady, only falling off four or five years ago; his business is now down by 60 per cent from its pre–1963 level. Before then he needed three clerks to wait on his customers, but now he employs only one who remains idle most of the time for lack of business. He also owned a neighboring store which sold cloth (*tecidos*) and dry goods, but he closed it in 1964 when sales fell off sharply. Unlike other areas of the county, business in the Vagalume does not increase during the coffee harvest in June; the small number of remaining trees require few additional workers for the harvest, and little money comes into the area from the sale of this crop. Sales are up by 40 to 50 per cent from February to April during the peanut and cotton harvest, but this will probably no longer happen once the eradication contracts expire and the land now planted in lavoura branca is turned into pasture. This store owner says that he will probably sell out before this occurs, to try to avoid ruin.

What have been local reactions to Ouro Verde's rapid change in economic base? Very few are pleased, while the vast majority view the increase of pasture and cattle with decided alarm. Pessimism concerning the county's future is widespread. One farmer commented, "The future here is only more cattle, more pasture, and less coffee. Coffee can't last much longer because of the droughts and frosts and it costs too much to use fertilizer. You can already see what has happened in the Vagalume . . . houses abandoned, few people, no movimento. Within five years 90 per cent of the county will be like this. This is our only possible future." The owner of a small hotel in town said, "There was so much movimento here when we first came in 1954; so much coffee, so much activity. We never had a vacant room in the hotel. Now that is all in the past because of cattle. This place won't progress anymore [*não vai mais para frente*]." The company's agronomist noted the economic and social development that coffee had brought to northern Paraná, and he rued its demise: "Now we have schools and health services, but these things are going to waste as more and more people who can't find work leave the area. Socially speaking, the depopulation of the rural zone because of the introduction of cattle is a horrible thing."

One fazendeiro had a more hopeful outlook. He thought it was a good thing that other frontier areas would now reap the benefits of coffee cultivation that northern Paraná has already had: "Why was Londrina built? Coffee. Why was Maringá built? Coffee. Why were the roads, hospitals, and schools of northern Paraná built? Coffee. If it weren't for coffee this would still be a virgin forest. The government wants to spread this development to other areas of the country so they are encouraging coffee cultivation in Pará and Mato Grosso. It only seems fair. We have already benefited so much by it here." A farmer mentioned the added amount of work now needed to make the land produce: "When the land was first planted weeding was the only job that had to be done. Now to get the land to produce the farmer must treat it like a small child [*nem como uma criança pequena*]. For unless he gives it special care, always using fertilizer and insecticide, there will be no harvest." My main informant, Seu Laurenço, a retired sitiante, blamed the frosts for the extra expenses and work now involved in coffee cultivation: "Each time it freezes a little you must use fertilizer and prune the trees. But it's simply not worth it anymore. It is better to plant 1,000 trees on new land where it doesn't freeze and you can harvest 200 sacks, than to have 10,000 trees here, which will produce the same 200 sacks." The problems of frosts and low prices are a constant refrain: "This place is castigated [*castigada*] by the frosts. They ruined this whole region and created unemployment." But a fazendeiro took a different view: "The reason we have cattle now is the low price which the government was paying us for our coffee. When the farmer was allowed to sell his crop directly to the exporter without the government intervening, he made money. Now we earn nothing."

A few residents are more optimistic about the future of Ouro Verde and coffee's role in it. The current mayor, although not noted for the accuracy of his information on the county, said, "As you know where cattle enter, man exits. Still, coffee will survive here. The trees which we now have produce well, and the worst ones have already been cut down. I don't think that Ouro Verde will ever have more than half of its land planted in pasture." Still, he admitted, things had been better in the past: "Coffee used to be everywhere in Ouro Verde, even up to the doors of the houses. Then men depended only on coffee, but after the two big frosts they decided they had to diversify. Now the sitiante has his pig, his chickens, and his lavoura branca. This is all he needs to live."

Despite all the problems and hardships that local farmers and sharecroppers have had with coffee, they still firmly believe in its ultimate value, and almost invariably say they would plant it again if the land were fertile. A local agronomist emphasized this point: "Coffee is Brazil's greatest wealth. Commercial enterprises don't give as much profit as good coffee trees do. Productive trees enrich not only the landowner, but also his sharecroppers and day laborers who can earn a lot in the harvest. With good trees you can get credit in the bank. They are as good as cash. But with lavoura branca, no. It is too risky. Only coffee gives real security." And from the local bank manager: "There is no other crop that can give the farmer profits like coffee does. But coffee involves risk. Planting it is like a man who rides a bicycle. He goes and goes and goes, but then can go no farther. The bicycle falls and he along with it. So it is with coffee cultivation."

4. The Role of the Town in an Agricultural Economy

THE ECONOMIC life and health of the town are heavily dependent upon the agricultural enterprises in the rural zone of the county. There are three fairly distinct aspects to this relationship. The town is the residence of many people who earn their livelihood in agriculture: in a house-to-house census which covered about 90 per cent of the town's inhabitants, close to one-third of the household heads were employed in agriculture, as sítio and chácara owners, sharecroppers, renters, or day laborers. The largest businesses in town are those that deal in the processing of crops: there are two coffee processors who employ up to 20 workers each during the harvest, and a number of smaller enterprises which process rice and peanuts. The third link is the fact that over 50 per cent of the sales in the local shops, general stores, fruit stands, bars, and so on are made to rural residents who come to town once or twice a week to make their purchases. Since the population of the rural area (8,500) is far larger than that of the town (2,129), the heavy reliance on rural customers is readily apparent.

Aside from town residents directly involved in agriculture, there are also many store owners and merchants whose income is at least indirectly dependent upon the state of the county's agriculture.

Depopulation and unemployment have had adverse effects on the rural general stores and similar consequences in town. In addition to shopkeepers, many motoristas (drivers) are influenced by the rural agricultural economy. Since a large part of their business is transporting crops from local farms to town and neighboring counties, small harvests and crop failures cut severely the size and number of jobs for which they can contract. A final group of town residents whose well-being is partly related to agriculture are the *serventes,* irregularly employed handymen who work on the county's roads, in the town hall, or in construction, doing all manner of odd jobs. These men, whose income throughout the year is uncertain, take advantage of the money to be earned in the cotton, peanut, and coffee harvests from February through August. But when the harvests are small and require few hands, serventes lose an important source of income. Actually, the only town residents unaffected by agricultural changes are white-collar workers in the bank and town hall, schoolteachers, store employees, and self-employed carpenters, bricklayers, builders, and artisans. Even those in the last group sometimes find that business falls off during years of poor harvests when people simply do not have the money to pay for their services.

At one time there were three coffee-processing machines in Ouro Verde, but one closed down five years ago for lack of business. Of the remaining, one changed hands, because, as its former owner stated, "It just didn't provide me with a profit any more." This plant has the capacity to sort and hull (*beneficiar*) up to 1,500 sacks of coffee beans a day, but in 1967 it processed a total of 20,000 sacks and was in operation only two months. In 1965, in contrast, 60,000 sacks were cleaned and hulled and the machine was in operation for half the year. The other plant has a somewhat larger capacity and is financially more sound because it is owned by a large coffee export firm based in Santos. The company also owns a coffee-processing plant of similar size in the nearby county of Santa Maria, as well as a large coffee and cattle fazenda in Ouro Verde. During the 1966–67 harvest, the Ouro Verde facilities processed 48,000 sacks of coffee, although the year before only 15,000 sacks were cleaned due to the high incidence of broca in the county at that time. This plant also processes peanuts in February, but remains idle during the six months of the year no crops are harvested.

Between 60 and 70 per cent of the coffee processed by these two firms is grown in Ouro Verde, the rest coming from neighboring

Weighing coffee before it is brought to the processing plant

Hulling and sorting coffee beans at a local processing plant

counties. A law passed under the Castelo Branco regime[1] has encouraged farmers to have their coffee processed by companies in their own counties to aid municipal development by keeping local income within the community. If the coffee is sent to another county for cleaning and hulling, a 15 per cent tax (*imposto de circulação*) is placed on it by the government.

The coffee processors buy the uncleaned coffee (café em côco) directly from the sitiantes, fazendeiros, and sharecroppers in the county. The cultivators are paid according to the quality of their crop; 1968 prices ranged from CrN$ 13,00 to CrN$ 16,00 per 40-kilo sack. After the coffee is cleaned and hulled, it is sold to the Instituto Brasileiro de Café or to a coffee exporter, but one of the firms in Ouro Verde has an export license to sell coffee directly abroad. The processors received an average of CrN$ 50,60 per 40-kilo sack of processed coffee (café limpo) in 1968. The processors' profits are not as great as they may seem, since, on the average, it takes three sacks of café em côco to produce one sack of café limpo.

In 1968 there were no sítios or fazendas in Ouro Verde with processing facilities on the premises, although until six years before at least three large holdings cleaned and hulled their coffee and sold it to an exporter or the IBC, avoiding the expense of paying to have it processed. Some of the large fazendas in neighboring counties still have cleaning and sorting machines, but they are becoming rare as coffee declines in importance and is replaced with pasture and cattle. Since 1960, nearly twenty processing plants in the vicinity of Ouro Verde have gone out of business; the most extreme example of this is in nearby Paranacity which once had twelve processing plants, but in 1968 had only two in operation.

The larger of the two companies in Ouro Verde employs about twenty workers during the harvest and eight throughout the rest of the year. Those hired for the harvest run the machines, weigh and sack the coffee, and load it onto trucks. They are usually serventes and volantes with irregular jobs, and since the company pays them a fixed daily wage, this work is much sought after. The year-round employees include a resident manager, a bookkeeper, a night watchman, and five mechanics. In addition, a number of poor families are given sacks of coffee to *catar*, that is, to separate the whole well-formed beans from the broken ones. Although machines can do

1. Castelo Branco became president of Brazil immediately after the 1964 coup in which army officers overthrew the government of João Goulart.

this work more rapidly and efficiently, the owner of the processing firm explained that it was cheaper to have it done manually.

There are currently three rice-processing machines (*máquinas de arroz*) in Ouro Verde, although there were once four. They hull rice and turn corn into *fubá* (maize flour). The *maquinistas* (owners of the processing machines) buy rice from sitiantes, process it, and sell it to the local general stores. Sometimes they store it, waiting for the price to go up before selling it. Most farmers grow only enough rice for subsistence, however, and after having it processed use it for family consumption. Whether or not they sell it depends largely on the size of the crop that year, and when crops fail, they may even be forced to buy it when their harvest is insufficient for subsistence needs. The processing is usually not paid for in cash; instead the maquinista keeps 30 kilos for every 70 kilos processed. He often sells it directly to town residents at a somewhat lower price (about CrN$,10 less per kilo) than the general stores. In 1968, as a result of the crop failure, the county did not produce enough rice to meet its own needs, and rice had to be imported from as far away as Minas Gerais. The price shot up, and many farmers who usually grow enough rice for subsistence were forced to buy it from the maquinista or general stores. The higher price and greater demand for store-bought rice created a minor boom for the rice processors who were not at all unhappy with the situation.

There are twelve general stores of varying sizes in town and seven in the rural area of the county. All are about equally affected by the seasonality of an economy based largely on agriculture. As in the rural areas, there is a "dead season" in town from October through January. The owner of an armazem in town estimated that from February to May his sales averaged CrN$ 4,000,00 to CrN$ 4,500,00 a month; they rose to CrN$ 6,000,00 a month during the coffee harvest, from June to August, then fell to CrN$ 3,000,00 a month from October to January. He said that all his profits were made during the harvests and that if he did not do well then, he could not make it through the rest of the year. Another shopkeeper sells food on credit during the slow season, to encourage business, but during the harvests he accepts only cash payments. Only one shopkeeper, a Japanese, claimed that his volume of sales remained about the same throughout the year ("People always have to eat"). His sales rise sharply on Saturdays, as do those of all the store owners in town, when farmers come in from the rural area to make their weekly purchases. The Japanese noted that on Saturdays he employs eight clerks to take care of his customers, while during the week three can do the job. Unlike most other store owners (*armazenistas*), he does not sell on credit, but his prices are somewhat lower, which explains his large volume of business.

Most store owners mentioned that different types of items sell during the two seasons of the year. One armazenista sold forty-two beds and twenty-seven mattresses over a two-month period at the height of the cotton harvest, more than during the preceding eight months. Household goods, such as pots, pans, dishes, and glassware, and decorative items, such as bric-à-brac and plastic flowers, are much in demand during the cotton and coffee harvests but sell little the rest of the year. Sitiantes and sharecroppers tend to buy the same amount and type of food (mainly rice, beans, coffee, and sugar) during the harvests, but they buy meat more frequently then than during the dead season. Even when they have cash to spend, they rarely buy expensive canned goods, which are purchased only by the wealthier fazendeiros and town residents.

On Saturdays there is a small market (*feira*) set up near the bus station at the entrance of town.[2] It has five stands, three selling meat, one selling cheese and sweets (*doces*), and one selling combs, soap, thread, pins, and other odds and ends. The meat stalls are owned by farmers who have a few head of cattle, one of which they slaughter each week to sell at the market. The activity in the feira is slight, most people preferring to shop at the general stores where they can buy on credit. The market in the neighboring county of Paranacity, also held on Saturdays, is a good deal larger; fruit and vegetables are also sold. Many of Ouro Verde's residents prefer shopping there (it is only three kilometers away) since the selection is greater and the prices about the same.

There is general agreement among Ouro Verde's shopkeepers as to which crop, coffee or cotton, now produces the most movimento in their stores. One butcher in town said that when he first bought his store three years ago, his best months were from June to August, during the coffee harvest, but now this is a slow period and business is only good from March to May, during the cotton harvest. He claimed that at that time his sales increase by about 30 per cent over the average for the rest of the year. An armazenista agreed: "It

2. In comparison to many Brazilian towns, particularly those in the Northeast, Ouro Verde's market is very small and is not an important center of business activity.

The weekly market

Cleaned coffee ready for transport

is only cotton which brings business to my store. Coffee doesn't do this anymore. Cotton is even riskier than coffee though and I fear a drought almost as much as cotton growers do. If one comes my business may fail."

Prices in the general stores in town vary slightly, with only one refusing to permit credit buying (see Table 13). Prices in the two butcher shops in town were identical for a kilo of meat: first quality beef was CrN$ 2,00, beefsteak CrN$ 1,70, beef ribs CrN$ 1,30, hearts CrN$ 1,50, and jerked meat CrN$ 2,00.

TABLE 13. Prices in Seven General Stores in Town (April 1968)[a]

	Price (CrN$)						
Item (1 kilo unless specified)	#1	#2	#3	#4	#5	#6	#7
Beans	,55	,50	,45	,45	,50	,50	,50
Rice	.85	,85	,75	,85	,90		,85
Coffee	,84	,80	,80	,84	,84	,84	,84
Sugar	,40	,35	,35	,35	,38	,40	,40
Salt	,20	,20	,20	,20	,20	,20	,20
Onions	1,00	1,00	1,00	,80	1,00	1,00	1,00
Potatoes	,25	,30	,25	,20	,20	,20	,30
Manioc flour	,35	,35	,35	,30	,30	,35	,35
Wheat flour	,70	,75	,70	,70	,70	,70	,70
Corn flour					,35	,35	,40
Pork fat	2,00	1,80	2,00	1,75	1,75	2,00	2,00
Dried meat					2,00	2,00	2,00
Spaghetti	,75	,70	,75	,75	,70	,75	,70
Margarine (½ kilo)	1,50	1,30	1,50	1,50	1,20	1,40	1,30
Cooking oil (liter)	1,70	1,60	1,60	1,60	1,70	1,60	1,80
Kerosene (liter)	,40	,40	,40	,40	,40	,35	,40
Bread (1 roll)	,15			,15		,15	,15

a. The exchange rate at that time was CrN$ 3,20 to U.S. $1.00.

In addition to the general stores, there are three *bazares,* stores selling ready-made clothes, shoes, dishes, stationary, school supplies, and small household items, and one *casa de tecidos,* selling bolts of cloth. Until five years ago Ouro Verde had four casas de tecidos, but the others closed down for lack of business. Like the general stores, these small enterprises are affected by the state of agriculture in the county and the seasonal variations in volume of sales resulting from it. The owner of one bazar estimated that his sales varied as much as 50 per cent between the slack season and the peak of the cotton harvest. He has been in Ouro Verde for twelve years, but has not noted any significant decline in business over this period. Until five years ago he was competing with three other stores of the same type, but their closing did not increase the movimento in his own bazar. This would seem to suggest that total sales have fallen off, even though this particular shopkeeper has been unaffected by the trend because of the loss of some of his former competitors. A Japanese bazar owner was delighted with the movimento produced by the unusually large cotton harvest in 1968. Her sales had increased by 60 per cent over those of the preceding month, and she was now taking in up to CrN$ 200,00 (about U.S. $60) on very busy days. All bazar owners agreed that they sell virtually no clothing to farmers and sharecroppers during the dead season, since the cash needed to purchase these items is not available until harvest time.

There are five bars in town, two of which sell ice cream as well as beer, hard liquor, candy, and soft drinks. Only some of the bar owners, those who depend on a rural clientele, are affected by seasonal variations in the economy. The rest claim to do more or less the same amount of business all year round, mostly on Saturdays and Sundays when rural residents flock to town. The men usually drop into the bars to have a few shots of cachaça with their friends, leaving their wives and children outside. The bars vary in size and number of regular customers. The bar in the bus station caters mainly to town residents and has at least one or two customers at all hours of the day and evening. A smaller bar which sells only cachaça, Cinzano, and soft drinks takes in at times only CrN$ 1,00 (about $.40) a day, but on Saturdays and Sundays averages CrN$ 15,00 to CrN$ 20,00. There are fewer customers during the slack season and they tend to drink less, but movimento picks up in April during the cotton harvest. This bar owner said that his sales varied by as much as 50 per cent during different times of the year, and this is undoubtedly true because most of his regular customers are sitiantes and volantes who have little money to spend during the months when there are no harvests. Another bar owner noted a 10 per cent variation in business between the slack and harvest seasons, but added that he barely made ends meet all year round: "For six months of the year business comes to a halt [*está parado*], and we have nothing to do but sell a little cachaça now and then. The time from October to January is really slow. Why? Because only agriculture produces business [*o que faz o comércio é só a lavoura*]."

The few other town enterprises also feel the effects of the agricultural cycle. The owner of the local tailor shop particularly stressed his lack of orders during the dead season. His busiest months are March to May, during the cotton harvest, but sales decline at the end of June because "people are afraid of a possible frost and they want to hang on to their money."[3] Even though this period is the start of low winter temperatures, many are reluctant to spend money for warm clothes; if their coffee trees freeze, their financial situations will be very precarious.

Even the two town barbers witness a notable decline in business during the slack season, about 50 per cent fewer customers than during the harvest months. One of them said that his busiest time was during the cotton harvest when farmers, sharecroppers, and day laborers frequent his shop, while in May and June movimento tends to fall off since "only the fazendeiros reap the benefits of the coffee harvest."

About the only enterprise in town that is little affected by variations in the agricultural sector is the civil registry (*cartório*), owned by a former mayor of the county. Its main functions are to record the births, marriages, and deaths of Ouro Verde residents, and to draw up and notarize contracts of various sorts. Most of the marriages in the county occur in May and September, in part because these months are considered lucky,[4] and in part because they correspond to the end of the cotton and coffee harvests, respectively, when local residents have more money to spend on weddings. About 60 per cent of the marriages recorded in the county in 1967 took place during these two months.

One town enterprise, the agricultural post, services the entire county. It is under the direction of the Secretary of Agriculture in Curitiba and has one local salaried employee. He is a successful coffee farmer whose advice in agricultural matters is respected locally, although he has no formal training in agronomy. He explains the applications of each product before it is sold to a prospective customer, and encourages farmers to participate in the federal campaign to combat hoof and mouth disease (*aftosa*). He is paid by the prefeitura and also receives a commission on the sale of seeds.

The busiest time at the agricultural post is during the nonharvest months from late August to December when farmers and sharecroppers purchase seed, insecticide, and fertilizer for the plant-

3. Frosts almost always occur in July or early August.
4. May is the month of the Virgin and September is the start of spring.

ing and growing seasons. The slowest months are from January to March immediately before the harvests begin when cash is in short supply. Sales fall off by 90 per cent during this period.

Agricultural tools and vaccines for cattle are sent to the post directly from the Secretary of Agriculture, while seed, animal feed, insecticide, and fertilizer are bought from private companies. No tax is placed on any of the products sold at the post in order to keep prices down and encourage sales. Fertilizer and insecticide can be bought on credit through intermediaries, but they are not tax exempt and their prices are higher than at the post. Still, many farmers and sharecroppers without money on hand must buy these products on credit, but cannot do so at the post which has a policy of selling only for cash. This policy, formulated by the State Secretary of Agriculture, is the chief complaint against the post. As one renter said, "It [the post] isn't worth anything to us. When we need products we don't have the money, and we can't buy them *fiado* [on credit]. Oh, things are sold for one or two cruzeiros less, but what good is it?"

Many cultivators of small farms say that the post will begin servicing their needs only when it allows them to pay for its products at the time of the harvest. As it stands now, the only ones who benefit from the lower prices are the wealthier sitiantes and fazendeiros who can pay in cash. Although the manager of the post sympathizes with the viewpoint of the poorer farmers, he can do nothing about the situation. He does occasionally permit old friends to buy on credit, but if they do not pay their debts he has to make up the loss out of his pocket. He claims that no credit buying is allowed because agriculture is a risky business, crop failures are common, and the state which supports the post would *tomar prejuízo* (be hurt) if it were allowed. But, he concedes, the way the post is currently run accommodates only a minority of the cultivators in the county, and he adds, "We still don't have any real support for agriculture here."

The Town's Credit Role

One of the most important links between the town and the rural area of Ouro Verde is the credit and loan functions which the former supplies to the latter. There is the Banco Comercial do Paraná (Bancial), a private bank with a branch in town. The nearest office of the Banco do Brasil, which is federally controlled, is in the neighboring county of Nova Esperança, 22 kilometers away, but it is frequented by many Ouro Verde inhabitants. In addition, most of the intermediaries and armazem owners who buy crops from the local farmers and sharecroppers and give them short-term loans live in town.

A majority of the agriculturalists in the community depend on one of the town's credit and loan facilities. Out of a sample of eighty-two sitiantes, fazendeiros, sharecroppers, and renters, fifty-one borrowed money from a bank or intermediary. Tables 14–16 show the type of cultivator who borrows from each of these sources, the amount of land owned, rented or sharecropped by the borrowers, and the uses to which the loans are put.

TABLE 14. Loan Sources and Economic Status of Borrowers

Borrowers	Bank of Brazil	Bancial	Intermediary	No financing
Landowners	25	3[a]	1	23
Sharecroppers	3	5	9	7
Renters		1	4	1
Total	28	9	14	31

a. Two of these also borrow from the Bank of Brazil.

Although there seems to be a disproportionately large number of landowners in the sample, this in fact reflects the actual makeup of the county's cultivators. From the tables it becomes clear that the Bank of Brazil is the most important source of loans for landowners, while most sharecroppers and renters receive financial assistance from intermediaries. While loans granted by the Bank of Brazil are used mainly for agriculture, those from the intermediaries are more often used for household expenses. A large minority of the county's agriculturalists do not rely on any of these sources, either because they are unable to secure loans from them or they do not need any.

The Bank of Brazil, which charges an interest rate of 1 per cent per month on all agricultural loans, is clearly the most desirable place from which to receive financing, since the interest rates covered by Bancial and the intermediaries are considerably higher. In addition to the basic interest, both banks charge an additional 10 per cent or more annually for the services of the assessor and the expenses of the paper work involved in making loans. One fairly wealthy landowner, for example, borrowed U.S. $10,000 from the Bank of Brazil for one year. He used the money for insecticide, fertilizer, and wages for his workers, enabling him to obtain the low

1 per cent interest rate for agricultural loans. At the end of the year he estimated that he had paid the bank a total of U.S. $13,000; the additional $3,000 represented interest and extra charges of various kinds.

Although the Bank of Brazil is the best source of low-interest loans, many sitiantes complain about the difficulties they encounter in trying to borrow money there. In one case, a chácara owner with 5 alqueires planted in coffee and lavoura branca sought to borrow CrN$ 200,00 (about U.S. $60). The bank *fiscal* (assessor) was sent to look over the property, but denied him the loan, ex-

TABLE 15. Loan Sources and Sizes of Borrowers' Holdings

Number of alqueires	Bank of Brazil	Bancial	Intermediary	No financing
5 or less[a]	9	7	12	13
6–10	6		2	9
11–20	6	1		2
21–30	3			
31–40	1			2
41–50	2	1		1
over 50	1			4[b]

a. Owned, rented, or sharecropped.
b. These owners of large amounts of land do not have bank financing because they have planted pasture and the banks do not make low interest loans to subsidize cattle.

plaining that the land to be used as collateral was of too little value. The following week the same owner was offered $10,000,00 by a prospective buyer for his holding. One of the commonest ways to secure a loan is to bribe the bank manager or the fiscal.[5] In one instance, a sitiante with 10 alqueires was refused a small loan. But when he requested it again, he asked the fiscal what he wanted. The fiscal pointed to a young calf; the sitiante gave it to him as a "present," and has since enjoyed almost unlimited credit at the bank. Bribes of this sort are difficult for the farmer who may only want to borrow CrN$ 100,00 or CrN$ 150,00, since the pay-off to the manager or fiscal may nearly equal the size of the loan!

Many sitiantes remarked about the shabby treatment they receive at the Bank of Brazil. They are invariably obliged to wait in line many hours before they are called in to fill out the complicated

5. The willingness of loan recipients to bribe bank officials may be explained by the fact that, given the rate of inflation in Brazil during this period, real interest rates were negative.

forms required for loans. Farmers are often unable to spend this time away from their land and so are forced to seek financial aid elsewhere. The fazendeiro, on the other hand, who is frequently a personal friend of the bank manager, has immediate access to his office and is quickly granted a loan. I witnessed one incident which illustrates this. When a wealthy landowner with holdings of over 200 alqueires arrived at the bank, there were about thirty men milling about on the porch outside waiting for admittance. The fazendeiro brushed past them and went to the bank manager who greeted him warmly and proceeded to discuss his financial needs. In the words of one farmer, "The sitiante is generally unknown to

TABLE 16. Uses of Loans

Use	Bank of Brazil	Bancial	Intermediary
Coffee	10	4	1
Cotton	4	2	6
Peanuts	2		1
More than one of these crops	10	1	
Household expenses	1	2	5
Other	1		1

the people in the bank so that they don't want to finance him. Also the Bank of Brazil highly values a tie [*vale muito a gravata*]. They will quickly give loans to the rich fazendeiros who have lots of land and dress well."

Another problem which the sitiante often encounters is the long waiting period before his loan is granted. Sometimes weeks pass before the Bank of Brazil's assessor visits his property to evaluate it and decide whether or not to approve the loan. Sitiantes usually need cash immediately either for household expenses or to buy insecticide or fertilizer which must be applied to the crops at a specific time. The days drag on, and often by the time the loan is granted it may no longer be needed.

For all these reasons, the sitiante often tries to secure credit from another source. The Bancial grants loans almost immediately and does not send out an assessor to evaluate the prospective borrower's crops and land. There are fewer forms to fill out, a blessing to the semiliterate farmer who frequently knows only how to sign his name. Still, these advantages are costly since interest rates at the private banks are high, usually 5 per cent a month plus service charges. However, a recently enacted federal law has made it illegal for banks to charge an interest rate of more than 3 per cent a month. As a result the private banks have become increasingly reluctant to lend small sums of money since the returns on it are greatly reduced. This has been a blow to the sitiante who has had an important source of financial aid closed to him.

The Bank of Brazil will grant agricultural loans at the low interest rates only for specified crops. It will finance seed, insecticide, and fertilizer for all types of lavoura branca, and will lend money to those who are trying to improve the size and quality of their coffee yields. There is a strict prohibition, however, against loans for financing new coffee plantings, in accord with the government's effort to limit the spread of coffee on marginal lands. The bank does grant loans for the purchase of cattle, but many sitiantes interested in increasing their herds have only small holdings planted in pasture; these are unacceptable to the bank as collateral.

Renters and sharecroppers with written contracts also have the right to borrow money from the bank if their employers or other landowners endorse the loan. A renter or sharecropper working for an absentee landlord will usually ask a friend or relative who owns some land to co-sign for him. Loans to nonlandowners must always be guaranteed in this way. It is frequently in the patrão's interest to help his sharecroppers borrow money from the bank. Part of the loan may aid in meeting household expenses, but part is usually used to purchase insecticide and fertilizer to improve the quality and quantity of the crops. Since the landowner receives a fixed percentage of the harvest, he clearly benefits when yields are large, so he encourages his sharecroppers to apply insecticide and fertilizer.

The landowner can make low-interest loans from the bank in the name of his sharecroppers with the provision that the money will be used to improve their crops. When loans are taken out this way, the sharecropper must come to the bank personally to pick up the money. This is to prevent his patrão's relending the money to him at a higher interest rate than the bank's. Some landowners who have contracts with a large number of renters and sharecroppers borrow a single large sum from the bank in their own names, and then distribute it to their workers. In this case, they can legally charge higher interest rates than the bank, thus creating a small profit.

Landowners frequently manage to get around the stipulation requiring the sharecroppers presence through their friendship with and "gifts" to the bank manager. Not uncommonly sharecroppers who have had loans taken out in their names never see a single cruzeiro of the money. Their patrões take advantage of the low interest rate obtained through them, and then spend the money in whatever way they wish. Many landowners keep the written contracts they have made with their sharecroppers so that the latter cannot go to the bank and demand the low-interest loans to which they are entitled. A few of the better known and more prosperous sharecroppers and renters in town avoid this potential chicanery by convincing friends or relatives who are sitiantes and shopkeepers to co-sign their loans, thus ending dependence on their patrões.

The importance of bank loans to the maintenance of the agricultural structure cannot be overestimated. A large number of sharecroppers and landowners would not be able to pay for their basic cultivation expenses if it were not for the banks. Many take out annual loans, usually just managing to pay them off but never having more than a small profit because of the money that goes to interest and other fees. The importance of the banks was dramatically expressed by one fazendeiro: "The only God around here is the Bank of Brazil. Oh yes, and the private banks are the saints." One sitiante prided himself on the fact that he had always managed to get by without bank financing: "What good are loans when the harvests aren't even big enough to pay off the interest? They can only hurt you in the end. Loans and interest are cancers. They just keep growing and there is no cure for them."

Borrowing money from an intermediary presents fewer problems to the renter and sharecropper: no co-signer is required, there are no forms to fill out, and the cash and/or credit is available immediately. The prospective borrower need only sign his name on the contract or affix a thumbprint if he is illiterate. There are four principal intermediaries in Ouro Verde, all of whom own land and have small warehouses or armazens for the storage of crops. They deal only in peanuts and cotton; coffee is highly regulated and must be sold to the IBC, and other crops (corn, rice, beans, and manioc) are produced on a small scale in the county and sell for comparatively low prices.

The following is a typical account of the dealings between a renter and an intermediary. Before the renter harvests his peanut crop, he is deeply in debt to a local armazem where he has purchased food and supplies on credit. He is anxious to sell the crop in order to pay off the debt, and goes to the armazem owner who claims that the price that peanuts are currently selling for is not yet known. Still, the latter offers to pay for the transport and storage of the renter's crop. At this time the price for peanuts may or may not be known locally, but if the renter finds out what it is, and then wants to sell his crops to a local processor, the armazenista demands immediate payment and interest for transport and storage. The renter still has no cash since his crop has not yet been sold. The armazem owner offers to buy it from him at a price lower than the going rate, and the renter has no choice but to sell. He cannot borrow money from the bank to pay off the armazenista for the bank will not accept crops stored in a warehouse as collateral; the fact that they are there implies that a debt already exists.

Any intermediary will have similar dealings with a number of renters. He buys their crops and, when he has a sufficient quantity, he contacts a peanut-processing plant in Maringá which sends a truck to pick them up. The individual renter cannot sell his crop directly to the plant since it only accepts truckloads, with a minimum of four hundred sacks of peanuts, and will not buy small lots from individual cultivators. Needless to say, renters lose a considerable amount of money in this process since they must pay for transport and storage, and they receive lower prices for their crops from an intermediary than they would from a processor. The only way for renters to extricate themselves from this system is through the formation of a cooperative which would sell crops directly to a processor and bypass the expense of the middleman. So far, cooperatives of this sort do not exist in Ouro Verde.

One of my best informants noted that not all renters and sharecroppers go to intermediaries for loans: "The more experienced [*experto*] cultivators pay their debts with part of their crop and store the rest in their own houses instead of bringing it to an armazem. The bank will finance renters and sharecroppers who do this if they can get someone to endorse their loan. These people get along [*vai bem*]. They are independent. They own wagons and transport their crops themselves. When they need cash they sell a chicken or a pig and don't go running to an intermediary to borrow money at high interest rates. They give their patrão his share of the crop as soon as it is harvested so that they are free and clear." But of those who use intermediaries, he said, "The new and less experienced cultivators don't yet understand this system. Anyway, they don't know people who will co-sign bank loans for them. These are the ones who go to the armazenista to borrow money.

They don't understand that this will hurt them for they are novices [*novatos*] and don't know the system here."

Some sitiantes also sell their crops to intermediaries since they too lack sufficient quantities to sell directly to the processing plants. But, unlike sharecroppers and renters, the sitiante rarely borrows money from an intermediary since, as a landowner, he has less difficulty securing a bank loan. He generally receives a better price for his crop than the renter does, for he is not in debt to the intermediary and therefore is not obliged to sell his crops to him.

Another common practice involves the intermediary and the renter's patrão. The patrão will direct the renters under contract to him to sell their crops to a particular intermediary. In return, the patrão receives either a small percentage of the crop from the intermediary or favorable terms when borrowing money from him, such as a 90-day loan with interest covering only 70 days. The patrão holds another advantage: renters who are in debt to an intermediary cannot legally leave their current jobs. Thus, landowners have the assurance and advantage of a stable work force. They are certain of having sufficient labor for planting and harvesting. If they can retain a sizable percentage of workers from year to year, they avoid the bother and expense of finding and hiring new workers, of paying their moving expenses, and of drawing up new labor contracts. It is clear, then, why patrões do not discourage their workers from dealing with intermediaries.

Another frequent practice involving intermediaries, renters, sharecroppers, and their employers is a worker's patrão arranging credit for him at one of the local armazens. During the slack season before the harvests begin, many renters and sharecroppers run out of cash and are forced to buy food and supplies on credit. A worker's patrão will agree to guarantee his debts up to a specific amount. The employer and employee will go to a general store, and the patrão will tell the armazenista that this worker can charge up to CrN$ 100,00 worth of food for a 90-day period.[6] The worker receives a small notebook in which are listed all of his purchases. When he has spent the predetermined sum, the armazenista will not allow him to charge anything more unless his employer agrees to guarantee additional credit. Although a few store owners charge interest on these debts, most do not, since these arrangements bring them a great deal of extra business.

6. Amounts usually range from CrN$ 50,00 to CrN$ $300,00 and ninety days is the usual length of time for which credit is given.

At the time of the harvest, the renter or sharecropper pays off his debt, either in cash or with part of the crop (corn, beans, or rice) equal to the amount of money owed. Since repayment can be made either way and there is no paper work or waiting involved when money or credit is given by an intermediary, this system is far more widely used than bank financing among sharecroppers. There is a drawback, though: their purchases must be restricted to the armazem where they have credit, even though prices may be lower elsewhere.

A final credit system will be dealt with briefly and discussed more fully in chapter 5. It is confined to men who rent large tracts of land, usually from absentee landowners, and subcontract the land to cultivators who do the actual planting and harvesting.[7] These renters serve as intermediaries to their subcontractors. Some of them own armazens in town and are engaged in the other credit systems mentioned. The renter-intermediaries have written contracts with the landowners, but not with their subrenters, thus making it impossible for the latter to receive bank financing. The renter-intermediary "furnishes" (*fornece*) the cultivators working under him credit for food and agricultural supplies at his own or another local armazem, and he may also rent them a tractor for clearing the land, all at high interest rates. Intermediaries who subcontract land are virtually the only ones who charge interest on food bought on credit. If the renter-intermediary owns a store, he can take out a loan at the Bank of Brazil and then relend the money to his subcontractors at a higher interest rate (usually 4 per cent a month for eight months) than he paid. The subrenters must accept these terms since bank financing is unavailable to them. In at least one case, the renter-intermediary gives scrip (*vales*) rather than cash or credit to his subrenters, who can exchange it for food at only one armazem in town where prices are quite high.

After the harvest, the renter-intermediary buys his subcontractors' crops under much the same terms as he purchases those of independent renters and sharecroppers. That is, he offers the subcontractor a price below the current rate, and the former is forced to accept it since he is deeply in debt by that time. The renter-intermediary adds his subcontractors' produce to that which he has bought elsewhere and sells the entire lot directly to a processor in Maringá.

7. These men will be referred to as renter-intermediaries, for lack of a better term.

The Town as a Center of Social Life

There is no doubt that the residents of the rural area of the county view the town as the locus of the community's social and religious activities. Sharecroppers, day laborers, and farmers, living fairly isolated lives on rural sítios and fazendas during the week, look forward to visiting town on Saturdays and Sundays to shop, meet friends and relatives, and attend church services. The town is seen as the center of movimento. The noise of cars, trucks, and wagons, and the bustling atmosphere which overtakes the town on weekends present a striking contrast to the quiet existence which most rural residents lead. Nearly all of them try to come to town at least once a week. Early Saturday morning they begin to arrive on foot, by wagon, or in trucks and jeeps. Whole families dressed in their Sunday best start descending on the town just after dawn, and by mid-morning there is a hum of activity. Stores and bars are filled to capacity and the town square, a tranquil spot during the week, is transformed by milling throngs and laughing children. Local residents seem also to enjoy this burst of activity, a relief from the usual slow pace of town life. On Sundays, movimento subsides somewhat since the stores are closed and the day is spent in church or with family and friends.

The town is the site of most of Ouro Verde's religious activities since, with only two exceptions, all of the county's churches are located there. The community is overwhelmingly Catholic, although there are a number of Protestant denominations, each with at least a handful of adherents. Out of 162 town residents covered in a preliminary survey, 142 said they were Catholics, 9 belonged to the Cristão do Brasil Church, 5 were Adventists, and 8 were members of other denominations including Baptist, Methodist, and Assembly of God. In a sample of 75 household heads in the rural area, 58 said they were Catholics, 6 were Cristões do Brasil, 4 were Adventists, 2 belonged to the Assembly of God, 2 were Buddhists, 1 was a Spiritist, and 1 professed atheism.[8]

The one Catholic priest in the county, Padre Antonio, is a Spanish immigrant who has lived in Brazil for over twenty years. He resides in Ouro Verde, but he also ministers to the neighboring counties of Uniflor and Paranacity. Aside from the large wooden church in

8. Both Buddhists were born in Japan and occasionally go to services at the small temple in the nearby county of Nova Esperança. The atheist was a German university student temporarily administering his father's cattle ranch.

town, there are five small chapels scattered throughout the rural area where the Padre says mass from time to time. In addition to his religious duties, he teaches French and history at the local *ginásio* (junior high school), and oversees the activities of various church groups. These include the *Congregação Mariana,* with a membership of fifty-six men who sponsor *festas* (parties) to raise money for the church, the *Filhas de Maria,* a similar organization for women, the *Apostelado de Oração,* a prayer group which also helps organize festas, and the *Vincentinos,* a charitable group with fourteen male members.

The Marianas attend mass together the first Sunday of each month, and then meet to plan festas and discuss other means of raising money to complete the new church which has been under construction since 1963. Festas are held three or four times a year, followed by a cattle auction (*leilão*). The cattle are donated by a few of the county's more prosperous Catholic families, and the proceeds of the sale go to the church. Until about a year ago, the church was in charge of distributing Alliance for Progress (*Aliança para Progresso*) milk to a hundred poor families in town, but for reasons that are not known, Aliança products no longer reach the area. The membership of the Marianas is diverse and includes local businessmen, farmers, and sharecroppers. No day laborers belong, for it was explained that one must be a permanent resident of the community in order to be a member and volantes are "here today and gone tomorrow."

The Vicentinos raise about CrN$ 5,00 ($1.60) a week which is distributed among five or six of the poorest families in town. On occasion, food and milk are also supplied and, in emergencies, money for medicine and consultations with the local doctor. Of the families who regularly receive charitable assistance, two are headed by widowed mothers and the rest by men permanently unable to work because of illness. In one instance, the Vicentinos raised money to send a young girl to the state capital where she could receive free medical treatment. All of the regular recipients of aid live in town, since resources are scarce and the groups that provide charity cannot even begin to cope with the far greater problem of rural poverty. The families of impoverished day laborers did receive Aliança produce when it was available, but now they get no help of any kind.

Padre Antonio claims that church attendance has varied little over the last ten years or so, although there are now fewer people at services due to general population decline. Also, for this reason, the average number of baptisms has decreased; according to the Padre, this is a good index of population loss since everyone, even nominal Catholics, has his children baptized. Women attend church more frequently than men and are more likely to say confession and take communion. Old people go to mass more often than younger ones, and attendance is particularly high among the aged of Spanish and Italian descent. Town residents go to mass with less regularity than those who live in the rural area, even though the latter live at a greater distance, making it more difficult for them to attend. Men in town rarely visit church, and the Padre explains this by saying that they are "too preoccupied with business." Perhaps a better explanation for higher rural attendance is the fact that church-going is one of the few communal activities open to farmers and sharecroppers who live isolated lives throughout the week.

Padre Antonio claims that there is no friction between Catholics and Protestants (*crentes*) in the community, and that there are many interfaith friendships. He noted that poor Protestant families were also given the Alliance food distributed by the church, and mentioned his having awarded a small scholarship for school supplies to a needy Protestant boy. Still, a number of crentes with whom I spoke expressed hostility towards Padre Antonio and Catholics in general. One Adventist claimed that it was not true that Protestants were given Aliança products when they were available, nor do they ever receive charitable aid from the Church. An old woman who belongs to the Cristão do Brasil Church criticized the Padre for drinking cachaça and "wearing a long skirt." She added that Catholics are usually "untrustworthy" since, unlike Cristões, they drink and gamble.

Membership in most of the Protestant churches in Ouro Verde has remained fairly stable over the last ten years, aside from the losses due to general population decline. The largest Protestant group is the Cristão do Brasil with over 150 adherents in 37 families. About three decades ago the Cristões split away from the parent Assembly of God Church whose headquarters are in the United States. There is one Cristão church in town and two in the rural area, one of which is located on a member's farm. Almost all of the church's members are employed in agriculture as sitiantes,[9] sharecroppers, and renters. Only one day laborer belongs, and there are no Cristões who work in business or commerce. The membership is

9. No Cristão has a holding of more than 10 alqueires.

mixed in ethnic origin (Brazilian, Italian, and Spanish) and in place of birth (the Northeast, São Paulo, and Minas Gerais). Although most of the Cristões were converted before coming to Ouro Verde, a few converts, usually relatives and friends of members, were made within the county.

The Adventists are the second largest Protestant group in Ouro Verde. They are divided into two sects, the Seventh Day Adventists, who are affiliated with the North American church of the same name, and the Adventistas da Promessa, a splinter group native to Brazil, having no connections with the international Adventist movement. The Seventh Day Adventists have five families in Ouro Verde, four in town and one in the rural area. The town families include those of the postmaster, two chácara owners, and one construction worker. All but one of the families were already Adventists when they came to the county, and the local Adventist church was established fourteen years ago. At one time there were over fifty members, many of whom were sharecroppers, but as work became scarce a number moved away.

The Adventistas da Promessa have four families in the county, three of which are related to each other. Three of the family heads work as volantes and one is the owner of a small sítio. Since the sect is very small, it has no local chuch and members meet informally once a week in members' homes. There are Adventistas de Promessa churches in Maringá and Paranavaí which the county's adherents visit whenever possible. There is no difference in religious doctrine or observance between the two Adventist groups.

Eight families in Ouro Verde belong to the Assembly of God Church (*Assembleía de Deus*). The sect was founded in Brazil about forty years ago by an American missionary, but, unlike the Cristão de Brasil Church, it is still affiliated with the parent organization in the United States. The religious beliefs and practices of the two groups are virtually indistinguishable, with the exception that the Assembleistas have a full-time, salaried pastor. Most of the Assembly of God members in Ouro Verde are sharecroppers and renters, and only one landowner belongs to the sect. Four of the eight families are related, all of them having converted from Catholicism in their native Espiríto Santo. At one time, thirteen families belonged to the Assembleía, but five were forced to leave the county when the farms on which they sharecropped coffee were turned into pasture. The sect has no church or pastor in Ouro Verde, and members attend services in Paranacity.

The Methodists are the last Protestant group of any size in the county and the five families who are members are all related. They are town residents with white-collar jobs, one of whom was elected mayor.[10] There were four more families who belonged to this church, but they left the county about six years ago when sharecropping positions became increasingly difficult to secure. There is no Methodist church in Ouro Verde, and services are attended in Nova Esperança.

Aside from religious activities, the town is also the site of the various holiday commemorations held in Ouro Verde during the year. Brazilian Independence Day on September 7 is marked by a parade of school children and speeches by the mayor and town councilmen. In 1967, the occasion was used to dedicate the newly completed junior high school, the first in the county. December 14, the date of Ouro Verde's founding, is County Day (*Dia do Município*). Stores are closed and most workers are given a holiday. Aside from a brief speech given by the mayor at the town hall, the occasion is otherwise uncelebrated. In 1966, however, the county's tenth anniversary, the state governor and mayors from nearby municípios participated in more elaborate commemoration ceremonies. Christmas is not nearly as important a holiday in Brazil as it is in the United States and Northern Europe, and in Ouro Verde it is celebrated only by a few of the more prosperous families who exchange gifts. Of more note is Carnaval, the start of Lent at the end of February, which is marked by parades and parties throughout Brazil. In Ouro Verde, a Carnaval dance is held at a local warehouse festooned with balloons and paper streamers. A small band from a nearby county is often hired and the festivities continue into the early hours of morning. The last important holiday of the spring season is the Festival of São João at the end of June. Bonfires dot the countryside, special church services are held, and a dance in which the participants come dressed as *caipiras* (hicks or hillbillies) is sponsored by the municipal government.

Perhaps the most important centers of social activity in Ouro Verde are the town bars. They are filled to capacity on weekends when rural residents come to town to shop and attend church. Even on weekday nights, four or five male customers can be seen talking and drinking until closing time at 11:00 or 11:30. Women are rarely seen in bars, except those that sell ice cream, and should one enter,

10. Personal communication. He was elected in November 1968, the only candidate running for that office.

conversation comes to an immediate halt and all eyes are turned toward her. Some of the bars have billiard tables where two or three players are often surrounded by a dozen onlookers, and one bar has a backroom where card games are held. The bars are the only meeting places in town since there are no clubs or other establishments for informal social gatherings. They are frequented by men of all strata, and are not segregated on the basis of wealth or occupation. Farmers and sharecroppers do tend to go to the same bars, however, where conversation often turns to the prospects of the next coffee harvest or the current price of cattle. Likewise, town residents usually frequent particular bars in which topics of mutual interest are discussed.

The Town as an Educational Center

The educational facilities of the community are about evenly divided between the town and the rural area. The town is the site of a kindergarten (*jardim da infância*), a primary school (*grupo escolar*), a junior high school (ginásio), and adult literacy classes.[11] There are fifteen additional primary schools in the rural area. The county employs thirty-six teachers, seventeen in town and nineteen in the countryside, and nine school administrators and directors. The kindergarten and literacy classes are financed by municipal taxes, while the primary and secondary schools are supported by the state.

The kindergarten, with forty-three four- and five-year-olds, occupies a single classroom in the newly completed junior high school building. It was started in 1967, and its directress claims that some parents are unwilling to send their children there since they are not yet used to the idea of having them start school at such an early age. A more likely explanation is that they lack the money to buy the required smocks and school supplies. This inability, combined with the fact that the kindergarten is located in town, has meant that its enrollment consists largely of the children of the more prosperous town families.

Primary classes are held in a rather small wooden building which has eight classrooms. The recent influx of farmers into town has

11. It is unusual for a community the size of Ouro Verde to have a secondary school. Most towns of equivalent population, particularly in the Northeast, have at most one or two primary schools. In northern Paraná, however, much public construction is financed by the municipal government with funds received from the Commodity Transfer Tax (ICM) collected on exported produce. This, in fact, was the way in which Ouro Verde's ginásio was built.

increased school enrollments so that the building cannot adequately house the extra classes that have been formed. There are 480 children in the four grades of the town primary school, and they have been placed on triple session to make up for the lack of facilities.

About two hundred students attend the three grades of the town's junior high school. Morning and evening sessions are held, the latter for students in the rural area who must work during the day. In addition, thirty-seven students are enrolled in the three-year teacher training program (*curso normal*) for which classes are held in the afternoon, and five students from Ouro Verde attend university level courses at the new teachers' college in the town of Paranavaí.

Literacy classes for adults are given in the ginásio five nights a week. The curriculum is identical with that of the primary school, but only persons fourteen years or older may attend. In 1968, those enrolled ranged in age from fourteen to forty-one. A majority of the younger students are farmers' sons who help their fathers during the day and can only go to school in the evening. Most of the older men are employed as volantes in the rural area; there are no landowners or sharecroppers in the classes. All of the women live in town or at a maximum distance of three kilometers, since it is deemed neither safe nor proper for a woman to travel very far at night. At the beginning of the semester, enrollment is large, but attendance falls off as many of the students, particularly those who work as volantes, leave the county to seek work elsewhere. Every year, four or five former illiterates complete the four-year course and go on to attend the evening session of secondary classes.

The educational situation in the rural area of the county is not nearly as favorable as it is in town. Approximately 750 children attend classes in fifteen rural one-room schoolhouses. The curriculum of the first three primary grades[12] is taught in morning and afternoon sessions by a total of nineteen teachers. Although the directress of the county school system claims that no rural child is more than five kilometers from a school, I encountered children who had to walk ten to twelve kilometers to the nearest classroom. This is especially true for those living on the more isolated cattle ranches at the outskirts of the county where population density is low. Thus far, four schoolhouses have been dismantled in areas which

12. There are only three primary grades in the rural area due to the lack of teachers and classrooms.

once were planted in coffee but are now given over to cattle ranching. However, there are plans to reconstruct them in regions with a large number of school-age children and inadequate classrooms facilities.

At least 20 per cent of the children in the rural area never attend school, and a far larger percentage of those who are enrolled go to classes on an irregular basis. Absenteeism is particularly high from March to May and June through August, during the cotton and coffee harvests, since children often help out in both. But variations in the number of absences from year to year is directly correlated with the size of the harvest. Absences also rise during the rainy season when roads become muddy and difficult to pass and parents are reluctant to let their children travel on them. Since few children in town work in the harvests and none lives far from school, their rate of absenteeism is far lower.

On one occasion I asked ten school-age children on a large fazenda how many of them attended school. Only one replied affirmatively, the others explaining that they had to help out in the harvest. Although there is a schoolhouse not too far away, the children said that they probably would not go to it even after the harvest was completed. According to one highly reliable informant, many fazendeiros discourage their workers' children from attending school, preferring to have them on hand at all times to do small tasks. For this reason, many landowners refuse to allow vacant buildings on their property to be used as classrooms, even when the prefeitura agrees to supply a teacher.

The children of volantes frequently do not attend school at all. Since they usually live in Ouro Verde only for the duration of the harvest, it seems impractical to enroll them in school for such a short period of time. Moreover, many volantes' children are kept home from school because their parents cannot afford the necessary supplies, clothes, and shoes. For these reasons, most of the illiterate children and adolescents in the county are children of volantes. Similarly, since many sharecroppers do not stay in the county for more than one year, they are often lax about enrolling their children in school. Sitiantes, on the other hand, almost always send their children to school, although their attendance records may be poor since their help is needed on the land. Boys tend to miss classes more often than girls because they are more likely to help their fathers during the harvests, but in some families there is a feeling that girls require little education and that their time is better spent helping their mothers at home. The principal factor in determining absenteeism is the degree to which a child's labor is needed at home, and this, in turn, depends largely on whether the family has sufficient resources to hire outside help.

Even those rural children who do attend school regularly do not often go for more than three years because the fourth year of primary school is taught only in town. Some of the more prosperous farmers make arrangements to board their children with relatives or friends in town so that their schooling can be continued there. By the end of third grade, most children can read and write well enough to meet the educational requirements of rural life, and many parents feel it unnecessary for them to continue beyond the third year, especially when their help is needed on the land. Although many illiterate parents make a special effort to send their children to school so that they can learn to read and write, others take the attitude of this farmer: "I got along without knowing how to read and write and I am not any worse for it. So will my children."

Literate parents take it for granted that their children will learn to read and write, and since adult literacy is correlated with economic well-being, they are usually able to send their children to school for as long as they think necessary. A few farmers expressed the wish that their sons could study agronomy since this type of training would have immediate practical value. One put it this way: "It is not enough to just know how to read and write. You need a diploma to have any success in this world. Because we are without education, we plant manioc where we should plant potatoes, and we only notice plant pests when the crops are dying and it is too late to use insecticide."

County Health Services

All of Ouro Verde's health services are located in town. They consist of a private hospital owned and operated by a doctor trained in surgery in Rio de Janeiro, a public health clinic (*centro de saúde*) which, although completed in early 1967, was not open to patients in 1968, and a dental office run by a Japanese chácara owner who has had no formal courses in dentistry.[13] The hospital is staffed by a

13. Ouro Verde has remarkably good health services compared to other communities of its size in Brazil. See Harris (1956) and Wagley (1964). While the local hospital is privately owned, the public health clinic was built with ICM funds.

nurse and two orderlies who supervise it when the doctor is in his São Paulo office. It is a fairly small wooden building equipped with an operating room, an X-ray machine, and a dispensary with a large assortment of drugs. There are ten rooms for patients, in addition to rooms for the staff and a kitchen where meals are prepared.

The doctor enjoys an excellent reputation throughout the area and patients from neighboring counties often come to him for consultations. He practices general medicine as well as surgery, and says that he came to northern Paraná as a young medical school graduate to "earn a reputation and build a lucrative practice." He has succeeded in both, and has invested his earnings in two coffee and cattle fazendas in the county. His financial success is at least partly due to his rigid rules about fee payments. All patients are charged CrN$ 10,00 per consultation, and the price never varies in accordance with ability to pay. A sharecropper or day laborer without cash on hand must get a written guarantee from his patrão or other property owner that the fee will be paid. Since some patrões are unwilling to be responsible for their workers' debts, particularly those of their day laborers, the latter often go untreated. Sometimes the doctor allows poorer farmers to pay in installments, especially if the bills are large and cover operating and hospital room charges.

The doctor has worked out an informal system for evaluating the financial ability of prospective patients. When one arrives at the hospital, the nurse comes out to greet him, then reports to the doctor how he is dressed and whether he came to the hospital by jeep, in a wagon, or on foot. After hearing the nurse's description, the doctor is "out for the day" to those he expects will be unable to pay, unless they have a note from their patrões stating that their medical bills will be covered. This system is used principally with patients from the rural area, since the doctor is acquainted with most town residents and their financial situations. Although the doctor claims that many rural people distrust him and avoid going to him because they are "ignorant," a more logical explanation is that they lack the money and know that they will be untreated without it. For this reason, roughly 30 per cent of the townspeople and a far larger number of rural residents frequent one of the local *curandeiras* (curers) or *rezadores* (prayers) to be helped through the use of herbs and prayers when they are sick. Not uncommonly, both curer and doctor will be consulted for serious illness.

About 30 per cent of the women in the county give birth to their babies in the hospital, while another 30 per cent are attended by one of the three midwives (*parteiras*) in town. There are also a number of parteiras in the rural area who charge between CrN$ 15,00 and CrN$ 20,00 for their services. They only bring their patients to the doctor if there are complications or if a Caesarean section is necessary. The doctor charges between CrN$ 90,00 and CrN$ 120,00 for a simple delivery and CrN$ 200,00 for a Caesarean. In addition, the patient pays about 20 per cent of the cost of delivery for her two- or three-day stay in the hospital; for an additional 10 per cent she may have her mother or another female relative stay in the room with her. These fees include monthly prenatal examinations, but women who use the services of parteiras only come to them at the onset of labor and receive no prenatal care of any kind.

Birth control pills are the only modern method of contraception used in the community and are available at both of the pharmacies in town. They cost about CrN$ 8,00 for a month's supply. Their use is limited almost entirely to women who live in town, but even there it is confined to those in the middle class. The poorer women do not take them, not for lack of knowledge or desire, but because of the expense involved. If one only earns the minimum wage of CrN$ 80,00 a month, eight cruzeiros is a great deal of money. In the rural area, modern methods of birth control are little known or used. There is a common belief that nursing women remain infertile, so that many nurse their children as long as possible, usually until they conceive again. Herbal teas (*erva cidreira* and camomile) are sometimes taken to terminate unwanted pregnancies since they are thought to act as abortifacient.

Without doubt, the greatest health problem in Ouro Verde is malnutrition, especially among children. While outright starvation is not common, there was at least one case of it while I was living in the county. An unconscious three-year-old girl was brought to the hospital. The daughter of a volante who had not been able to find work for weeks, she was extremely thin with a grotesquely distended stomach. The family had had nothing to eat but *farinha* (manioc flour) and beans for weeks, and the doctor was unable to save her. Malnutrition is particularly common among the children of day laborers living in the rural area, who, unlike renters and sharecroppers, have no subsistence plots (*roças*) and must buy all of their food. Their diet largely consists of farinha and beans,[14]

14. Rice, a staple in many parts of Brazil, has risen greatly in price in Ouro Verde and is now beyond the means of the poorest families.

but virtually no meat or fowl since they rarely own pigs or chickens. In town, the problem is not as acute because of the prefeitura's policy of loaning small vacant plots of land to the very poorest families for subsistence cultivation.

While amoebiasis is not common in Ouro Verde, the doctor estimated that about 90 per cent of the county's children have worms. Only the newest and best appointed houses have indoor sanitary facilities, and there is almost a complete lack of deep outdoor latrines. These factors have aggravated the problem, facilitating the ease with which parasites pass from animal to human hosts and back again.

Although fairly modern medical facilities do exist in the community, it is clear that they are used by only the relatively small percentage of the population who can afford them. The public health clinic, should it ever open, will ameliorate this situation to some extent, since medical care will be far less expensive there than in the hospital. By 1968, however, the prefeitura had been unable to find a doctor willing to operate the clinic for the relatively small salary being offered by the municipal government.

The Town as County Seat

Since its separation from the county of Nova Esperança on December 14, 1957, Ouro Verde has been an independent município. Technically the town is a *cidade municipal* (county seat), but the entire county still belongs to the judicial district (*comarca*) of Nova Esperança. The município is not subdivided into smaller districts (*distritos de paz*), as is common throughout Brazil, for its small area makes further political subdivisions both impractical and unnecessary.[15] The county is governed by an elected mayor (*prefeito*) and nine councilmen (*vereadores*). Elections for these offices are held every four years, although in the last election, soon after the "Revolution of 1964," there was only one mayoral candidate and the councilmen were subsequently appointed by him. He belongs to the *Aliança Renovadora Nacional,* or ARENA (National Renovating Alliance), the party of the generals then heading the federal government. The mayor before him was a member of the *Partido Trabalhista Brasileiro,* or PTB (Brazilian Labor Party).

With two exceptions, the men now serving as vereadores have landholdings in the county. Some of them also own stores or serve

15. The average area of municípios in Paraná, 969 square miles, is considerably smaller than the national mean of 1,725 square miles. See Smith 1963:632.

as intermediaries, and all have resided in Ouro Verde for at least ten years. Their ethnic backgrounds reflect the whole community: two are Northeasterners, two are of Japanese descent, two of Italian descent, two of Spanish descent, and one is a naturalized Brazilian born on the Portuguese island of Madeira. The mayor owns one of the two pharmacies in town, as well as a small coffee fazenda.

The major function of the mayor and councilmen is the allocation of municipal revenues. The imposition of the *Imposto de Circulação de Mercadoria,* or ICM (Commodity Transfer Tax) in 1964, whereby the county government receives 50 per cent of the taxes placed on all local products sold outside of the município,[16] has given the community funds never before available. An important aspect of the tax is that the amount of state funds received by any given county is directly dependent upon the size of its contribution to the state treasury. Since the tax was imposed four years ago, the money collected from it and from the state has been used to build a junior high school, an artesian well, a new town hall, a landscaped square, a health clinic, and a new bus station. The mayor also used this money to purchase an electric mimeograph machine imported from the United States at a cost of CrN$ 3,000,00 (about U.S. $950)! In addition, there are plans to construct a new primary school and a few small houses which will be loaned rent free to some of the indigent families in town.

This vast amount of new construction is not a reflection of the community's current economic condition; one must not fail to realize that it actually has been made possible through the use of these newly acquired funds. The money also has allowed local officials to indulge in the peculiarly Brazilian "great works complex." This is the custom in which impressive structures are built with a view to aggrandizing the men or political party in power. While some of these works may be necessary and useful, others are extravagances which demonstrate an odd sense of priorities on the part of local officials. In Ouro Verde, the mayor's name and his political affiliation are displayed prominently on all the buildings erected during his administration.

The creation of the ICM tax has had another important consequence. Although Ouro Verde currently belongs to the comarca of Nova Esperança which receives 10 per cent of its ICM taxes, there has been a movement to remove the county from this judicial district

16. The comarca of Nova Esperança receives 10 per cent of ICM and the remaining 40 per cent is divided between the state and federal governments.

and place it in the comarca of Paranacity. The mayor and councilmen of Ouro Verde are resisting this change for a number of reasons. Paranacity's agricultural production, both in coffee and lavoura branca, is far below that of Ouro Verde. The county has a severe lack of water resources, and sparsely growing pasture covers much of its land. It has no coffee processing facilities and its single industry is a small sawmill. Since it is outside of the area settled by the CMNP, large fazendas owned by absentee landlords predominate. Unlike Nova Esperança, the town of Paranacity has a rustic Wild West atmosphere with muddy unpaved streets and little movimento. And, at this point, the county is in such financial straits that its local officials receive salaries on an irregular basis. It is widely felt in Ouro Verde that it would be a "step backward" to become part of such a poor undeveloped comarca which has minimal influence in the state legislature. The lone advantage that this change in affiliation would have is that the residents of Ouro Verde would be closer to the *sede da comarca* (seat of the judicial district), since Paranacity is only 3 kilometers from town and Nova Esperança is 22 kilometers away. Needless to say, the mayor and councilmen of Paranacity would very much like Ouro Verde to come under their jurisdiction, for the latter's ICM tax would greatly increase municipal revenues. The matter is now being debated in the state legislature in Curitiba, with both sides trying to influence the decision.

There is notable absence in Ouro Verde of the political divisiveness so frequently found in small Brazilian communities (Harris 1956). Party affiliations often split rural towns into two factions whose antagonisms reach fever pitch during local elections. The lack of this phenomenon in Ouro Verde may be traced to two factors. The settlement of the county is very recent in comparison to most other areas of Brazil. Powerful upper-class cliques who might control local politics have not yet been formed, since most of Ouro Verde's residents are of humble origin, and the few men of considerable wealth who own land in the county live in the cities of northern Paraná and São Paulo and have little interest in community life. In addition, the generals involved in the "Revolution of 1964" outlawed all political parties save their own, ARENA,[17] so that whatever incipient divisions there may have been along party lines in Ouro Verde have disappeared.

17. An official "opposition party," the *Movimento Democratíco Brasileiro*, or MDB, has recently been formed with the consent of the generals in power.

The only potential political split in the community is based on religious rather than party affiliation. One of the two mayoral candidates who ran for election in November 1968 is a Methodist, the other a Catholic. The Padre and some of the most prosperous Catholic landowners supported the latter even though his qualifications were highly questionable. He is barely literate and has had almost no contact with the residents of the community, preferring to spend his time in seclusion on his farm. The other candidate was secretary to the mayor, and has always been involved in the operations of the municipal government. The Catholics' principal objection to him was that he had promised a more equitable distribution of the money donated by the prefeitura to local religious institutions. In the past, all of these funds were given to the Catholic Church, with the various Protestant groups receiving no part of them at all.[18]

In 1968 there were 3,200 electors in Ouro Verde. Although Brazilian law has a literacy requirement (defined as the ability to sign one's name) for voting eligibility, this has barred relatively few people in the county from participation in the political process. Out of 120 adult men in a sample, only 20 were unable to sign their names.[19] A far larger number were illiterate, but could vote since they could sign the registration rolls. Somewhat fewer women are able to sign their names, but even among those who are eligible to vote, only about 20 per cent actually do so. The aim of the current literacy campaign financed by the prefeitura is to increase the size of the electorate, since the more electors there are in a given county, the more state aid it receives.

Effects of Coffee's Decline on the Town

The prosperity of the town is closely linked to agricultural conditions in the countryside; thus, the changes now taking place in the rural economy have had important effects on town life. Within the last few years, the town's population has grown by one-third, from 800 in 1965 to 1,200 in 1968, at the same time that the population of the whole county decreased. The reasons for this phenomenon are quite specific. As coffee production declined and farmers found that they could no longer make ends meet on the income de-

18. I learned through a personal communication that the conflict was resolved when all parties agreed that the Methodist candidate would serve as mayor and the Catholic candidate as assistant mayor.

19. Eight are volantes, six are sharecroppers, four are shopkeepers, and two are self-employed artisans.

rived solely from their crops, many sold their land and moved to town. These moves were facilitated by the fact that a number of fazendeiros sought more land for their growing cattle herds, and readily offered reasonable prices for small sítios near or adjacent to their own holdings. Other farmers retained their land, but moved to town to educate their children. They contracted sharecroppers or hired volantes to cultivate the crops, and they themselves served as administrators, visiting their farms once or twice a week. Sharecroppers, renters, and day laborers who could no longer find work in the rural area also added to the increasing town population. Some became self-employed carpenters and builders; others found odd jobs in the prefeitura and on road construction.[20] Many of them still work in agriculture during the cotton and coffee harvests. The movement from the countryside to town cannot be underestimated. Of fifty-two town residents in a sample, twenty-one had moved to their present homes from the rural area within the last six years. But in a sample of seventy-five rural household heads, only two, both day laborers, had formerly lived in town.

Aside from this movement, a significant number of town residents are leaving the county entirely and settling in other parts of Paraná and São Paulo. At least twenty families who once lived in Ouro Verde have moved to Maringá. Many of them are employed in one of the crop-processing plants in that city. A few moved to the state capital of Curitiba; others are now residing in the city of São Paulo. Some work in factories there; others have opened stalls in the city's markets. One town resident who owns a chácara said that he planned to move to São Paulo this year if his coffee freezes, but will wait until next year if it does not so that he can receive money from the sale of one more crop. His sons will work as taxi drivers or in industry in the city, and once there he hopes to be able to retire. Aside from the movement to urban areas, at least six town families from Ouro Verde have bought land in the Paraná sertão within the last year. As noted earlier, the move to the frontier is even more common among sitiantes who own land in the rural area of the county.

Many of the town residents who are moving to the cities are the sons of prosperous landowners and shopkeepers. Although they can

20. It should be noted that the town economy is not expanding despite increased population. For this reason, I believe that the "rural-urban" migration will be a short-lived phenomenon, for the town simply cannot support its increasing numbers. See chap. 7.

find jobs in the county, working in the bank, in the prefeitura, or on their father's land, many expressed the view that "Ouro Verde has no future. It won't progress any more (*não vai mais para frente*). So why should we stay here?" The movimento and excitement that stemmed from the settling of a frontier region are long past. The boom-town atmosphere is gone, for there is no longer the opportunity to prosper through agriculture.[21] Many young men prefer to try their luck in the cities, and the move there is facilitated by their fathers' usual willingness to support them until they find work.

Town businesses have also been affected by the decline of coffee and the increasing importance of cattle in the county. As one store owner put it, "There is no solution to the mess that businesses are in now, especially if it freezes again." While noting that movimento always varied from season to season during the year, the owner of a butcher shop remarked on the decline in business during the last few coffee harvests, compared to those of the past: "Ten years ago when I first bought the store there was tremendous movimento. On Saturdays there was a line of people around the block waiting to get in. In one day I killed two, sometimes three cows to fill all the orders. Now customers come in and ask for 100 cruzeiros worth of bones! At first I sold an average of three or four cows a week, then it went down to two. But in the last three years or so what have I sold? Sometimes not even one cow in ten days!"

Between 1967 and 1968, two of the town's general stores closed for lack of business. One store, which has branches throughout northern Paraná, was particularly hard hit, for its stock largely consisted of canned goods, beer, and wine, all luxury items which are only in demand during times of unusually good harvests. Many of the other armazens have changed hands three or four times over the past few years, with none of the owners being able to make ends meet.

A bazar owner who sells ready-made clothes and small household items said that she nearly had to close shop for lack of customers, but 1968's excellent cotton harvest saved her and her sales went up to 50 per cent. But her view of the future was dim: "What will happen in a year or two when there is no more cotton? I will be back in the same position as I was before. Why, when

21. While it is true that, in comparison to many Brazilian towns, Ouro Verde seems to have a great deal of movimento, it should be realized that the current pessimism expressed by local residents is relative to the tremendous activity and optimism which suffused the county during its first years of settlement.

I first opened the store in 1955, I did so well I was able to buy a house, a jeep, and a chácara. But that kind of movimento is all in the past. Things can never be the same here again." The owner of a tailer shop in town also rued his current economic situation. At one time he had four employees; today, he alone does all the tailoring. Until five years ago he was in competition with another tailor who has since moved away, but even at that time he received more orders than he does now. Perhaps the owners of the hotel in town have been most affected by the changing patterns of agriculture in the county, for their business is heavily dependent on crop buyers from outside of the county and truck drivers who transport the crops to warehouses and the ports of Santos and Paranaguá. This year's cotton harvest did not improve matters; most of the crop was brought to Maringá in trucks owned by the processing companies there, and since the round trip can be made in a few hours the drivers did not have to spend the night in Ouro Verde. It is not unusual now for the hotel to have no customers for weeks at a time. Its owners are anxious to sell it, but as yet they have had not been able to find a buyer. The other hotel in town has changed hands five times in the last six years, and remained closed for many months before its last owner was able to sell it.

The single town enterprise that has benefited from the changeover from coffee to cattle is the civil registry. Since much of its work consists of drawing up sales contracts and land titles, business picks up when a large number of landholdings are put on the market. Every time a frost occurs and farmers decide to sell their land, the registry has to hire additional employees to do all the paper work involved in transferring land titles. Business was particularly brisk from 1963 to 1968 as more and more farmers sold their small holdings and moved to town or away from the county entirely.

The final effect of the malaise in agriculture on the town, the decline in movimento, was mentioned over and over again. The air of excitement and hope that marked the first years of settlement has disappeared. Fewer people with less money to spend are transforming the town from a place of bustling activity to a sleepy backwater which seems to have been bypassed by the world.

Changes in the rural economy resulting from the decline of coffee are recent phenomena and the town, therefore, is just beginning to feel the effects. New construction is going on, a result of the availability of ICM funds, and population is on the increase due to migration from rural area, but this growth will be short lived. As more land is converted to pasture, as unemployment increases, as municipal funds fall off due to lowered agricultural output, and as emigration from the county to the frontier and to the cities of Paraná and São Paulo gains momentum, the town's social and economic life will be more seriously affected. The proliferation of construction activity will come to a halt, additional small businesses will shutter their doors, existing social services will decline in quality and number, and even the current slackened pace of town life will decrease still further.

5. Rural Life

THE Northern Paraná Land Improvement Company, which surveyed Ouro Verde and a large part of the northern area of the state, used three classifications for the holdings it sold. Chácaras, small farms of 1–5 alqueires situated immediately adjacent to town, were the smallest plots for sale. According to the company's plan, the chácara owners would supply town residents with a variety of food crops and would cultivate coffee only as a subsidiary activity. Sítios range from 6 to 49 alqueires and are located throughout most of the rural area; there were to be none in the "suburban zone" next to town. The company subclassified sítios by size: small sítios from 6 to 10 alqueires, medium from 11 to 29 alqueires, and large from 30 to 49 alqueires. Fazendas, holdings of 50 alqueires or more, were to be located exclusively at the county's outer margins, at the farthest possible distance from town. These terms are used by the residents of Ouro Verde, except that large sítios of over 30 alqueires are often referred to as *fazendinhas* (small fazendas).

Since the land divisions were first surveyed in the early 1950s, the map of the county has changed radically. Large fazendas are now found throughout the rural area, and sítios are frequently located adjacent to town. In addition, chácaras are now found throughout the countryside, not just in the suburban zone next to town. The company's plan for these small holdings, to supply basic food crops to the nonagriculturalists in town, has not succeeded. Coffee has proved to be more profitable than corn, rice, and beans, and, while all of these crops are grown in small quantities to meet subsistence needs, there is rarely a surplus for sale on the market. Since similar problems and solutions are encountered on holdings of this size, regardless of distance from town, all farms of 5 alqueires or less will be called chácaras and dealt with as a unit.[1]

TABLE 17. Number of Landholdings by Size in Ouro Verde in 1966

Type of landholding	Number
Chácara (1–5 alqueires)	120
Sítio	
Small (6–10 alqueires)	142
Medium (11–29 alqueires)	110
Large (30–49 alqueires)	24
Fazenda	
Small (50–99 alqueires)	36
Large (100 or more alqueires)	29

According to data collected by the *Instituto Brasileira de Reforma Agrária* (Brazilian Institute of Land Reform), there were 461 landowners in Ouro Verde in 1966 (IBRA 1966).[2] There is reason to believe that their number has decreased since the survey, as land consolidation has continued into the present. Table 17 lists the number of landholdings in each category in 1966. As can be seen, small landholdings still clearly predominate in Ouro Verde but the data do not give a full picture of the changes currently taking place. Sixty-two per cent of the landholdings ranging from 30 to 100 alqueires or more are actually made up of small farms which have been consolidated since the early 1960s. While a number of those in the category of large sítios may consist of only two or three holdings of 10 and 15 alqueires apiece, quite a few of the large fazendas have been formed from as many as 24 small farms. Slightly over half of the small fazendas are made up of single sítios now in the hands of one owner.

A clearer pattern of land distribution emerges if we look at the

1. A chácara's location, insofar as soil quality and the area's subjection to frosts are concerned, is the important variable here.

2. All local farmers had to fill out questionnaires for the Land Reform Institute detailing land usage, size of holding, work systems, and so on.

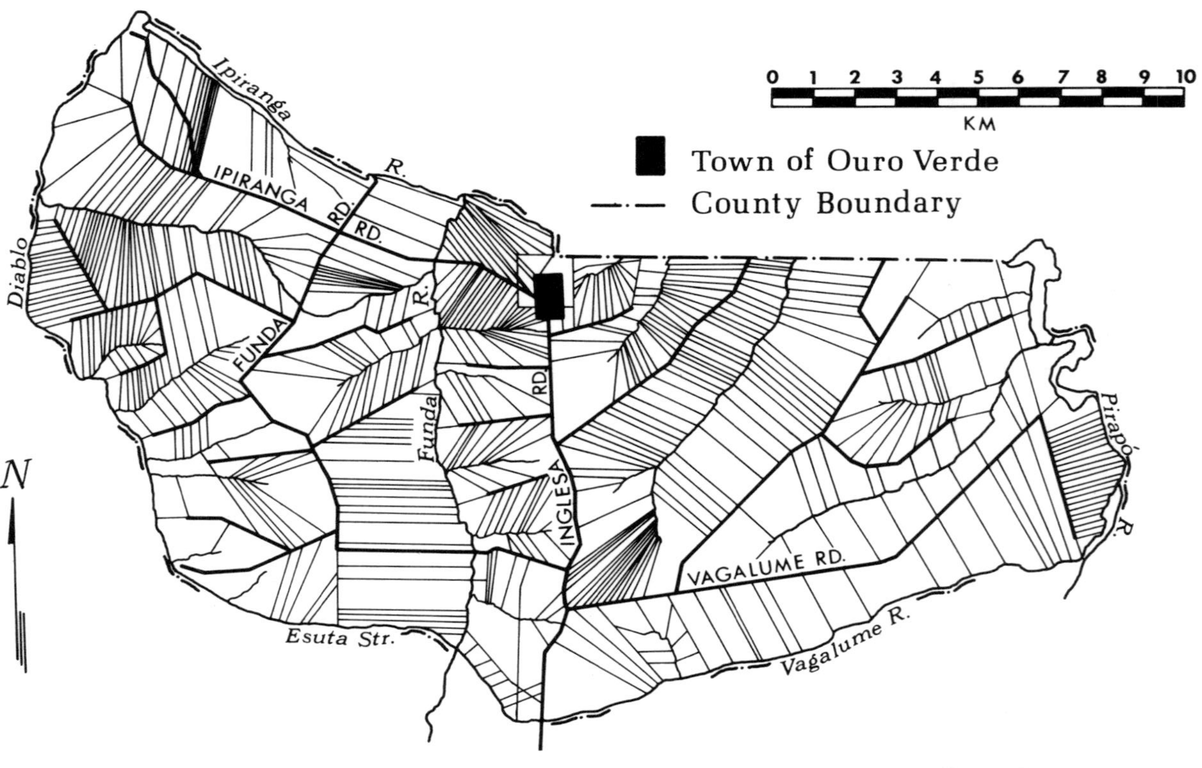

7. Rural land division

total amount of land cultivated and the percentage of it in large holdings. There are 11,076 alqueires under cultivation in the county. The 29 owners of large fazendas possess 4,264 alqueires. Thus, 6 per cent of the landowners hold slightly over 38 per cent of the area under cultivation. In addition, the 36 holders of small fazendas own 2,207 alqueires, that is, nearly 8 per cent of the owners hold approximately 20 per cent of the land. These two groups make up 14 per cent of the county's population but own 58 per cent of its cultivated land. In contrast, the remaining 86 per cent of Ouro Verde's cultivators, those with from 1 to 49 alqueires, own 42 per cent of its land.[3]

Labor Arrangements in Agriculture

One striking feature of rural life in Ouro Verde and the surrounding regions of northern Paraná is the diversity of labor systems employed in agriculture. Even within a particular category, the variations in individual arrangements between landowner and worker seem almost infinite.

There are three kinds of labor arrangements, which, although once common throughout the county, have largely fallen into disuse. Two of these, *formadores de café* (literally, coffee formers) and empreiteiros (labor contractors), were widespread in the county in the first years of settlement. Both systems are well suited to the requirements of opening frontier lands, and tend to be used only until full settlement has taken place. The colono system, common in the coffee regions of São Paulo, was never employed on a large scale in Ouro Verde or the neighboring areas of northern Paraná.

The role of empreiteiros and their peões in clearing the land around Ouro Verde for settlement has been described. The labor contractor signed a written agreement with the company or a landowner to clear a given area of land at a predetermined price, usually so much per alqueire. He gathered together a labor gang of young, unmarried men, often recently arrived from the Northeast, and paid them with part of the money received from the landowner, always keeping a healthy percentage for himself. Labor contractors frequently provided their men with food and cachaça at inflated prices and deducted these items from the agreed-upon wage. Labor gangs tended to break up once a job was completed,

3. Land distribution in Ouro Verde actually compares favorably with Brazil as a whole, where 83.4 per cent of the cultivators own 16.6 per cent of the land and 0.5 per cent own 36.4 per cent of the land (Smith 1963:334).

although many empreiteiros had peões who worked for them on a regular basis. One resident of Maringá who was a labor contractor in Ouro Verde and the surrounding counties had as many as four hundred men working under him at one time. He claims that they sought him out when in need of work, and he frequently had more requests for positions than he could fill.

Labor contracting in this form no longer exists in Ouro Verde and the nearby counties because the forests have disappeared and the land is completely settled. Empreiteiros are still common, however, in the more western areas of the state that are being opened up for cultivation. Labor gangs are now employed occasionally in Ouro Verde on fazendas which require a large number of hands to work on a specific job for a short period of time, for example, to harvest the coffee crop, to weed pasture, to build fences, or to dismantle abandoned barns and workers' quarters. It is difficult to estimate the number of peões in the county since they move from farm to farm, often crossing into neighboring municípios in the process.

Today the gangs are formed either through the services of an empreiteiro or by the landowner himself, who travels to nearby towns, gathering a group of unemployed men found around the local rooming houses and bus stations. Debt servitude is not uncommon under certain circumstances. The following account was supplied by a local fazendeiro: "I went to one of the *pensões* [rooming houses] in Nova Esperança looking for 20 workers to help harvest my coffee crop. Since the peões are always in debt to the owner of the pensão, he keeps their *galos*[4] as security. I 'bought' 20 galos from the pensão owner, an amount equal to the number of workers I needed. The cost of each one corresponded to the size of its owner's debt to the pensão. I took the sacks to my fazenda and the peões followed closely behind, unwilling to part with their few worldly possessions. I put them to work in the harvest so that they could buy back their galos from me, and then I paid them in cash for any wages they earned beyond the purchase price of their sacks. This is a good system—very common here—for it guarantees a fazendeiro enough men to work in his harvest."

Landowners often travel to the bus station in Maringá where

4. *Galos*, literally "roosters," are sacks in which workers keep their few personal belongings—some clothes, a saint's picture, and perhaps a photograph of their family. They are called galos for they are large sacks with little in them, and have long necks making them resemble roosters.

there are always a large number of unemployed men willing to take jobs for small wages. The local police frequently collaborate in this system. Men are picked up for vagrancy and may be hauled off to jail if they are without any apparent source of income. At this point both landowners and empreiteiros intercede "on the men's behalf" by offering them work and paying off the police for having conveniently rounded up a labor force. One peão told me that he reluctantly accepted an offer from an empreiteiro, even though he sought other work, for he feared that he would be picked up by the police if he remained unemployed for any time.

From the landowners' point of view, there are numerous advantages to employing labor gangs rather than individual day laborers. One fazendeiro said, "It is a great blessing that the peões never have their families with them. I can house them all together in an abandoned farm which would be unsuitable for women and children. They never come pestering me for money to buy medicine for their wives and children. Also since I pay the empreiteiro in one lump sum I end up saving money. You have to pay more, maybe CrN$ 2,50 or CrN$ 3,00 to an individual worker who earns by the day. But the biggest advantage of using peões is that the empreiteiro does all the work for me. He recruits the men, sees that they are fed, sometimes lends them money, and is responsible for getting the job done. Me—I only deal with him, and have no headaches about the personal problems of the workers."

Still, there are some drawbacks to using peões, particularly in coffee cultivation. Since they are always paid according to the number of trees they harvest, it is to their advantage to pick as many as possible in the shortest period of time. This often results in partially harvested trees with branches damaged by rough treatment. Some landowners refuse to employ peões for this reason: "Peões? Never!! Their work is badly done [*fazem serviço de qualquer jeito*]. Any fazendeiro who uses them has to pay a heavy price. He thinks he is saving money but he really loses in the end."

The wages and living conditions of peões vary from one fazenda to another, but as a group they are the most poorly paid agricultural workers in the county. The peões working on the mayor's landholding are typical. An empreiteiro who was contracted by the mayor hired ten men to harvest the latter's coffee crop. Four of the men were brothers who had left their wives and children in Minas Gerais and had come to Paraná seeking work. The rest were young, unmarried men from the Northeast and São Paulo. All the

Paulistas and Mineiros had had previous experience in harvesting coffee, and some came to Paraná from their home states every year. The empreiteiro who located the men at the bus station in Nova Esperança agreed to pay them CrN$,12 (about U.S. $ .04) per tree harvested and to give them one free meal a day. The mayor, in turn, paid the empreiteiro CrN$,24 per tree harvested, double the amount received by the peões. The men lived in a large ramshackle barn on the mayor's property and were served dinner by the empreiteiro's wife at 4:00 P.M. daily. If they were not hungry at that hour, they had to forego the meal and purchase their food independently. The empreiteiro sold the men cachaça at CrN$,30 a shot, cigarettes at CrN$ 1,00 a pack, and matches at CrN$,10 a box.[5] He refused to advance them cash so that they could make purchases at the stores in town. All of the peões agreed that by working at a steady pace they could harvest a maximum of a hundred trees a day, giving them a daily wage of CrN$ 1,20 (about U.S. $ .40). They were not paid on rainy days when the harvest came to a halt, and, on one occasion, the empreiteiro deducted CrN$ 3,00 from a peão's wages after he had refused to work on his Saint's Day, even though none of the men ever earned half that amount for a full day's labor. All of the peões on the mayor's fazenda expressed a desire to find jobs elsewhere, but since they were not too familiar with the region, they did not know where to go to secure work and feared that without it they would be picked up for vagrancy.

In their attitudes toward peões, employers clearly seek to justify this continuing exploitation. One labor contractor said, "I never pay my peões in cash while they are still working on a job. Why? They would rush off to town and spend it all in one night on whores and cachaça. And I'd never see or hear from them again. It is easier for me to sell them liquor here on the farm where I can at least keep an eye on them." A fazendeiro held much the same view: "Peões never stop wandering. They only work for a short time to get enough money so they can go off on a binge [*fazer uma farra*]. They really don't want to live any differently. They are happy with their lives as they are."

Apparently when the region was first being opened up for settlement, peões fared somewhat better than they do now, and most of them were able to save enough money to return to their homes in

5. Average prices for these items at the local stores are CrN$,15, CrN$,60, and CrN$,05, respectively.

the Northeast. This is rarely possible today since bus fares have risen sharply and it is far more difficult to secure steady work. Those that do come south are rarely able to return to their homes, and they often migrate instead to western Paraná, Mato Grosso, and Paraguay, all frontier areas where jobs are still fairly abundant. Very few Northeasterners are arriving in the more settled regions of northern Paraná, for word has filtered back that employment is scarce and wages are low. The *Gato Preto* (Black Cat), the only empreiteiro still residing in Ouro Verde, complained about the current situation: "Today I hardly earn enough to eat. Before I had an easy life. The fazendeiros were always after me and my peões. We had more work than we could handle. But now everything is different. No more forests, no more men. Sometimes I have to travel for days to get a labor crew together. And the tractors coming in![6] They are also taking away jobs that my peões used to do. And when I do get a contract here, the fazendeiros sometimes don't have the money to pay me and I have to take it out of my own pocket to pay off my men. Everyone has gone off to Mato Grosso and Paraguay. That's where a man can really earn money. A man gets CrN$ 5,00 a day there, but only CrN$ 2,00 here. Paraguay is the land of the future, and that's where I'm going as soon as I can."

Another type of laborer very common in Ouro Verde during the first years of its settlement, the formador de café,[7] has almost disappeared. After the forests were felled and the land burned off in preparation for planting, the landowner who did not want to open up the property himself signed contracts with formadores de café. The contracts varied according to the length of time for which they were made and the amount of assistance supplied by the landowner. They generally took three forms. The formador with a four-year contract and the right to 100 per cent of the fourth year's harvest[8] received the land completely cleared of underbrush with the *covas,* small carefully spaced holes in which coffee seeds are placed, already prepared.[9] Under this contract the formador only

6. Many landowners now use tractors to clear their land before planting pasture.

7. What are described as formadores de café here are often termed colonos in São Paulo.

8. The fourth year's harvest is usually small, and the trees do not start to produce large yields until the fifth and sixth years after planting.

9. Sometimes peões were contracted to dig covas after they had cleared the land.

had to plant the seeds and care for the young trees for four years. In addition, he was generally given the use of a house and some money, the amount of which depended upon the number of trees under his care. Under a five-year contract the formador was allowed to keep all of the fourth and fifth harvests. The land was cleared and burned before he received it, but he dug the covas himself. No house and very little money, if any, were provided for in the contract. The formador with a six-year contract kept the entire harvests of the fourth, fifth, and sixth years after planting. He cleared the land himself, dug the covas, and planted and cared for the trees. He did not receive a house or any cash.

In all of these cases, the formadores were permitted, for the duration of their contracts, to plant subsistence crops between the rows of coffee trees. The kind and amount of each crop were usually specified, with decreasing allowances as the trees grew toward maturity. This prevented diminishing the coffee harvests, which sometimes occurs when other crops compete with the trees for nutriment. In most cases the landowner supplied the seeds and tools needed for planting and caring for the coffee trees.

This labor system had advantages for formador and landowner alike. The latter expended capital on land but not labor, while the former was given the opportunity to acquire a substantial sum of money through the sale of two or three coffee harvests. Not a few formadores were able to purchase small sítios with the money earned in this manner. If the formador wanted to terminate his contract before it expired, he could, with the landowner's permission, arrange to have someone take it over from him. Contracts were sometimes transferred after a frost when it became apparent that the harvests to which the formador was entitled would be small. Many formadores suffered serious setbacks when the trees which they had cultivated for four or five years froze and their yields were minimal or nonexistent. Landowners also profited from this system since they did not have to contend with the hardships of the frontier. All of the inconveniences of living in the hinterland and opening up virgin forests were left to the formadores, and by the time the landowners came to reside on their properties, most basic services (roads, schools, and so on) were established.

Still, certain minimal resources were needed in order to enter into a five- or six-year contract. Since little was earned from subsistence crops and no money was forthcoming from the landowner, a prospective formador had to have some savings to tide him over until the coffee trees came into production and the crop could be sold. For this reason, peões and other workers who earned subsistence wages rarely became formadores, and these positions were usually filled by families of at least modest means.

The colono system, never very common in Ouro Verde, is found today on only one fazenda in the county. Since small holdings cultivated by the landowner and his family always predominated, colonos were rarely contracted on a large scale. This is not the situation in the older coffee regions of São Paulo where large fazendas requiring many hands were the rule (James 1959:441). The classic colono contract, so widespread in São Paulo and parts of northern Paraná during the first half of this century, was designed to protect European immigrants working in agriculture from the abuses of greedy landlords. The colono was contracted for one year and received a fixed monthly salary, the size of which depended on the number of trees under his care. He was paid separately, usually so much per sack, for harvesting the crop. The colono was permitted to plant subsistence crops between the rows of coffee trees, but, unlike the formador, he was compensated in cash and had no right to any part of the coffee harvest. In addition, the written contract set out a number of fringe benefits—free housing, the right to use a small area of pasture, free coffee for household consumption, and the use of a hulling machine for processing rice. While on many fazendas some of these stipulations were never fulfilled, the colono did have definite job security in that the landlord could not fire him before his contract expired.

There is general agreement among landowners on the reasons for the decline of the colono system in Ouro Verde and the surrounding areas. Since colonos are protected under the law and are supposed to have written contracts, it is difficult to avoid paying them the regional minimum wage because their salaries must be specified in writing. It is simply cheaper and less complicated for fazendeiros to employ day laborers who are not under the same protective labor legislation. Colonos must be paid whether they are able to work or not (due to illness or bad weather), whereas volantes who are paid by the task only earn money for work actually done. In addition, the fazendeiro is not free to dismiss the colono, but the volante can be fired without notice. The frequent frosts and subsequent decline in coffee yields in Ouro Verde have made it uneconomical for a landowner to employ workers on an annual basis with a fixed salary. If the trees freeze and the harvest is small, he still has to pay their wages even if there is little or no work to be done. He can cut down on expenses by employing volantes to do only the essential tasks necessary for the maintenance of the trees.

While all of these labor systems still are used occasionally in Ouro Verde, the total number of agricultural workers involved in them is small. The two types of labor arrangements most common in the county today are sharecropping and the use of day laborers. In addition, renting or tenant farming is fairly widespread in areas given over to the cultivation of cotton and peanuts, and mensalistas, workers paid a fixed monthly wage, are employed on many of the county's cattle fazendas.

There are two kinds of sharecroppers, *meeiros,*[10] those that sharecrop coffee and receive up to 50 per cent of the harvest, and *percenteiros,* workers who sharecrop cotton, peanuts, and rice, and keep over 50 per cent of the harvest. In local usage, coffee sharecroppers are referred to by both terms, while cultivators of lavoura branca are always called percenteiros. Within each system there is great variation in individual agreements between sharecroppers and landowners.

Since coffee always receives a higher price than any other crop, prospective sharecroppers will readily agree to contracts in which they receive only half of the harvest or less, a percentage that would be unacceptable for cotton, peanuts, or rice because of their lower market value. Sharecropping contracts may be written or oral, and they are rarely made for more than one year. This is to protect both landowner and sharecropper. The former may be displeased with the work of the latter and wish to dismiss him after the harvest, while the latter may be able to secure a better position on another holding. Before entering into a contract, most sharecroppers will examine carefully the trees that will be under their care, noting their height, the fullness of their branches, and the color and quality of the soil. They will question the landowner about the size of his harvests over the past few years and the incidence of coffee pests in an attempt to insure that the trees will give at least reasonable yields, since the attractiveness of a particular sharecropping position is almost completely dependent on the quality of the trees. Sharecroppers frequently travel from farm to farm in an effort to find trees that produce well.

The actual percentage of the harvest that the sharecropper is allowed to keep is directly related to the size of the harvest that

10. From *meia*, meaning "half."

the trees on a given holding are expected to produce. If their yields are generally high (more than 100 sacks per 1,000 trees is considered excellent in this region), the sharecropper will receive 30 or 40 per cent of the harvest. If the yields are expected to be low (less than 30 or 40 sacks per 1,000 trees), the sharecropper will receive 50 per cent of the harvest. Another reason landowners are reluctant to contract sharecroppers for more than one year is that yields do vary from one harvest to another. If two-year contracts were signed and the second year's harvest was larger than the first, the landowner would stand to lose, since he could not adjust the sharecropper's percentage downward in keeping with the size of the crop.

Sharecroppers are well aware of the pitfalls of accepting a position in which the landowner agrees to give them half of the harvest: "I know right away that if a fazendeiro offers me 50 per cent of the harvest that his coffee trees are no good any more [*não presta mais*]. If they produce less than 40 sacks per 1,000 trees it doesn't pay to take the position for I wind up with only 20 sacks and my expenses will be high. I prefer to get 40 or 45 per cent on good trees since I really can earn more money that way." Many sharecroppers complained of the difficulty in securing positions on fazendas with excellent coffee trees; landowners are unwilling to divide their large harvests and prefer employing day laborers who are paid in cash and receive no part of the crop.

Before a sharecropper signs a contract with a landowner, he estimates the number of trees he will be able to care for on the basis of the number of working members in his family and/or the number of outside workers he can afford to hire. In general, one adult can care for 2,000 coffee trees (1 alqueire) annually, although he may have to hire volantes for a large harvest. Since all sharecroppers till subsistence crops and many are also percenteiros of cotton or peanuts on the same landholding, they must figure out their available manpower in terms of these crops as well. For example, one man who sharecrops 4 alqueires of coffee and cotton is aided only by his wife since his children are very young. He therefore hires one day laborer who works for him year round, and ten to twelve additional hands for the cotton and coffee harvests. A sharecropper who cares for 12,000 trees and cultivates rice as well almost never requires hired laborers, since he has five sons who work with him. A sharecropper with two grown children cultivates 7,000 coffee trees along with intertilled subsistence crops, and he only needs extra workers when the coffee harvest is unusually large.

An important determinant of the percentage of the crop to which a sharecropper is entitled is the amount of cultivation expenses he agrees to assume. In general, the sharecropper who pays for all or a large part of the costs of fertilizer and insecticide keeps a bigger percentage of the harvest than does one who contributes nothing toward the expenses of cultivation. A sharecropper who receives 50 per cent of the coffee crop pays for insecticide and fertilizer; another who keeps 45 per cent of the harvest pays for half of the cultivation expenses. When the sharecropper does not have cash to pay for his part of the expenses, the landowner may take out a bank loan in his name or finance him privately, usually charging a sizable interest rate. Sharecroppers may also receive financing for household expenses either from their patrões or from an intermediary.

Another varying aspect of sharecropping is the way in which the crop is sold. Usually when the landlord resides on his property or in a neighboring town, he personally sells the crop to a local processor and then gives the sharecropper his portion of the returns, or he may buy the sharecropper's part of the harvest and sell it along with his own. In the case of absentee landowners who have no resident administrators on their property, the sharecropper decides where he will sell the crop and then gives the landowner his share of the money when he visits the holding.

With few exceptions, the sharecroppers in Ouro Verde are permitted to intertill subsistence crops between the rows of coffee trees in their care, and they rarely have to give any part of these harvests to their patrão. As with colonos, the kind and amount of crops which may be planted is usually specified in the contract if it is written, but in no instance are mamona (castor beans) or cotton allowed near the trees, as both rob the soil of its nutriments.

Frequently, married sons and sons-in-law of owners of small farms work as meieiros on their fathers' or father-in-laws' farms. This is one solution when there is sufficient land to support another family but not enough cash to invest in a separate holding. The sharecropping arrangements here are usually the same as those mentioned, although written contracts between father and son are rare. Sons who sharecrop on their fathers' farms also often work for other landowners as volantes during the coffee and cotton harvests. Likewise, most sharecroppers in the county supplement their incomes by working part time as day laborers and doing odd jobs.

Sharecropping positions, like those of formadores de café, are not available to every agricultural worker in Ouro Verde. Before agreeing to contract an individual to sharecrop coffee, the landowner first questions him about his finances. He tries to find out if the prospective sharecropper is in debt to anyone, if he has sufficient savings to support himself and his family until the crop is harvested, and if he has any money to pay for his share of the cultivation expenses. Landowners are loath to contract men with large families and no resources since they will need a considerable amount of financing. Sharecroppers who become heavily in debt to their patrões are considered bad risks, for it is feared that they will abandon their positions once the debt exceeds the value of their share of the harvest.

Landowners with little money to spend on cultivation look for sharecroppers who are willing to use their own savings to buy insecticide and fertilizer. One sharecropper with a capital of CrN$ 2,000,00 (about U.S. $750) invested a good part of this in the trees under his care. His patrão, a man of meager resources, had clearly hired him because he had little money of his own to spend on cultivation. The sharecropper, who was illiterate, had unwittingly agreed to a one-year contract; after that time the landowner dismissed him, claiming that he had neglected the trees. The sharecropper's investment had benefited his patrão's land and had enabled him to remain solvent at least for another year.

Usually far less money is needed to secure a sharecropping position, particularly one in which the landowner agrees to pay for the expenses of cultivation. The minimum savings for a family of five to see them through the seven months prior to the coffee harvest is about CrN$ 150,00 (U.S. $48); this is to purchase food for the three months before their subsistence crops are harvested. The figure is based on the assumption that they pay nothing toward insecticide and fertilizer, that they live very frugally on a diet largely of beans and manioc flour, and that no medical expenses are incurred. But even this small sum is beyond the means of a large portion of the agricultural workers in the county, so that sharecropping positions are rarely or never filled by day laborers or others who earn subsistence wages.

September 1 is the end of the agricultural year and the date on which sharecroppers who are not staying for the following harvest must vacate their houses. Before leaving the property they are obliged to clear the land which was used for lavoura branca and subsistence crops and ready it for the next planting. This enables the new sharecroppers to plant their own crops immediately on arrival and then begin caring for the coffee trees.[11]

The term percenteiro usually refers to workers who sharecrop cotton, peanuts, and rice, and its meaning here will be limited to that use. Percenteiros keep between 60 and 70 per cent of the harvest, giving the remainder to the landowner. The actual percentage retained by the percenteiro depends on the proportion of cultivation expenses he assumes. In some cases, he gives his patrão a predetermined percentage of only one crop; in others, he may be obliged to give him a portion of all the crops that he cultivates. Sharecroppers of cotton and peanuts require more capital than coffee meieiros do. Since subsistence crops may not be planted among the cotton and peanuts, percenteiros have to purchase all of their food.

There are various arrangements between landowner and percenteiro. A sharecropper on one farm gave his patrão 30 per cent of all the crops (corn, cotton, and rice) harvested. He assumed responsibility for all cultivation expenses, but the patrão advanced him money to buy cotton seed and insecticide. This debt was then deducted from the portion of the cotton harvest to which the sharecropper was entitled, leaving him with 65 per cent of the crop. The sharecropper also paid the wages of the eight men whom he hired to help harvest the cotton. A percenteiro who sharecropped 1½ alqueires of cotton and peanuts only kept 50 per cent of the harvest, since the landowner paid him CrN$ 50,00 a month toward household and cultivation expenses. Another sharecropped 3 alqueires of cotton and rice on his brother's farm, giving the latter 25 per cent of both crops.

As with coffee meeiros, sharecroppers of cotton and peanuts may sell their portions of the harvest to their patrões or sell them independently to an intermediary. They must vacate their houses at the end of May after the cotton harvest, but, unlike meieiros, they are usually not required to clear the land and ready it for replanting.

Renting land or tenant farming, a recent innovation in Ouro Verde, has become more common as lavoura branca continues to replace coffee. Since coffee is a perennial and takes four years to come into production, it is never cultivated by renters (*arrendá-*

11. Sharecroppers are allowed to devote the first two weeks to their own crops before turning their attention to the coffee trees.

tarios) whose contracts are for one year. Unlike sharecroppers who give the landowner a certain percentage of the harvest, renters pay him a fixed, predetermined sum, independent of the size of the yields. This may be in cash, but more commonly payment is part of the crop, so many arrôbas of cotton or peanuts per alqueire of rented land. During abundant harvests this arrangement benefits the renter who may have to give only a small fraction of his crop in payment. But when yields are small, the amount given the landowner as rent may be a considerable percentage of the total harvest.

Renters generally are thought to have more independence than sharecroppers. Since the patrão who receives a fixed rental on his land is little concerned with the size of the crop, renters are able to work when and how they wish. They may plant whatever supplementary crops they desire, as long as they also cultivate the crop, most often cotton, that will be used to pay their rent. The landowner receives no part of these other crops, whether they are for subsistence or for sale. Still, the amount of land that a renter may plant in crops other than the one being used for payment is limited by the fact that he must be sure that the rental crop's yields are sufficient to meet his obligations to the landowner.

The renter pays for all cultivation expenses, although the landowner may advance him money, usually at an interest rate of 3 per cent a month. Some renters are financed up to six months by private banks if their patrões are willing to endorse their loans. In either case, the renter pays off his debt after the crop is harvested and sold. Frequently, the landowner will sell the renter seed and insecticide at inflated prices. In one instance, a renter paid CrN$ 15,00 for a sack of cotton seed which could be purchased for CrN$ 10,00 in town. Lacking cash, he was forced to buy at the higher price on credit.

One fazendeiro suggested that renters could avoid paying interest charges for agricultural supplies if they purchased them with cash after the harvest, instead of relying on their patrões to finance the necessary items. Unfortunately, this "rational solution" is not practical for most renters. The money they receive from the sale of the cotton crop in April and May must be used to support themselves and their families through the following November.[12] Not only are they without cash to buy seed and insecticide during this period,

12. Landowners usually start advancing renters money for cultivation and household expenses in November.

but most of them work as day laborers just to be able to pay for necessities.

Landowners are concerned with the financial status of prospective renters. A man with enough savings to support his family for only one or two months will usually be denied a rental contract. But renters with sufficient capital to pay for cultivation and household expenses for at least three months are considered "good risks," and will not have difficulty renting land. While many landowners are willing to finance renters for two or three months, most are reluctant to hire men who will have to receive assistance for the entire duration of the contract. One fazendeiro complained, "I lost CrN$ 3,000,00 this year on renters who couldn't pay off their debts to me after the [peanut] harvest failed. I loaned them money for food, clothing, seeds, and insecticide. This year I will be wiser. No more household expenses! If they can't support themselves then I won't rent them land!"

Last year the average rental in the county for an alqueire of land was 50 arrôbas of cotton. The yields, unusually large, averaged 200 arrôbas per alqueire, and often reached 350 arrôbas. Thus, a man with 1 alqueire of rented land and an average size harvest paid a rental of 25 per cent of the crop. This is considerably less than a sharecropper with the same area of land who would have to pay his patrão between 30 and 40 per cent of the harvest, or 60 to 80 arrôbas of cotton. Since yields vary greatly from one harvest to another, landowners are reluctant to contract renters for more than one year. This is made clear in the words of one fazendeiro: "I rented 25 alqueires to six men last year and charged them 60 arrôbas per alqueire. Well, do you know what the average yields turned out to be? Three hundred arrôbas per alqueire! This year I made sure that I got a better deal. I charged 80 arrôbas per alqueire,[13] and they agreed to pay it for they knew my land was good. But now yields are averaging 250 arrôbas so that the renters are not doing as well as before."

Areas of 1–5 alqueires are usually contracted to individual renters,[14] the actual amount varying with the number of workers in the family. Almost without exception, renters have to hire volantes to assist in the cotton harvest which requires an intensive labor input, especially when yields are large. One man who rents 4 alqueires, 3½ of which are planted in cotton, is aided by his four sons, but

13. This is the highest rental I came across in the county.
14. Intermediaries rent far larger areas of land.

he still must employ ten to twelve day laborers during the harvest, all additional hands paid by the renter rather than the landowner.

In general, the renter gives the landowner his share of the crop and then sells the remainder independently. Sometimes, however, when the renter is heavily in debt to his patrão, the latter sells the crop and gives the renter his portion of it, less the amount previously loaned. In these cases, it is not uncommon for the landowner to act as middleman in the sale; he keeps an extra percentage of the crop for himself and pays the renter less per arrôba than the rate paid by the processors.

Renters are most frequently employed in those regions of the county which are changing over from coffee to cattle. They are hired to plant lavoura branca for two or three years, thus enabling the landowner to fulfill the terms of his eradication contract. In the Vagalume, 90 per cent of those engaged in cotton and peanut cultivation are renters. Since the planting of these crops is often an intermediate stage between the exit of coffee and the entrance of cattle, many rental contracts contain clauses requiring renters to plant pasture before leaving the property. In at least two cases, the land was given rent free in exchange for this task. The employment of renters saves the landowner from the necessity of hiring day laborers to plant lavoura branca in the intervening period, and it lessens his expenses since renters assume the burden of cultivation costs. In addition, at the termination of the rental contract the land, planted in pasture, is ready for the introduction of cattle.

Subrenting and subsharecropping, arrangements in which workers are contracted by an intermediary or middleman rather than by the landowner, are found only on the large fazendas in the county. Intermediaries are most often administrators on holdings with absentee owners, or crop buyers who have some connection with a particular property. In all instances the intermediary must have some capital; CrN$ 500,00 is the usual minimum, with which to "furnish" seed and insecticide to his subrenters, as well as a tractor which he can rent them.

The administrator on one large holding rents 50 alqueires from the landowners at a cost of 30 arrôbas of cotton per alqueire and, in turn, subrents the land to ten or twelve men for 50 arrôbas of cotton per alqueire. He sells the subrenters seed, at CrN$ 10,00 more per sack than it costs at any of the stores in town, and insecticide for the cotton crop, but will not advance them money for food or other household expenses. In addition, he owns a tractor which the subrenters may use for plowing at a cost of CrN$ 130,00 (about U.S. $40) per alqueire. The sub-renters pay the administrator for the use of the land with a part of the cotton crop, while the debts owed him (for seed, tractor rental, and so on) are paid in cash after the harvest is sold.

The following accounts of two subrenters illustrate practices typical of those in the county.

José rented 2½ alqueires of land from Antonio, the administrator of Fazenda Boa Vista. He did not choose the particular piece he was to cultivate, and complained that the administrator assigned him to an area which produced poor yields. The quality of land on this fazenda varies greatly, but on parts of it yields may reach 350 arrôbas or more per alqueire. José claimed that the poorer land was given to him because he had less capital than some of the other renters, and therefore required more financing (*aqueles que são ruim de vida o intermediário dá terra peor*).[15] He received the land in early July and had to begin immediately to prepare it for planting, so that he was not able to earn extra money as a volante in the coffee harvest as he had done in the past. The few subrenters who were contracted in May prepared their land right away and were free to harvest coffee until late August when the cotton crop was ready for planting.

José planted 2 alqueires of cotton and a half alqueire of corn, rice, and beans. Both the rice and bean crops failed because of drought, and he was forced to buy these items in town to meet his family's needs. His cotton yields were very small, the 2 alqueires producing only 190 arrôbas. After paying a rent of 100 arrôbas of cotton to the administrator, he sold the remainder at CrN$ 6,50 an arrôba, or CrN$ 585,00 for his share of the cotton crop.

His expenses were CrN$ 260,00 to Antonio for the use of the tractor to plow 2 alqueires, CrN$ 100,00 for the wages of volantes who assisted in the harvest, CrN$ 202,00 for insecticide, and CrN$ 120,00 for eight sacks of cotton seed. The last two items were paid for with cash earned by José and his two young sons[16] when they

15. It is a common practice to assign the least desirable land to those renters who have little savings, and have no choice but to accept it, since they would encounter difficulties in renting land elsewhere. On the other hand, subrenters with more capital find many positions open to them, and can select their land.

16. The sons, ages nine and ten, were unable to attend school since their labor was needed on the land.

worked intermittently as day laborers, thus avoiding the inflated prices that Antonio charges for seed and insecticide, although money was borrowed from him to pay the day laborers used during the harvest. José's total cultivation expenses came to CrN$ 682,00, leaving him in debt to Antonio for CrN$ 97,00. When the latter insisted on immediate payment and suggested that José sell his horse in order to raise the money, José took the case to the *promotor público* (labor mediator) in Nova Esperança. The promotor público ruled that the debt could be paid off the following harvest if José agreed to remain as a renter on the same holding. Although José had planned to leave Fazenda Boa Vista and search for better land to sharecrop or rent, he was forced to remain because of the debt.

João, another subrenter with 4 alqueires on the same fazenda, fared better. He lives in town where he owns eight small parcels of land and has rented and sharecropped on various holdings in the county for the past eleven years. Since he had some savings with which to pay for cultivation expenses, Antonio allowed him to choose the best land on the fazenda. He planted the entire area in cotton, explaining that he didn't want to "waste" it on subsistence crops.[17] João received no financing from Antonio, preferring instead to take out a small bank loan to help pay for the seed and insecticide. A friend in town who owns a sítio agreed to co-sign the loan.

João harvested an average of 200 arrôbas of cotton per alqueire, a total of 800 arrôbas. Two hundred arrôbas were given to Antonio for rent, and the remainder were sold in town for CrN$ 6,50 each, or CrN$ 3,900,00 for the sale of his cotton.

During the year, only João and his grown son worked on the land, but for the harvest, day laborers were employed at a cost of CrN$ $250,00. His other cultivation expenses were CrN$ 520,00 for the rental of Antonio's tractor, CrN$ 270,00 for cotton seed, and CrN$ 450,00 for insecticide. Thus, João's net profit on his rented land was CrN$ 2,410,00. He plans to save as much of this money as possible, rent the same land for another year, and invest the profits from the two harvests in a small sítio on the frontier.

Subsharecropping operates much as subrenting does, except that the subsharecropper pays a predetermined percentage of the harvest rather than a fixed rental to the intermediary. In both cases, the worker has dealings only with the intermediary, and often

17. Since João is well known in town, he was able to buy food on credit at one of the local stores.

does not know or has never met the actual landowner, who usually lives in an urban area of Paraná or São Paulo and visits his property once or twice a year. Subsharecropping is less common than subrenting; in the latter, the intermediary is assured of receiving payment for the use of the land no matter what the size of the harvest. Since he in turn must pay the landowner a fixed rental, this system has definite advantages over one in which a precise return is not guaranteed. Still, under certain circumstances, subsharecropping can be a highly profitable venture for the intermediary.

Chico is a crop buyer in town and a brother-in-law of an administrator of Fazenda San Giorgio, the largest property in Ouro Verde. He rented 40 alqueires on the fazenda for a cash payment of CrN$ 100,00 per alqueire,[18] and then turned the land over to ten men to sharecrop. The case of one of these subsharecroppers is similar to all of those working on this holding. Luis was sharecropping peanuts on a fazenda in a neighboring county when he met Chico, who offered to rent him 2 alqueires of land in return for 40 arrôbas of cotton per alqueire. Since the rental was relatively low, Luis' parents and brothers also agreed to the offer and arranged to rent 8 additional alqueires. Chico paid the entire family's moving expenses, but when they arrived at San Giorgio he backed down on the original agreement and insisted they sharecrop the land instead of renting it, and give him 30 per cent of the harvest. At this point he mentioned that he would charge them an interest rate of 30 per cent on all loans for cultivation and household expenses, and would not advance them any cash. Since neither Luis nor his parents had a written contract and they were already in debt to Chico for the costs of moving, they reluctantly accepted his new terms.

Both families arrived on San Giorgio a full month before the cotton planting season, and Chico put them to work clearing land and harvesting coffee during the interim. None of the subsharecroppers received any payment for these tasks. Unlike most other sharecroppers, they were not permitted to plant subsistence crops on their land and so were forced to buy all of their food. Since none of the families working under Chico had any savings, they all required financing for 100 per cent of their household and cultivation expenses. Chico patently refused to advance them money with which to make purchases in town. Instead, at first he personally

18. This is a very low rental and was undoubtedly given to Chico for this price because of his relationship to the fazenda's administrator.

sold them food, clothing, seed, and insecticide, then later gave them credit at his brother's store where they could charge these items, spending up to a specified amount. The only cash outlay he gave the subsharecroppers was for the wages of volantes employed in the harvest. In addition to all of this, Chico rented his tractor for plowing at a charge of CrN$ 150,00 per alqueire. These loans were made for periods of three to four months, with a 30 per cent interest rate covering everything, including the money owed on the tractor rental. At the end of the harvest, Chico gave Luis an itemized list of charges:

Cultivation Expenses		
Two sacks of FTP insecticide	CrN$	76,00
Three sacks of ZP insecticide		120,00
Transport for volantes in harvest		30,00
Volantes' wages		132,00
Scale to weight cotton		20,00[19]
Tractor rental (2 alqueires)		300,00
Total cultivation expenses		678,00

Household Expenses		
Medicine	CrN$	26,00
Dentist		5,00
One month's food		59,00
One month's food		79,00
One month's food		73,00
Cash (for haircut)		1,00
Five kilos of potatoes		1,25
Nine kilos of rice		8,10
Clothing		35,00
Moving expenses		105,00
Total household expenses		392,35
Total owed to Chico		1,070,35
Plus 30 per cent interest		321,11
Total debt including interest		1,391,46

In order to indicate individual prices charged for some of the food purchases, Chico presented a list to Luis' father. It represents

19. Scales of this type are sold for CrN$ 5,00 in town.

food for a family of five for one month. The average prices for the same quantity of these items in seven stores in town are in parentheses.

Item		Charged	Town average
Fifty kilos of rice	CrN$	40,00	(CrN$ 35,00)
Sixty kilos of sugar		22,00	(22,80)
Ten kilos of wheat farinha		6,50	(6,50)
Seven kilos of salt		2,10	(1,40)
Five kilos of dried meat		12,50	(10,00)
Ten kilos of beans		8,00	(4,90)
Two packages of matches		1,00	(,70)
One can of kerosene		6,00	(4,00)
Charges at brother's store		44,18	
Total food bill		142,28	
30 per cent interest		42,68	
Debt for food, including interest		184,96	

Luis harvested a total of 400 arrôbas of cotton on the 2 alqueires he sharecropped and gave 30 per cent, 120 arrôbas, to Chico. Along with this, Luis received 76 arrôbas in compensation for planting and harvesting cotton on Chico's land, giving him a total of 356 arrôbas. As soon as the harvest was completed, Chico took Luis' cotton, locked it in a warehouse, and gave him a receipt for it. He then offered to pay CrN$ 6,25 per arrôba which Luis was forced to accept, even though he certainly would have received a better price had he sold the crop in town. Thus, for the sale of his cotton Luis was paid CrN$ 2,225,00, of which he owed CrN$ 1,391,00 to Chico, leaving him with a net profit of CrN$ 834,00 (U.S. $261) for nearly nine months of work.

Luis commented on his experience at Fazenda San Giorgio: "The other [ten subsharecropping] families working for Chico could tell you exactly the same story. He charged them the same interest and then bought their cotton for a low price. But the two renters who worked for him did better [*saiu melhor*]. They had their own money when they came and didn't take loans except to pay their volantes' wages. Their harvests were big and since they were not heavily in debt to Chico, they were able to buy small sítios in Cruzeiro d'Oeste [on the Paraná frontier]. And now what does Chico do? He goes around town bragging that these men made a lot of money working for him. But he never mentions the other ten families he exploited. What a joke!"

The use of intermediaries has definite advantages for the landowner. When land is subrented through an intermediary rather than by the landowner, the latter is able to skirt a series of labor laws which deal with renters and sharecroppers. These laws state that the landowner must finance his workers' cultivation expenses by taking out low-interest bank loans in their names. But the fazendeiro who rents to an intermediary has a contract with him, not with the men who actually work on the land, so that legally he is not required to finance them. Similarly, since these laws only pertain to landowners, the intermediary who only leases land is not bound by them, and in any case, has no right to take out bank loans for his subcontractors.

Volantes[20] or day laborers are the most numerous and the most disadvantaged group of agricultural workers in Ouro Verde. They are paid either by the day or by the task, the latter arrangement being particularly common in coffee cultivation. While most volantes live on the property where they are employed, quite a few are semipermanent residents of the county and reside in town.

The large majority of volantes in Ouro Verde hold short-term positions on the sítios and fazendas where they work. They may be employed, for example, to prune the coffee trees or to harvest a crop, afterward moving to another holding where again they are hired to do a specific task. Many volantes never remain on any one property for more than the time it takes to complete the harvest. It is this group that is most affected by the seasonality of agricultural employment. One volante has worked in six different counties over the past twelve years. On only one occasion during this period did he remain on a fazenda for more than nine months, and he estimates that he has worked on over ninety properties since coming to the area.

Another group of volantes may be distinguished from the majority by the greater length of time they stay on a particular sítio or fazenda. I encountered a few who had been working for the same patrão for four or five years, although most only remain for a year or two. The living and working conditions of the men in this group are hardly adequate, but they do have more job security than those who continually go from one fazenda to another in

20. Volantes, literally fliers, comes from the verb *voar,* to fly. They are called this because they are continually on the move.

search of work. In addition, they are occasionally given small areas of land on which to grow subsistence crops, a privilege never extended to the highly mobile volante. Many of the semipermanent volantes live in town. They are well known and have less difficulty securing positions than those who are relatively new to the area. One town resident who has lived in the county for six years works regularly on four or five of the neighboring chácaras, and rarely lacks employment for any length of time. Another worked under a local empreiteiro for a few years until he became acquainted with a number of landowners who offered him fairly steady jobs. In his words, "Thank God I have always been able to find work, even from September to December [the slack season]. Before, I worked for an empreiteiro who kept half of my wages, but since I made friends here I don't have too much trouble finding jobs on my own. I still make very little, often only CrN$ 2,00 a day,[21] but at least now it is all mine."

When volantes move, they are frequently accompanied by relatives. The usual practice is for one nuclear family to seek work on another property and send back word describing their living conditions and wages, perhaps suggesting that their relatives join them. The groups which travel together are not highly stable. A married couple and their children may work alone on a number of fazendas in a neighboring county for a year or more without ever being joined by their relatives in the region. The kinsmen who work together do not seem to fall into any particular category. I found cases of brothers, father and son, nephew and uncle, brothers-in-law, and father and son-in-law who were employed on the same holding and tried to secure jobs together whenever possible.

Just before the coffee harvest begins in early June, the movement of volantes throughout the region gains momentum and becomes even more pronounced than during the rest of the year. Families travel among fazendas in search of coffee trees laden with berries. Since they are paid by the number of sacks picked, it is advantageous to locate trees which promise large yields and can be harvested in a short period of time. Landowners whose trees give low yields are almost invariably forced to pay their workers a higher price per sack to compensate for the smaller returns.

Landowners almost always pay their volantes' moving expenses and then deduct the amount from their wages. A truck is hired and

21. This falls considerably below the legal minimum wage for the region, which is CrN$ 117,00 (about U.S. $33) per month.

loaded with the volante's few personal possessions which are brought to the fazenda where he will work. Prices vary according to distance and size of the load. A move of two or three kilometers will cost the volante about CrN$ 10,00–15,00, while one to the vicinity of Maringá, about 50 kilometers, will cost CrN$ 50,00–60,00. In order to comprehend just how costly this is, one must remember that a worker rarely earns more than CrN$ 2,00 for a full day's labor. Volantes are forced to spend a large part of their wages on moving expenses; if there are no jobs available in a particular county, they must secure work elsewhere in order to survive.

Volantes are plagued by the seasonality of employment in agriculture. From September through December there is little work to be had; no crops are being planted or harvested and the few tasks to be done rarely require additional hands. With luck, the volante may find a semipermanent position tending coffee trees (weeding, pruning, applying insecticide and fertilizer) during the slack season. But this type of work requires far less labor than the heavy input necessary during the cotton and coffee harvests, and many volantes remain unemployed. Some work a few days a week on construction, repairing roads, and doing all manner of odd jobs, but none of these positions is long term. Those volantes who are unable to find any work in the vicinity of Ouro Verde move to more distant counties in hope of locating employment.

Starting in January, with the onset of the peanut harvest, the situation eases somewhat. When the cotton harvest begins in February, still more jobs become available and unemployment is greatly reduced. Soon after the cotton harvest ends in May, the coffee harvest gets under way, so that jobs are plentiful until late August when the last berries have been picked. Then the cycle begins again and many volantes are without jobs by early September.

Volantes' wages vary throughout the county, according to the quality of the crop (the larger the yields, the lower the pay) and the urgency with which the landowner's labor requirement must be met. Certain tasks are consistently higher paying than others: in the cotton harvest, volantes are paid between CrN$ 1,50 and CrN$ 2,00 per arrôba, and in the coffee harvest between CrN$ 1,50 and CrN$ 3,00 per 40-kilo sack. For tending coffee trees during the year volantes are paid either on a piecework (*por empreita*) or daily (*por dia*) basis. Piecework payments for a specific task (applying insecticide and fertilizer, weeding, clearing debris from under the trees) may be per tree or per 1,000 trees. Wages paid on a daily

Worker's house on a cattle fazenda

Volante's house on a large coffee fazenda

basis range from CrN$ 1,50 to CrN$ 3,00. Basically, the number of working members in a volante's family determines the size of his monthly income. With five or six hands weeding coffee trees, for example, the family may earn up to CrN$ 120,00 a month; a family with only two or three workers will make between CrN$ 50,00 and CrN$ 70,00. The income of volantes who work por empreita is increased by the assistance of their children in cultivation tasks, but those who work por dia do not benefit from this help unless their children are paid a separate wage, which is rare.

The children of volantes have the highest rates of school absenteeism in the county. One rural teacher estimated that the six children of day laborers in her class were not in attendance more than 50 per cent of the time. Absenteeism is most pronounced among these children during the cotton harvest when payment is for the number of arrôbas picked. Children are used in harvesting cotton because their short stature makes picking the cotton bolls a somewhat less arduous task than it is for adults. The children of volantes not only attend classes irregularly but often are not enrolled in school at all when their parents work in a place for a short period of time. Even those children with three or four years of schooling are usually illiterate, although most have learned how to sign their names.

Working conditions also vary from one fazenda or sítio to another. In general, volantes employed by landowners and sharecroppers on small farms tend to be better off than those working for resident administrators on large properties owned by absentee landlords. On a small holding, the patrão may supply the volante and his family with free milk, wood, and housing, a subsistence plot, and small loans in times of emergency. The volante is usually permitted to spend his free time working on other farms in the area in order to earn extra money. In addition, volante and patrão are often *compadres,* and have a friendly, face-to-face relationship, with little of the deferential behavior found between people of different socioeconomic groups.

On large holdings volantes are never given subsistence plots, and very rarely receive loans for food and medicine. Three to five cruzeiros a week are deducted from their wages for the housing and wood which are supplied by the fazenda. Since there is always some work to be done on properties with vast acreages, volantes are not free to work on other holdings in the area for extra income. Fazenda administrators make a point of not serving as compadres to the volantes they hire, for this would involve reciprocal obligations of which they want no part. The actual landlord, of course, visits his property only intermittently, and never has any direct dealings with the day laborers he employs.

Since most volantes have no subsistence plots and all earn very low wages, the purchase of food often becomes a problem. Some fazendas allow their workers to charge a specified amount of food and other items at a particular store and then deduct the expenditures from their pay at the end of the week. Storeowners almost unanimously refuse to allow volantes to buy on credit unless their patrões guarantee payment. In the words of one shopkeeper, "I never sell fiado [on credit] to volantes. I used to, but I lost so much money on their unpaid bills that I no longer do it. A volante will leave at a moment's notice and no one can keep him in one place. And if I don't let him go, his debts only keep getting bigger. But if he can't find anyone to sell him fiado, he goes hungry." Sometimes volantes will hire themselves out in exchange for food rather than cash. One man who was out of work and had no money to buy food agreed to weed coffee trees for one week on a shopkeeper's sítio in return for a sack of rice. A few volantes fish in their spare time and then go from farm to farm trading their catch for milk and eggs.

In all cases, the volantes' diet is sparse and has little variety. Manioc flour and beans are the staples, with small quantities of rice mixed in for added bulk. Meat of any kind is a rare luxury. One volante commented, "Our daily meat is pumpkin [*A nossa carne diário é abóbora*]. I can only afford a kilo of *carne sêca* [sun-dried meat] once a month, and then only during the coffee and cotton harvests." Another volante explained why he did not earn enough to live on: "I make maybe CrN$ 15,00 a week and have a wife and three children to feed. Rice costs CrN$ 1,00 a kilo, coffee CrN$,84 and beans CrN$,50. How can I pay for these things on my wages? I buy food for the week on Saturday and by Wednesday it is almost all gone!"

From the landowners' point of view, there are both advantages and disadvantages in employing volantes. Since day laborers are not covered by the labor laws which pertain to other agricultural workers and they never have written contracts, they can be dismissed at will.[22] Even volantes who have worked for the same patrão

22. For a detailed explanation of why a stable labor force is often considered undesirable by landowners, see Knight 1969.

for a year or more can be fired without notice when their services are no longer required. Volantes are powerless to do anything about the situation, since they are not unionized, and landowners invariably win any cases brought before the local promotor público. For the same reason, minimum wage laws are easily skirted by patrões. If a volante does not earn the legal monthly minimum, the landowner simply claims that he did not work as many hours as required or that he took "vacations" without permission. One fazendeiro explained, "Sure I will pay the minimum wage if the volante will work eight hours a day during the week and until noon on Saturdays. If they don't they must make up the time on Sundays and holidays. But which one of them does this? So maybe I don't pay the minimum, but it is their fault, not mine. Two cruzeiros a day is low, but they are willing to work for it, aren't they? They are not interested in making more than this."

The drawbacks of employing volantes regularly are also sizable. Just as day laborers can be dismissed at any time, they also can leave a property without notice if they find better paying work elsewhere. During the peanut, cotton, and coffee harvests, which must be completed in a short time so that the crops will not be endangered by heavy rains or drought, a sudden mass exodus of volantes can prove disastrous for the landowners. Since volantes are paid by the day or by the task, they have little to gain from doing a particularly good job, and may, in fact, stand to lose by being overly careful in their work. When a volante works on a piecework basis he increases his wages by weeding a large number of coffee trees or picking many arrôbas of cotton in a short period of time. But work done with great haste is often slipshod and may actually do damage to the crop. One frequently hears complaints about partially harvested coffee trees, broken branches, and damaged berries. All this contrasts sharply with the situation of sharecroppers who directly benefit from the care given to the trees since they keep a percentage of the harvest. In addition, volantes are fairly independent; they can work when they so choose, taking time off at their own discretion, and the landowner can do little about it short of firing them. Hiring volantes also involves the added expense of employing foremen (*fiscais*) to oversee their work, assign them tasks, and keep accounts of the wages owed. In the case of sharecroppers, who work independently and receive no cash compensation, all that is needed in a case of absentee ownership is a general administrator who sees to it that the fazenda runs smoothly.

Mensalistas, workers who are paid a fixed monthly salary, are relatively new in Ouro Verde. The growth in their numbers is directly linked to the increasing areas in the county used for pasture and cattle raising, since they are involved exclusively in this enterprise. Still, at present, mensalistas comprise only a small part, perhaps 5 per cent, of all rural workers, due to the fact that the labor requirements for cattle raising are low and a handful of workers can care for large herds on vast expanses of land. Mensalistas are usually *campeiros* (cowhands); they round up the cattle, brand them, milk them, and deliver their young. They are never given subsistence plots since the fazendas on which they work are planted largely in pasture. Thus, their only compensation is a fixed monthly wage,[23] ranging from CrN$ 80,00 for an inexperienced cowhand to CrN$ 130,00 or more for those who specialize in caring for recently birthed cows and their calves. Although campeiros rarely have written contracts, they enjoy somewhat more job security than volantes, since, unlike agriculture, cattle raising requires approximately the same number of hands all year round.

Fazenda foremen and administrators are also paid a fixed monthly salary, but, unlike campeiros, they receive other benefits as well. Administrators often may use small areas of land on the property in any way they see fit. On one fazenda of 100 alqueires, the administrator received 3 alqueires which he chose to plant in cotton. He contracted two sharecroppers to cultivate it for him and was not obliged to give the landowner any part of the harvest. Where larger areas of land are involved, they are given to the administrator on a rental or sharecropping basis. The common pattern in these cases is for the administrator to subcontract workers to do the actual cultivation. Intermediary arrangements of this sort can be highly profitable, and administrators usually derive the bulk of their income from them since their salaries are small.

Foremen employed to oversee volantes are either given free use of 1 or 2 alqueires for planting subsistence crops or somewhat more land if they wish to rent or sharecrop. Unlike administrators, fazenda foremen usually do not have sufficient capital to serve as intermediaries and are more likely to do the cultivation themselves.

The Chácara, Sítio, and Fazenda

Rural properties in Ouro Verde show marked differences in the use of land and labor, in the technology employed, and in the size

23. The fazenda usually supplies campeiros with free milk.

of crop production. Variations in the first two factors and in average yields are functions of the size of the holding and its location within the county; differences in agricultural technology are more directly linked with the economic well-being of the landowner.

Chácaras, small holdings of 1–5 alqueires immediately adjacent to town, were intended by the company to supply basic food crops to the nonagriculturalists in the county. But this plan was never carried out; the chácara owners preferred to cultivate coffee. Until five or six years ago nearly all of the chácaras in Ouro Verde had between 75 and 95 per cent of their land planted in coffee, with the remaining areas given over to small patches of pasture and intertilled subsistence crops. After the frost of 1963, however, many chacristas were forced to abandon coffee as their principal cash crop, cut down the most badly damaged trees, and replace them with lavoura branca, predominately cotton and peanuts. Today, approximately 40 per cent of the chácaras in the county have less than one-quarter of their land in coffee. Most of the holdings that made the changeover are located in the upper Vagalume region which was hard hit by that frost. One chacrista whose 5 alqueires were planted in 10,000 coffee trees prior to 1963 now has 2,000 trees, with four-fifths of his land given over to peanuts, cotton, and castor beans.

Even on those chácaras planted largely in coffee, the percentage of land reserved for nonintertilled lavoura branca has been increasing. Farmers cannot afford to risk everything in the event of another frost, so they have taken the precautionary measure of reducing their dependence on coffee and substituting other cash crops. Cotton and peanuts are not subject to frost because their agricultural cycles fall outside of the coldest months.

Subsistence crops, particularly corn, rice, and beans, have always been and continue to be intertilled by holders of small amounts of land. There is widespread disagreement about the effects of this practice on the size of coffee yields, although most agronomists claim that it is harmful. Corn and castor beans affect the trees by competing for vital soil nutriments, particularly when the trees are less than four years old, and the cultivation of these crops can delay the first harvest by a year or more. When rice is intertilled with coffee, it is less harmful if its roots are extracted from the soil after harvesting, to prevent them from resprouting.

Owners of small landholdings have little choice but to intertill subsistence crops with coffee, for they lack sufficient acreage to

TABLE 18. Land Use and Size of Holding

Crop	Percentage of land in each crop	Number of chácaras (1–5 alq.)	Number of small sítios (6–10 alq.)	Number of medium sítios (11–29 alq.)	Number of large sítios (30–49 alq.)	Number of fazendas (50 or more alq.)
Coffee						
	25 or less	4	2	5	1	5
	26–50		4	3	2	1
	51–75	7	5	4	2	
	76–100	3	4	1		
Lavoura branca						
	25 or less	10	13	10	5	5
	26–50	2	2	2		1
	51–75	1		1		
	76–100	1				
Subsistence crops						
	25 or less	12	13	12	5	6
	26–50	2	2	1		
	51–75					
	76–100					
Pasture						
	25 or less	14	11	8	3	
	26–50		4	4	1	3
	51–75				1	1
	76–100			1		2

grow them separately. Although this practice may reduce coffee yields by as much as 30 per cent,[24] these crops of corn, rice, and beans form a large part of the local diet, and, in years of unusually good harvests, a portion will be sold, thus adding to the farmer's income.

Land usage on sítios of 6 to 49 alqueires shows even greater variation, depending on size and location, than it does on chácaras. On most small sítios (6–10 alqueires) coffee still predominates, but on nearly 40 per cent of the holdings in this category, coffee accounts for less than half of the land under cultivation. Medium sítios of 11 to 29 alqueires show a further decrease in the percentage of land in coffee, with a concomitant rise in pasturage. Less than half of the sítios of 30 to 49 alqueires have over 50 per cent of their land in coffee, and, here again, larger areas are reserved for pasture. Very few of the holdings in the sítio category are heavily dependent upon lavoura branca; less than 18 per cent have more than one-quarter of their cultivated land in cash crops other than coffee.

Fazendas (50 alqueires or more) have large expanses, never less than 25 per cent of their total acreages, planted in pasture. Virtually no large holding has more than half of its land in coffee; the majority have under 25 per cent in this crop. Lavoura branca also plays a small and temporary role here. In order to fulfill the terms of their eradication contracts, many fazendeiros have planted cotton and peanuts on land previously devoted to coffee, but this is a short-term arrangement and the land in question will soon be converted into pasture.

Most of the county's fazendas are currently going through a period of change. The owners no longer have nearly all of their land planted in coffee, as was the case six or eight years ago, and many have reached a temporary accommodation with areas given over to cotton and pasture as well as coffee. One large holding of 100 alqueires illustrates this trend: 40 per cent of the land is now planted in coffee, 30 per cent in pasture, and 20 per cent in lavoura branca. When the fazenda was purchased in 1962 by its present owner, 100,000 coffee trees covered 70 per cent of the holding. Under the eradication program, half were cut down and replaced with pasture and cotton. Cotton will be grown for one more year, and then pasture will be planted instead. Another large property

24. This is an estimate supplied by an agronomist with the Associação de Crédito e Assistencia Rural do Paraná.

is even farther along in this process: four-fifths of its 500,000 coffee trees were eradicated between 1960 and 1964, and 80 per cent of its land is currently given over to cattle raising.

A large majority of the fazendas in Ouro Verde have little or no land planted in subsistence crops. Those few landowners who employ sharecroppers allow small quantities of specified crops to be intertilled among the coffee trees. The cultivation of beans and peanuts is permitted, but never corn or castor beans because of deleterious effects on the size of coffee yields. One fazendeiro admitted that he had ulterior motives in allowing his workers to intertill rice and beans: "I let them plant a limited amount of their own crops between my trees, even though it may slightly reduce the yields, because the workers take better care of the coffee when their own crops are at stake. They work harder at weeding the base of the trees since weeds also harm their rice and beans. Also I guess there is a psychological aspect involved. The worker says to himself, 'I am caring for my own crops and not just the coffee of the son-of-a-bitch patrão.'"

About ten years ago, when land was plentiful and growing coffee was so lucrative that fazendeiros refused to prejudice the size of yields through intertilling, many gave their workers separate subsistence plots (roças) on which to grow food crops. With increased land values, however, and lowered coffee yields, the fazendeiro now utilizes every inch of available land for his own crops, and the practice of giving workers individual roças has disappeared.

The single most important factor in determining land usage on all holdings in the county, regardless of size, is location. The actual location of a given property is closely linked with the quality of its soil, which varies significantly within the county. Altitude and subjection to frosts are also related to location, and are even more important determinants of land usage. A case in point is the Vagalume region of Ouro Verde. Its soils, terra mista with only a slight sandy admixture, are among the richest in the county, but the Vagalume also has the lowest altitude of any area in the vicinity, some 20 meters below that of the town and the surrounding regions. It is therefore highly subject to frosts. Even a light frost which does not affect most parts of the county will "burn" the coffee trees in the Vagalume and lead to reduced yields in the following harvest. For this reason, despite their fine soils, the properties in the Vagalume have undergone the most radical change in economic base of any in Ouro Verde, and are closer than any others to the complete replacement of coffee cultivation by cattle raising.

But altitude alone does not determine land usage, as illustrated by the holdings along the Estrada Funda on the western border of the county. This area is fairly high and is affected only by severe frosts, but its soils are sandy and produce low yields. Without massive application of chemical fertilizers, an average harvest rarely exceeds 30 sacks per 1,000 trees. In this region, poor soils rather than susceptibility to frost have produced large-scale shifts from coffee to cattle, although to a slightly lesser degree than in the Vagalume.

The type of labor various landholdings in the county employ is closely related to their size, the economic well-being of their owners, and, to a smaller extent, the number of able-bodied workers in the owner's family. Altitude and soils indirectly affect labor usage in that they help determine the way in which the land will be utilized, and, therefore, the size and type of labor force needed. Coffee cultivation demands more hands year round than any other crop, and an added labor input during the harvest. Cotton and peanuts, the other two major cash crops grown in Ouro Verde, need fewer hands, but they too require a large number of additional workers for the harvest. Cattle raising has small manpower needs, and a handful of men can care for hundreds of head of cattle on vast expanses of land.

The labor requirements of coffee vary with the height of the trees and their productivity. Highly productive trees which yield an average of 150 sacks per 1,000 need fewer workers for their upkeep. Weeding operations on these trees are greatly reduced because little undergrowth develops around their trunks. Still, many hands are needed to harvest their large yields. Poorly producing trees, on the other hand, must be continually weeded if the undergrowth is not to diminish further the size of the harvests, but the harvest itself requires fewer hands. Because of these variations, it is difficult to estimate general manpower needs in coffee cultivation. For trees of average productivity, about 50 sacks per 1,000,[25] one worker can harvest two sacks of coffee over an eight-hour period, thus covering forty trees. One family with five workers harvests an average of ten sacks a day, or two hundred trees. Over a week's time they will harvest seventy sacks. On a 5-alqueire holding with 2,000 trees per

25. The average yield throughout northern Paraná is 60 sacks per 1,000 trees (Rowe 1963:38).

Coffee drying on a terreiro

Children picking coffee beans

alqueire, this same labor force will need approximately fifty days to complete the harvest. Twice the number of hands would be required on a property of 10 alqueires. Aside from the workers doing the actual picking, two additional hands are needed during the coffee harvest, one to carry the sacks of beans to the drying terrace (terreiro), and the other to continually rake the moist berries so that they will be exposed to the sun for drying. Thus, seven full-time workers are needed over a seven-week period to complete the coffee harvest on 5 alqueires of land.

Labor usage in coffee cultivation on chácaras of 5 alqueires or less is almost wholly determined by the number of workers in the owner's family. About half of the properties in this category in Ouro Verde rely solely on family labor throughout the year; the other half use volantes to help out in the harvest. In no instance are sharecroppers or renters contracted on holdings of this size; none employs year-round laborers; and there is not a single case of a nonresident owner. In general, children of eight years or older assist their parents in the coffee harvest. They are particularly adept at picking the low branches, and can reach the berries toward the center of the tree by crawling underneath, a difficult task for adults. One farmer stressed how important his children's labor was to him, then pointed to his three daughters and said, "They are my peões." Large families with no small children have a decided advantage in that they do not have to spend money for hiring extra hands for the harvest since the family itself is a sufficient labor force. Even adolescents who do a full day's work are compensated only with free room and board, never receiving cash wages.

One chacrista with 4 alqueires, one in pasture and three in coffee, is aided in caring for the trees by two sons; he resorts to outside help only for the harvest, when he hires three or four volantes, depending on the size of the yields. Another landowner works with his brother-in-law who receives a percentage of the crop as payment. These two men are able to care for and harvest 6,000 trees by themselves and never need outside assistance. When the brother of one chácara owner left for São Paulo, the latter was forced to hire a volante to replace him. He grumbled about this, complaining that paying even a small wage cut into his meager profits.

Cotton cultivation has similar labor requirements. Three workers can care for up to 5 alqueires of land planted in cotton, but day laborers must be employed for the harvest, the number depending upon the size of the yield. One chacrista with 4 alqueires of cotton

TABLE 19. Labor System and Size of Holding

Labor system	Chácaras (1–5 alq.)	Small sítios (6–10 alq.)	Medium sítios (11–29 alq.)	Large sítios (30–49 alq.)	Fazendas (over 50 alq.)
Family members only	7	2	3		
Family members and volantes for harvest	7	8	2		
Family members, sharecroppers, and volantes for harvest		1	6	3	
Sharecroppers[a] and volantes for harvest		4[b]	2	1	3
Day laborers and/or mensalistas				1	3

a. Renters are included under the category of sharecroppers in this table.

b. In these cases, the landowners live in town and own stores or have salaried incomes.
for aste up

works alone throughout the year, since his children are too young to be of any use, but he hires up to six volantes for the harvest. Another man with 2 alqueires of cotton cultivates his land by himself, and only his son-in-law aids in harvesting the crop.

When there is not sufficient land to support a large family, the landowner and/or his sons earn additional income by working as sharecroppers or day laborers on nearby properties. This practice is particularly common if the sons are married and have their own families to support. They usually live on their father's land and sharecrop 2 or 3 alqueires belonging to a neighbor, also working for daily wages during the harvest. Three variables are involved in determining whether a landowner and/or his sons will take outside jobs: the number of workers in a family in relation to the number of dependents (wives and small children), what crops are grown, and the size of the landholding in question. Landowners with over 10 alqueires rarely seek outside work since the cultivation of their own crops leaves them little free time. Outside sharecropping becomes necessary only if there are many sons and sons-in-law with large families residing on the property. But nearly 80 per cent of the owners of farms of 5 alqueires or less hold sharecropping positions, the few exceptions being those with young children who cannot help out on the land.[26]

The type of crops cultivated and the size of the yields are also important factors in determining outside employment. The income from 10 alqueires planted in moderately productive coffee (50 sacks per 1,000 trees) can support a man, his five married sons, and their families without any need for additional earnings from sharecropping. A holding of 5 alqueires planted in coffee can support up to three families. However, properties of similar size planted in lavoura branca can sustain only about half this number, so that their owners are more likely to hold outside jobs. One man who owned 6 alqueires, 1 in pasture and 5 in cotton and peanuts, also sharecropped 3 alqueires on a neighboring farm, while three of his five sons worked as day laborers. He recently sold his sítio in Ouro Verde and bought 10 alqueires on the frontier, a holding of sufficient size to supply work for his entire family.

Labor usage on small sítios of 6 to 10 alqueires presents some contrasts with that found on chácaras. Day laborers are far more likely to be employed in the harvest since only a small number of

26. Candido (1964) noted that all sitiantes with 5 alqueires or less in Rio Bonito, São Paulo, worked as sharecroppers on outside holdings.

holdings in this category rely solely on family labor throughout the year. Many small sítios belong to shopkeepers who live in town, making absentee ownership common. Unlike chácaras, nearly one-third of all small sítios in the county are cultivated by sharecroppers. This number is positively correlated with the number of holdings with nonresident owners. I encountered only one case in which a sitiante residing on his small property contracted a sharecropper to cultivate a portion of his land.

As with chácaras, the actual form of labor employed on small sítios is dependent upon the size of the family, the extent of the holding, and the way in which the land is used. One sitiante with 10 alqueires, 5 in lavoura branca, 3 in coffee, and 2 in pasture, has eight children and a brother-in-law, all of whom work full time on his property. Two of his married sons sharecrop for him, receiving half of all crops in payment. Because his family is large, he never has to hire outside help even for the harvest. Another farmer with the same amount of land is able to care for it with the aid of only a son and daughter and two volantes for the harvest. The labor needs of the holding are low since 60 per cent of it is in pasture, with the remaining area given over to peanuts and coffee. Before he cut down 6,000 coffee trees and planted pasture, one sharecropper was employed because the sitiante's family did not supply sufficient labor. In some cases, even on 10-alqueire holdings, there is an oversupply of labor in the owner's family and a few of its members are forced to sharecrop on neighboring farms. Four sons of one man work with him on his 10 alqueires, a third of which is planted in pasture, but a fifth son sharecrops an additional 2 alqueires on a sítio belonging to the local doctor.

Labor usage on medium-sized sítios (11 to 29 alqueires) closely resembles that on smaller holdings. In a few cases, only family members work on the property, but the vast majority use volantes for the harvest, and over two-thirds employ sharecroppers on a year-round basis. The most common pattern on sítios of this size is the contracting of one or more sharecroppers to cultivate a portion of the land, while the owner and his family care for the remainder. There are also a few instances of absentee ownership in which all of the land is sharecropped, but this is not nearly as frequent as on larger properties.

Sharecropping combined with family labor is more commonly found on farms of this size than on any others in Ouro Verde. Here again, the number of sharecroppers employed is related to the extent of the holding, the number of workers in the owner's family, and the use to which the land is put. The general rule is the fewer the potential workers in the owner's family and the larger the property, the greater the number of sharecroppers that will be employed. In no case, however, is there a sítio of over 25 alqueires that is cultivated exclusively by family labor.

The sitiante with insufficient labor and capital to maintain his holdings finds an excellent solution to his problems by contracting sharecroppers to plant and harvest a percentage of his land. He thus avoids the necessity of large cash outlays for cultivation expenses, as well as the costs that wage labor would entail. An additional advantage is that the sharecropper usually assumes the burden of paying volantes to harvest the crop. Of course, the landowner must pay for all these benefits in the long run, since he gives a percentage of his crop to the sharecropper as compensation; but without sharecroppers, many sitiantes with moderate-sized holdings but small families and little capital could not continue farming. Thus, whatever its drawbacks in decreased revenues from crop sales, sharecropping is sometimes a very real necessity.

There are relatively few large sítios (30 to 49 alqueires) in Ouro Verde. There is greater similarity, in terms of the forms of labor used on them, to fazenda-sized properties than to the predominately family-oriented forms so common on small sítios and chácaras. There are no farms in this category that rely solely on family labor or on family labor in combination with day laborers. As with slightly smaller holdings, the most common pattern is the use of sharecroppers and day laborers in addition to family members. But the landowner or his sons occasionally take on a new role: they sometimes serve in an administrative capacity, overseeing the workers and keeping accounts, rather than engaging in cultivation themselves. However, most resident landowners with large sítios continue to plant and harvest alongside their sharecroppers and day laborers and do not become "gentlemen farmers."

One Japanese sitiante has a mixed labor force on his 35-alqueire holding (18 in coffee, 10 in lavoura branca, and 7 in pasture). He and his two brothers and eight of their children care for about two-thirds of the land. Two families of sharecroppers are employed, a total of five workers, each family cultivating 2 alqueires of lavoura branca and 1 of coffee. One family of day laborers with five working members is hired to do odd jobs on the property on a year-round basis, and a minimum of two extra families of day laborers are employed during the harvests. On another large sítio, labor usage takes a different form because 22 of its 40 alqueires are planted in pasture. The landowner administers the holding and does not engage in cultivation himself. Five families of volantes who are paid by the task are employed year round to care for the 10 alqueires of coffee and 7 of cotton. Four or five additional families are hired for the harvests. Sharecroppers are no longer contracted, although they did constitute the principal source of labor before the eradication of 34,000 coffee trees on the property.

Large reductions in the number of workers employed have taken place over the past few years on this group of sítios. Large areas on many of these holdings have been converted into pasture, which requires fewer hands than coffee or lavoura branca, and many landowners with large sítios have attempted to cut down on their cultivation expenses by eliminating nonessential tasks, thus reducing the size of their labor needs. One German sitiante, a gentleman farmer who administers his holding, used to employ 15 families of day laborers, a total of 20 or 25 workers, on a year-round basis to care for and harvest the coffee trees. Today he employs only five permanent families, consisting of eight workers, even though he has eradicated none of his coffee trees which still cover about 80 per cent of his 35-alqueire holding. He gives the following explanation: "Today the price of coffee is low, much lower than it was ten years ago and we can no longer use manpower lavishly as we used to do. I can't afford to have anything done by hand anymore, so I bought four burros and three plows. Why didn't I use them before? Well, the price of coffee was so high that no one gave a thought to labor costs, which were cheaper then anyway. But now I use a burro and a plow which do the work of four or five men in the same period of time. In the past no one cared how much they spent, but now we are forced to economize if we are to make any profit at all on the crop." He went on to explain why he can no longer afford nonessential cultivation tasks: "I used to spend a lot of money caring for the trees. I had my workers treating them as though they were small children. Nothing was too good for my trees. The little extra services (constant weeding and pruning) were not absolutely necessary, but they increased the yields somewhat and when prices were high, that was the most important thing. But now labor is expensive, coffee prices have fallen, and I cannot afford these luxuries."

The use of labor on fazendas (50 alqueires or more) differs from that on most other properties in the county. With two exceptions, all of Ouro Verde's fazendas belong to nonresidents of the county. Most are owned by wealthy fazendeiros and businessmen from various parts of São Paulo and Paraná who bought their properties as investments when the region was opened up fourteen or fifteen years ago. These absentee owners rarely visit their land more than once or twice a year, and the day-to-day operations are entirely in the hands of resident administrators.

Even in cases where their lands are still largely planted in coffee and lavoura branca, fazendeiros are far less likely to employ sharecroppers than are the owners of small properties because they generally have the money to cover cultivation expenses, making it unnecessary for them to divide its costs with sharecroppers. By employing only low-wage volantes, fazendeiros avoid having to share their harvests but are still able to keep labor costs at a minimum. One absentee owner with 100 alqueires of land, over half of which is planted in pasture, employs fourteen families of day laborers on a permanent basis and they supply him with sufficient labor so that extra hands are not needed during the harvest. Another holding of 65 alqueires has six families of volantes who plant and harvest its 22 alqueires of coffee and cotton. Half of this area will be turned into pasture, and only two of the families and the administrator will remain.

The exceptions to this general pattern of relying exclusively on day laborers are found on large holdings whose owners have participated in the coffee eradication program. Since they are obliged to plant lavoura branca for three years before converting the land into pasture, many find it convenient to simply contract sharecroppers or renters to cultivate the specified crops for the required period of time. An extreme example of this is a 200-alqueire fazenda which is entirely cultivated by renters. All of its coffee trees were cut down, and the owner decided to rent the land in order to fulfill the lavoura branca stipulation in the contract. For over two years he has been collecting rent which he will use to buy cattle as soon as the contract expires and pasture is planted.

On large holdings devoted to cattle raising, only an administrator and a handful of campeiros are employed. Occasionally an empreiteiro will be contracted to round up men for a specific task such as building a fence or weeding pasture, but this group leaves the property once the job is completed. The third largest fazenda in Ouro Verde, over 400 alqueires, is entirely in pasture. Its 2,000 head of cattle are cared for by five workers who receive a fixed monthly salary. One of them also serves as administrator. Thus, this fazendeiro employs only one man for every 80 alqueires of land!

Even on small farms, cooperative forms of labor (*mutirão*) are not used. Mutirão is not found in Ouro Verde or in northern Paraná as a whole, unlike many other areas of Brazil.[27] Most informants from the Northeast and from Minas Gerais were familiar with cooperative labor in which groups of men get together to help harvest a neighbor's crop or do other tasks which require many hands, in exchange for reciprocal assistance at a future date. When asked why paid workers rather than some form of cooperative labor were used in the harvest, diverse reasons were given, not a few of which stressed the "individualism" of the northern Paranaense: "Mutirão? Oh no, here we are all individualists. Everyone is for himself, and God is for all." But most informants expressed the opinion that mutirão would involve them in unwanted obligations which would be difficult to fulfill. Since small farms rarely need more than a handful of extra workers for harvesting the crops, and an abundance of labor keeps wages relatively low, the formation of cooperative groups is unnecessary. In addition, because their harvests coincide, farmers cannot afford to spend the time away from their own land, a necessity if they engaged in reciprocal forms of labor.

The landowner in Ouro Verde may occupy one of three roles: farmer, administrator, or absentee. Of the 461 properties in the county, 170, or 36 per cent, are owned by absentee landlords.[28] Their places of residence outside of the county show 90 in neighboring counties,[29] 58 in other areas of Paraná, and 22 in São Paulo. Table 20 shows the pattern of absenteeism and residence according to the size of the properties.

There are two kinds of absentee ownership, that in which the landlord resides at some distance from Ouro Verde and visits his property once or twice a year, and that in which he lives in a neighboring county and makes frequent trips to his holding. In general, those who make their homes in São Paulo and distant towns and cities of Paraná are in the former category, while those who reside within a 50-mile radius of Ouro Verde are in the latter. There are exceptions to this rule; at least a few landowners who

27. See Martins 1962.
28. Data from the IBRA 1966.
29. Counties within a 50-kilometer radius of Ouro Verde.

live only 10 to 20 kilometers from their farms visit them rarely.

One Paulista resident with 160 alqueires in Ouro Verde has not been to his property since he inherited it from his father-in-law nearly two years ago. It is run by an administrator who complained that the owner was very lax about sending payments to cover the fazenda's expenses. He commented, "This could be a good fazenda, but now it is nearly abandoned [*largada*]. What it lacks is proper treatment and a patrão who cares about it. It is really a shame to let so much good land go to waste!"

One holding of 200 alqueires is owned by a fazendeiro who lives in São Paulo. He makes two trips annually to Ouro Verde, toward

TABLE 20. Type of Ownership and Size of Holding

Size of holding	Number of resident owners	Number of absentee owners
Chácara (1–5 alq.)	12	1
Small sítios (6–10 alq.)	12	3
Medium sítios (11–29 alq.)	9	4
Large sítios (30–49 alq.)	3	2
Fazendas (over 50 alq.)	1	5

the end of the cotton and coffee harvests, at which time he collects rent from the tenant farmers on his land and arranges contracts for the coming year. In contrast to this, another fazendeiro who makes his home in Maringá visits his property once a week and spends extended periods of time on it vacationing with his family. Since most of his 100 alqueires are planted in pasture and require little work, he oversees the fazenda himself and employs no administrator.

Most local residents agree that a large property run solely by an administrator, however capable, is bound to suffer some adverse consequences. The agronomist from ACARPA illustrated this point of view with a parable: "The presence of the landowner is indispensable to a property. For example, if you own a car you will drive it carefully and if there is a hole in the road, you will stop and go around it. But if you lend your car to someone, even a person that you trust, it will not receive the same treatment. If the person is in a rush he will drive right over that hole, and the car will be damaged. But if you are sitting next to him in the car he will be more careful for he knows that you are nearby. It is the same thing with a fazenda. No administrator cares as much about the land as its owner does. And what happens? The land must suffer." One fazendeiro was more understanding toward absentee landlords and explained why they often neglect their holdings: "Why should a lawyer or doctor spend much time on his property when he can earn so much more in his practice? Every hour away from it costs him more than he could ever make on his land. That is why it is always a good deal to buy land from *doutores*.[30] They make little on it and are willing to sell their fazendas for a lot less than those patrões who live and work on their properties."

A number of small holdings are owned by absentee landlords who live in town and do not themselves engage in agriculture. They contract the land to sharecroppers to cultivate, but usually make frequent trips to their properties, often serving as their own administrators. Still, the vast majority of farmers live and work on their holdings. In the Santa Maria region of the county, encompassing over fifty individual properties, only five are owned by absentee landlords, and on the Estrada Nova, another area in which small farms predominate, there are only seven nonresident patrões.

Since 1962 the number of absentee landlords in Ouro Verde has been increasing. When the county was first settled a handful of properties, perhaps five or ten, belonged to fazendeiros who resided elsewhere. Today, more than three times this number of absentee owners hold land in the Vagalume region alone, to say nothing of the number in the rest of the county. The principal factor in the recent growth of absenteeism is the consolidation of small sítios into large holdings. As this practice has become increasingly common, the number of absentee landlords has risen, since nearly all properties of 50 alqueires or more are owned by nonresidents of the county.

There are significant differences in the kinds of agricultural technology used on rural properties in Ouro Verde. Variations between holdings of different sizes form a continuum, however, and there is no clear correlation between the level of technology and the size of a sítio or fazenda.

Fertilizers for coffee are chemical or organic. The former, far more costly than the latter, is produced commercially and, if applied properly, can increase yields by as much as 50 per cent, barring frosts and droughts. One alqueire of coffee (2,000 trees) requires approximately 1,500 kilos of fertilizer annually, at a cost of CrN$ 222,00 to CrN$ 223,00 per 1,000 kilos, or about CrN$ 333,00

30. Doutores, or "doctors," refer to all college graduates in Brazil, whether they have their degrees in medicine, law, or engineering.

per alqueire. Many farmers use less than the recommended 200 grams of fertilizer per tree for they simply cannot afford the large sum of money involved. While even small applications help, the full benefits of chemical fertilizer are not realized unless the proper amount is applied.

The use of chemical fertilizer must be continual, for if it is employed only once, the trees suffer and the harvest will be greatly diminished, if not lost entirely. Chemical fertilizer can be applied in August or October; the best practice is to use it immediately after a small harvest so that the subsequent harvest, which is naturally larger, will increase even further in size. Fertilizer applied in August will actually augment yields, that is, more berries will grow on the trees; an October application secures the developing berries more firmly on the branches and eliminates the danger of their falling to the ground prematurely, a common occurrence on poor soils.

By far the most widely used organic fertilizers are the dried outer shells of processed coffee beans (*palha de café*). In the county, approximately 30 per cent of all farmers with less than 30 alqueires of land rely solely on palha to fertilize their coffee trees. Palha has advantages and disadvantages. Used without the addition of chemical fertilizer, palha must be applied in great quantities (one truckload for every 200 trees) to be of any value at all. It may be applied only once, then discontinued, without the soil damage that would occur if chemical fertilizer were used. The actual palha costs nothing since every farmer has the right to the waste products from the processing of his coffee beans. But transporting palha is costly, from CrN$ 15,00 to CrN$ 20,00 per truckload, depending upon the distance between processing plant and farm. Sufficient palha to fertilize 1 alqueire with 2,000 coffee trees would cost between CrN$ 150,00 and CrN$ 200,00 annually, far less than chemical fertilizers.

Many farmers are fearful of using chemical fertilizer; in the event of a frost or drought that destroys the berries, their entire investment is lost, since the fertilizer already applied will not benefit the subsequent harvests. One chácara owner with 4 alqueires of land put it this way: "I used Manah [a chemical fertilizer] for the last two years, but I am switching back to palha de café. Sure, the Manah improved the harvest, but what if there is another frost? Then I would lose the crop and the money I put into fertilizer as well. This way if a frost comes I will lose less. Also, Manah is very expensive and I have to pay interest on the money I borrow from the bank to pay for it. This is a big chunk which takes away my profits [*tira o lucro da gente*]."

Today approximately 70 per cent of all Ouro Verde landowners who cultivate coffee use chemical or organic fertilizer or both.

TABLE 21. Agricultural Technology and Size of Holding

	Chácaras (1–5 alq.)	Small sítios (6–10 alq.)	Medium sítios (11–29 alq.)	Large sítios (30–49 alq.)	Fazendas (over 50 alq.)
Fertilizer[a] for coffee (47 holdings)					
Chemical	5	6	5	4	4
Organic	2	4	3		
Neither	4	5	4	1	
Insecticide for coffee (47 holdings)					
Use	9	11	12	4	4
Don't use	2	4		1	
Type of drying terrace (47 holdings)					
Brick	1	7	7	5	4
Cement	4	2	3		
Earth	6	6	2		
Insecticide[b] for lavoura branca (29 holdings)					
Use	6	2	10	4	2
Don't use	2	2	1		
Agricultural tools (53 holdings)					
Hoe	3	1			
Plow	11	13	9	3	
Tractor		1	4	2	6

a. These and the other items related to coffee include only those holdings on which this crop is cultivated.

b. These include only holdings on which cotton and/or peanuts are cultivated.

This is a drastic change from ten or twelve years ago when virtually no one invested in these items. As with most newly planted lands, the soils were fertile and produced large yields without fertilizers. But, according to the local Secretary of Agriculture in Maringá, all coffee lands should be fertilized when they are first planted, even those with rich virgin terra roxa soils. Coffee gradually depletes the land of vital nutriments which can only be replaced through the use of chemical fertilizers.

Fertilizers for peanuts and cotton are employed on less than 10 per cent of all holdings on which these crops are cultivated. Many farmers plant cotton on land where castor beans were grown, since the latter serve as a natural fertilizer and increase the yields of annuals grown in the same area. Palha from castor beans and peanuts is also used occasionally to fertilize lavoura branca, but it is not nearly as effective as chemical fertilizers. About 800 kilos of chemical fertilizer are needed annually for 1 alqueire of cotton, at a cost of CrN$ 200,00. Since the cotton and peanut crops were very good in 1968, only the second year they were planted on a large scale in the county, virtually no one used chemical fertilizer. As the soil gradually loses natural fertility, fertilizers for lavoura branca will become a necessity, as they nearly have in the case of coffee.

Insecticides for both coffee and lavoura branca are more widely used than fertilizer. Eighty-five per cent of all farmers who cultivate coffee use insecticide against broca, while 82 per cent of those who grow cotton and peanuts employ insecticide to combat the various pests that attack these crops. Insecticides are relatively inexpensive compared to fertilizer, and farmers realize that the benefits to be derived are well worth the cost. Insecticide to eradicate broca must be sprayed on the coffee trees three times a year. Each application costs CrN$ 11,00, an annual cost of CrN$ 33,00 per alqueire. The same insecticide helps combat *praga mineira* (*Leucoptera coffeella*), a pest that attacks the beans and leaves. Insecticide for cotton is a good deal more expensive, but its use is essential since various insects, including the boll weevil, can destroy an entire crop. It is applied four or five times a year, a total cost of about CrN$ 125,00 per alqueire. Insecticide for peanuts is CrN$ 30,00 per alqueire and for rice CrN$ 10,00 per alqueire.

According to the agronomist employed by ACARPA, many farmers are ignorant about the amount of insecticide that should be applied to fight broca, and they use strong solutions that are dangerous both to the trees and to themselves. Since most dealers do not explain the method of application and are anxious to sell large quantities of their products, ACARPA has begun a campaign to instruct local farmers in the proper use of insecticides.

Only about 30 per cent of the landowners who cultivate cotton, peanuts, and corn buy selected hybrid seed at the Agricultural Post in town. The others use seed left over from their harvests of the preceding year, and this tends to lower the size and quality of their crops.

Very few coffee trees have been planted in Ouro Verde over the past ten years. The seedlings planted in the 1950s were predominately of the Bourbon and Caturra varieties which produce far smaller yields in terra arenosa and terra mista than in terra roxa. Sumatra, also known as Mundo Novo, is better adapted to sandy soils, but it was not in general use until 1950, so that only about 10 per cent of the coffee trees in the county are of this variety. Most early settlers from São Paulo and the older regions of northern Paraná were familiar only with Bourbon and Caturra, which they planted upon their arrival in Ouro Verde.

All three types of trees need fertilizer, although Sumatra gives a deceptive appearance without it; trees of this variety may be tall and full but actually produce few berries. Caturra gives large yields for four or five years without fertilizer, but on poor soils its subsequent harvests diminish rapidly. Likewise, Bourbon yields are high for six years, but decline quickly if fertilizer is not applied.

One problem found on many holdings in the county, both large and small, is that coffee trees are planted too close together. Since Ouro Verde's land is less fertile than that in many other areas of northern Paraná, the early settlers thought that they could compensate by planting more trees on the same amount of land. This proved to be a mistake, since a minimum area must be left between trees for good exposure to rain and sunlight. For this reason, the yield of a large number of crowded trees will be smaller than that of fewer trees that are properly spaced.

Contour planting (*curva de nível*), in which every tenth row of coffee trees is planted on a slight curve, is found on approximately 5 per cent of the holdings in Ouro Verde, all large fazendas. It helps prevent erosion and the wearing away of the topsoil by damming water as it runs downhill, but is not a necessity in northern Paraná since the gently rolling topography of the region does not usually erode. Agronomists with experience in the coffee-growing areas of São Paulo, where erosion has proved to be a problem, insist that trees always should be planted on a contour, but local experts familiar with conditions in Paraná argue that it is simply not worth the tremendous expense involved.

There are three types of coffee-drying terraces in Ouro Verde (see Table 21). Forty-eight per cent of the landholdings on which coffee is cultivated have brick drying terraces, 23 per cent have cement terraces, and 29 per cent have terraces of beaten earth. There are distinct differences between holdings of various sizes with regard to this item. No earth or cement terreiros are found on properties of 30 alqueires or more, while 47 per cent of the farms of 10 alqueires or less have only beaten earth drying terraces. Coffee beans set out to dry on brick terreiros require three to four days of sunlight before they are ready to be processed, but those on earth terreiros need ten days of sun to dry thoroughly, and involve more labor since they must be moved about more often. Another disadvantage of the latter is that the beans dried on them take on an earthen color which ultimately affects their taste. For this reason, the local processing plants pay between 10 and 20 per cent less for coffee beans which have been dried on earthen terreiros.

The use of hoes, plows, and tractors also correlates with the size of landholdings. While tractors are employed only on large holdings of 50 alqueires or more, with a single exception, they are absent on chácaras and small sítios of 10 alqueires or less. In 1966 there were eighty-five tractors in the county, but many fazendeiros own as many as three, so there are not that number of individual holdings with tractors.[31]

The animal-drawn plow is the most widely used agricultural tool in the county. It is found on large and small holdings alike, and even those farmers who own tractors also have a plow to do the more delicate tasks of cultivation. The few sitiantes who own only hoes rent plows from neighbors to weed the coffee trees and clear the land for planting. Day laborers are the only agricultural workers who make little use of plows. They usually have their own hoes and, when it is necessary, are supplied with a plow by the patrão. Over half of the sharecroppers in Ouro Verde have plows which they take with them when they move to a different sítio or fazenda.

Naturally, both tractors and plows have great advantages over hoes as labor-saving devices. One man driving a tractor can weed 4,000 coffee trees in an eight-hour period; the same man using a plow can cover 2,000 trees in the same time; with the exclusive use of a hoe, a man can weed a maximum of 200 trees in a full day. Both tractors and plows weed and turn over the soil in a single operation, but with a hoe each of these tasks must be done separately.

Tractors have very limited uses in local cultivation. They are employed to ready the land for seeding and to plant and weed pasture,

31. This is a large number of tractors compared to other areas in Brazil. For example, in 1950 there were only eighty-two tractors in the entire state of Bahia (Smith 1963:390).

Cleaning the beans with a peneira

Worker surrounded by unusually tall coffee trees

but there is always the fear that a heavy tractor will cut too deeply into the topsoil, with detrimental effects. Most farmers with medium-sized properties who own tractors are able to take full advantage of their investment by renting them out at high prices. Tractor rentals for clearing 1 alqueire of land generally range from CrN$ 90,00 to CrN$ 150,00. Tractors are also used for transportation when the roads become impassable after heavy rainfalls, to carry calves to market, and to transport crops and all types of heavy farm equipment. Still, the drawbacks of owning a tractor are numerous. Aside from their enormous cost, between CrN$ 15,000,00 and CrN$ 20,000,00 with bank financing, there are additional expenses for upkeep. Spare parts are sometimes difficult to find, and there is a severe shortage of experienced drivers in the area. One fazendeiro who sold his tractor remarked, "Sure it takes twice as long to do a job with a plow, but I had so many headaches with my tractor. It was always in the shop being repaired and I could never find anyone who knew how to drive it properly. My burros are more economical. At least they don't rust!"

Average crop yields are similar among holdings of various sizes in Ouro Verde. The most important factor in the size of harvests appears again to be location in the county, which, in turn, determines soil quality, altitude, and subjection to frosts. Although careful cultivation and the use of modern agricultural techniques are important, the overriding variables still seem to be climate and soil conditions.

Somewhat surprisingly, coffee yields on the fazenda-sized holdings in the sample fall toward the low end of the spectrum: no property of 50 alqueires or more averages even 51 to 75 sacks per 1,000 trees (see Table 22). A few of the chácaras, on the other hand, have high yields, with at least one of them averaging over 100 sacks of coffee per 1,000 trees. A possible explanation is that while all fazendeiros who cultivate coffee use chemical fertilizers, the very extent of their properties makes their soil qualities and altitudes highly variable. Even though a few thousand trees may be planted on low rich terra roxa and produce well, others cultivated in a different part of the holding, which is subject to frosts and has sandy soil, may have very low yields, reducing the average productivity of the trees. On chácaras, however, soil and altitude are quite uniform, so that small farms in areas of fertile land are often highly productive.

On terra mista and terra arenosa, the soils which predominate in Ouro Verde, yields of over 100 sacks of coffee per 1,000 trees are considered excellent. Average yields of 75 sacks per 1,000 trees are good, while mean yields in the county fall within the range of 26 to 50 sacks per 1,000 trees. Fully 63 per cent of the holdings in Ouro Verde produce yields which are in the latter category. The Bank of Brazil has a policy of refusing to finance any landowner whose coffee trees produce less than 40 sacks per 1,000 trees, since production below this level is considered a "bad risk." Approxi-

TABLE 22. Average Coffee Yields and Size of Holding[a]

Yield per 1,000 trees	Chácaras (1–5 alq.)	Small sítios (6–10 alq.)	Medium sítios (11–29 alq.)	Large sítios (30–49 alq.)	Fazendas (50 alq. or more)
Less than 25 sacks		3			1
26–50 sacks	8	7	8	4	3
51–75 sacks	1	5	3	1	
76–100 sacks	1				
Over 100 sacks	1		1		

a. These are average yields over a three-year period. For example, if a farmer harvested 30, 60, and 25 sacks per 1,000 trees per year, his average yields would be about 38 sacks per 1,000 trees for the three years.

mately 15 per cent of the farmers in the county are affected by this policy, although some, particularly wealthy fazendeiros, are able to secure financing by offering "gifts" to the bank's assessors.

The few holdings which have high average yields, over 76 sacks per 1,000 trees, are all near town in an area which has excellent soil. This region is affected by only the most severe frosts and is never touched by the geadas brancas which harm so many farms in the county. In addition, the owners of these properties have been using chemical fertilizers for at least five years, and while a few of them contract sharecroppers to do the actual cultivation, all live on their holdings and oversee the work themselves.

It should be kept in mind that all of these averages cover three-year periods, and actual yields vary greatly from year to year due to weather conditions and, still more important, the natural tendency of coffee trees to "rest" for one harvest after having produced well. Local farmers claim that their yields differ by as much as 100 per cent from one harvest to the next even when climatic conditions remain optimal. On the holding which produces the largest number of sacks per 1,000 trees in the county, the harvest of 1966 yielded an average of 50 sacks per 1,000 trees; in 1967, the same trees produced 180 sacks per 1,000 trees. In contrast, on a small sítio which produces 40 sacks per 1,000 trees during "good" harvests, yields sometimes fall to only 10 sacks per 1,000 trees.

There has been an overall decline in average coffee yields throughout Ouro Verde since 1960. Many farmers who regularly harvested 75 to 100 sacks per 1,000 trees without using fertilizer today take out only 50 or 60 sacks even though they now use this costly item. Declining yields have been particularly prevalent on the smaller holdings in the county, possibly because they are the ones on which subsistence crops are most frequently intertilled with coffee trees. The decreasing size of harvests must be largely attributed to the loss of soil fertility which has only recently been brought partially under control through the use of chemical fertilizers. There have also been increasingly frequent frosts, especially geadas brancas which do not damage the trees permanently but do substantially reduce the size of the harvest.

Cotton and peanut yields vary little from farm to farm, principally because these crops have been grown on a large scale for a relatively short period of time and the soils are still naturally fertile. The cotton harvest of 1968 was the largest in the county's history, due to a rare combination of optimal amounts of rainfall and sunshine at precisely the right periods in the growth cycle. Although past yields of 200 arrôbas per alqueire were considered good to excellent, production in 1968 often reached 300 to 400 arrôbas per alqueire. The near perfect conditions for cotton cultivation which prevailed that year will not be often duplicated, and as cotton continues to be grown on the same land, soil fertility will decrease and yields will decline substantially even if fertilizer is applied.

6. Social Class and Social Mobility

THE CLASS structure of Ouro Verde mirrors the residents' positions in relation to the community's most important strategic resource, land. In the rural area of the county, a person's socioeconomic status is determined not only by whether or not he owns land, but by the size of his holdings. The division between small-scale ownership (5 alqueires or less) and a profitable sharecropping position is blurred, since a number of sharecropping families are in better financial condition than neighboring chácara owners who barely eke out an existence tilling 1 or 2 alqueires of land. In the town, almost without exception, those in the highest socioeconomic positions own land either in the rural area of Ouro Verde or in one of the nearby counties. They may be shopkeepers or crop buyers by profession, but in most cases their major source of income is from the sale of agricultural produce cultivated on their holdings.

Town Classes

There are great similarities in the division of socioeconomic classes in the town and the rural area of the county, but they differ in two respects. The upper segment in town encompasses a wider variety of occupational groups than it does in the countryside, and the small number of wealthy absentee landowners has no equivalent social class in town. In Ouro Verde, unlike many Brazilian communities,[1] there is no clear correlation between rural residence and lower-class status. Members of the upper segment live in about equal proportions in both the rural and "urban" areas of the county. Town and rural classes will be treated separately only because the former have greater occupational variety which needs to be discussed in detail.

The residents of the town may be divided into three socioeconomic classes: the middle class (storeowners, farmers, crop buyers and processors, teachers, and other white-collar workers);[2] the lower class (store employees, self-employed artisans, sharecroppers, and renters); and the lower-lower class (day laborers and the indigent poor and unemployed). This threefold division is a slightly refined version of the residents' distinction between the poor (*os pobres*) and another class, variously termed the rich (*os ricos*), the middle class (*a classe média*), or "the people who have something" (*a gente que tem alguma coisa*). The residents' views of class differences will be presented later, and this tripartite scheme, a more accurate reflection of the actual socioeconomic division of the town, will be used here.

The so-called gentleman's complex,[3] the disdain and avoidance of manual labor, is not a major theme in Ouro Verde.[4] In many instances, farmers with considerable holdings work with the day laborers they employ, even though they could easily afford to hire additional hands to do all the tasks of cultivation. Thus, engagement in manual labor is not necessarily an accurate indicator of class rank, as it is in many parts of Brazil. It is true that all those belonging to the lowest stratum of local society do perform work of this type. The lack of widespread disdain for manual labor in Ouro Verde can be traced to the fact that nearly all of the early settlers cultivated at least part of their own holdings. Even when

1. Harris (1956) has noted that in Minas Velhas, a community in southern Bahia, there is an important distinction between rural and town residence and that the upper class resides only in the town. This phenomenon is common throughout Brazil except in the older plantation areas where owners of large landholdings reside on their land rather than in the neighboring towns. See Hutchinson 1957.

2. This group, with some very important differences, is roughly equivalent to what Wagley and Harris (1955) term the "local upper class."

3. This phrase was coined by Freyre (1964).

4. Disdain for manual labor has been noted by Wagley (1964), Harris (1956), and Hutchinson (1957), among others.

TABLE 23. Standard of Living: Town, Middle Class
(29 families)

	Crop processors or storeowners with landholdings	Landowners (6 alq. or more)	Chacristas (5 alq. or less)	Storeowners	White-collar workers
Meat consumption					
Daily	6	1		5[a]	1
Weekly	1	4	4	4	3
Less than weekly					
Radio					
Present	7	5	3	9	4
Absent			1		
Sewing machine					
Present	7	5	3	8	4
Absent			1	1	
Jeep and/or tractor					
Present	5	3		2	
Absent	2	2	4	7	4
Literacy[b]					
Literate	7	4	4	5	4
Illiterate		1		4[c]	

a. The high meat consumption in this group may be because they sell meat in their stores and pay wholesale rates for the meat their families eat.

b. Literacy is defined here as having a functional knowledge of reading and writing, not, as in the National Census, simply the ability to sign one's name.

c. In these four cases, the household head is illiterate; their wives are literate and keep the stores' accounts.

formadores were contracted to plant and care for the coffee trees for the first few years, the landowners took over or assisted in the tasks of cultivation when they moved to the county. The only exceptions to this rule are those with large holdings who bought land from the company as an investment but never took up residence in the community. The vast majority of farmers living in Ouro Verde today, prosperous or otherwise, have at some time been engaged in the cultivation of their own land, and the mystique surrounding "gentlemanly," nonmanual occupations has not had a chance to develop.

For these reasons, membership in Ouro Verde's middle class cannot be defined in terms of nonparticipation in manual tasks. In addition, the community has no social clubs or other groups with limited admission policies that might indicate divisions along class lines.

Middle class membership seems to be dependent upon four variables: landownership and the size of holdings, amount of income derived from nonagricultural pursuits (i.e., store ownership, teaching salaries, and so on),[5] general standard of living, including variety of diet, and literacy. Within these broad variables several levels must be distinguished. There appears to be a fairly sharp division between chacristas, those owning 5 alqueires or less, and owners of large holdings. Prosperous storeowners and crop processors must be distinguished from what will be termed "marginal proprietors," those owning very small bars and general stores with tiny inventories and little capital investment. The income derived from these highly marginal enterprises is very limited and unstable and their owners should be ranked within the lower class. While standards of living involve innumerable variables, those employed here (meat consumption, the presence or absence of a radio and sewing machine in the home, and ownership of a jeep, truck, and/or tractor) are directly correlated with income level (see Table 23). Meat prices are high in Ouro Verde (CrN$ 1,30 to CrN$ 2,00 per kilo), but meat is highly prized in the local diet and is purchased whenever possible. Both radios and sewing machines are much sought after, particularly the latter which allows families to avoid the purchase of expensive, ready-made clothing. Truck (or jeep) and/or tractor ownership is limited to a few landowners, crop processors, and motoristas, those who earn their living transporting

5. This applies only to members of the middle class in town since all rural residents are engaged in agriculture.

passengers and agricultural produce. Finally, literacy appears to have a high correlation with certain occupations, landownership, and a moderately high standard of living. The total number of years spent in school by the household head is less indicative of class membership than whether or not he has a minimal knowledge of reading and writing.

Within this amorphous middle class, there are considerable differences in wealth. With the exception of the absentee landowners in the rural area of the county, the most prosperous and influential group in the community are those men who own both land and general stores or crop-processing equipment, and act as intermediaries in the sale of agricultural produce. They serve as town councilmen and, in general, are the closest approximation to what Wagley and Harris (1955) term the "local upper class." It must be noted, however, that members of this group do not reside exclusively in town. A number of them live on their holdings in the countryside, but there is virtually no distinction between rural and "urban" segments. Unlike the absentee landowners, this group participates fully in the community's social and political life and, as was often stressed by local merchants, spends most of its income within the confines of the county.

Storeowners, chacristas, and white-collar workers enjoy somewhat lower standards of living, as indicated in Table 22, and with only two exceptions, none of the local political functionaries belong to these occupational groups. Still, with regard to literacy, diet, and income, they more closely approximate the wealthier landowners and crop processors than the lower socioeconomic stratum.

Place of residence within the town does not have a high positive correlation with social class. With the exception of a few well-appointed houses along the main street, the rest of the dwellings, both substantial and otherwise, are scattered in random fashion throughout town. A house's exterior is not always an accurate indicator of its owner's economic position in the community. Some of the more rustic wooden houses in town belong to the wealthiest crop processors and storeowners; they were constructed when the county was first settled, and simplicity was, at that time, a practical necessity. As these men prospered, additions were made to the houses, and their interior furnishings became more lavish[6] while their exteriors remained essentially the same.

6. They are furnished with a couch and one or two chairs with plastic upholstery, formica dining room sets, beds with spring mattresses, and shelves

The town lower class (see Table 24) consists of store employees, marginal proprietors, artisans (shoemakers, bricklayers, carpenters, and so on), and sharecroppers. With the exception of store employees, these occupations give unstable incomes with great seasonal variation. Carpenters and bricklayers usually have a great deal of work from April through August when the crops are being harvested and local residents use their additional income for house improvements, new furniture, and so on. The income from sharecropping also varies through the year. Thus, the standard of living among these groups, particularly the quality and variety of their diet, changes with the seasons. While most are able to purchase meat at least once a week when work is abundant, many residents remarked that during slack periods they were fortunate to have meat even monthly. A majority of those employed in these occupations own radios and sewing machines, but none has jeeps, trucks, or tractors. Their literacy rate is fairly high, even in comparison to the middle class, but artisans, whose work is not dependent upon a knowledge of reading and writing, are illiterate more often than not.

The quality of housing varies little among members of the lower class. A two- or three-room unpainted wooden dwelling with a cooking area in the back yard is standard. Unlike poorer houses in the rural zone, those in town have wooden rather than dirt floors. Furnishings are simple: a few benches, a table, a chest of drawers, perhaps a cabinet for pots and dishes, and wooden bedsteads with kapok-filled mattresses. Photographs of relatives and pictures of saints provide the only adornment.

The gap between the lower class and the very lowest stratum of town society, day laborers and the indigent poor, is very wide (see Tables 24, and 25). Day laborers have steady employment only about five months of the year (April through August), and even when they work, they receive far lower wages than any of the occupational groups in the lower class. The indigent poor are dependent largely upon charity and intermittant assistance from the prefeitura for survival.[7] The few day laborers and indigents

---

holding a variety of dishes, glasses, and bric-à-brac. Electric refrigerators and, more rarely, television sets are also found in these homes.

7. Thirty-two families in town are aided by the Church's São Vicente de Paulo Fund. Beans and rice are sometimes donated by the farmers in the county, and it is these families that receive Alliance for Progress produce when it is available. The prefeitura provides free housing for five families and occasionally pays for their medical expenses.

living in town are far better off than their rural counterparts who receive no assistance of any kind. All of the thirty-two families who receive charitable assistance and most day laborers in town have lived in the county for a minimum of three years. This contrasts with the highly transient volantes in the rural area who rarely remain in Ouro Verde for longer than the duration of a single harvest. There is an important difference between the families of indigents and those of day laborers. The former are headed by men unable to work for medical reasons, or by widows or women with small children whose husbands have abandoned them;[8] the latter are headed by males who have no regular jobs simply because none is available. Widows and women not living with their husbands often take in washing or hire out as maids. The older children in these families work as day laborers, but this source of income is never steady enough to provide full support. Both women and children from indigent households frequently are seen wandering

TABLE 24. Standard of Living: Town, Lower Classes[a]

	Sharecroppers[b]	Store employees	Artisans	Day laborers[c]
Meat consumption				
Daily				
Weekly	4	4	2	4
Less than weekly	2		2	8
Radio				
Present	5	4	4	3
Absent	1			9
Sewing machine				
Present	5	2	3	1
Absent	1	2	1	11
Jeep and/or tractor				
Present				
Absent	5	4	4	12
Literacy				
Literate	4	4[d]	1	2
Illiterate	2		3	10

a. Fourteen families are included in this sample, but this does not reflect the size of this class segment in the town population.

b. The majority of sharecroppers live in the rural areas of the county.

c. There are twelve families in this part of the sample, and they may be designated lower-lower class.

d. The high rate of literacy here is based on the fact that storeowners will not hire anyone who does not have a minimal knowledge of reading and writing in order to write receipts.

8. There is no divorce in Brazil, and, while there are legal separations (*desquites*), members of this class segment are far too poor to afford them.

from house to house begging alms and the children are occasionally taken in to be fed by sympathetic neighbors.

It is this group that fares worst by any index of living standards. Beans, manioc flour, and rice[9] are their only regular source of sustenance; meat of any kind is an extreme luxury, almost totally beyond their means. They rarely own radios and sewing machines, which are seen as basic necessities by the rest of the local population. Their illiteracy rate is far higher than that of any other class segment, and their children rarely attend school for more than a year or so since they must work to help support the family. Clearly, the lower-lower class consists of the hard-core poor and unemployed in the community.

TABLE 25. COMPARATIVE STANDARDS OF LIVING AMONG TOWN CLASSES (in percentages)

	Middle	Lower	Lower-lower
Meat consumption			
Daily	45		
Weekly	55	71	33
Less than weekly		29	67
Radio			
Present	97	93	25
Absent	3	7	75
Sewing machine			
Present	93	71	8
Absent	7	29	92
Jeep and/or tractor			
Present	34		
Absent	66	100	100
Literacy			
Literate	83	64	16
Illiterate	17	37	84

SOURCE: This table is based on data in Tables 23 and 24.

Rural Classes

Using the same criteria as in delineating town classes, the rural residents of Ouro Verde may be divided into three socioeconomic segments. Their outer margins are blurred since there are insignificant differences in the living standards, for example, of the poorest landowners and the most prosperous sharecroppers. In addition, the range within segments is wide, with the wealthier members

9. With the recent failure of the rice crop and the subsequent increase in prices, it is the lower-lower class that has been forced to cut down on its regular intake of this important dietary item.

of any given class enjoying a decidedly higher standard of living than the less fortunate in the same class. The three principal rural socioeconomic classes are the middle class (landowners with more than 5 alqueires of land), the lower class (holders of 5 alqueires or less, sharecroppers, and renters), and the lower-lower class (day laborers).

TABLE 26. Standard of Living: Rural, Middle Class[a]

	Owners of more than 40 alq.	Owners of 16–39 alq.	Owners of 6–15 alq.
Meat consumption			
Daily	4	2	3
Weekly	1	5	8
Less than weekly			2
Radio			
Present	5	7	13
Absent			
Sewing machine			
Present	5	7	13
Absent			
Wagon[b]			
Present	3	6	10
Absent	2	1	3
Tractor			
Present	4	2	2
Absent	1	5	11
Jeep or car			
Present	5	3	2
Absent		4	11
Literacy			
Literate	5	6	10
Illiterate		1	3

a. There are twenty-five families in this sample. The numbers of different-sized landholdings reflect, approximately, their actual proportions in the county.

b. Wagons are used to transport crops to processing plants and markets, and are, therefore, important for rural families. Whenever possible, farmers purchase wagons. If they do not own one, they must either rent one or receive less money for their crops from the processors who deduct the cost of transportation from the price paid for produce. The only agriculturalists in the county who do not own wagons are those too poor to buy them and the few landowners who own tractors, which serve the same purpose.

The small upper-class segment of absentee landowners with large fazendas in the rural area should be distinguished from resident landowners who are members of the local middle class. The former own the largest holdings in the county, but, properly speaking, they are in the community but not of it. Their homes are elsewhere in Paraná or in the state of São Paulo, they rarely visit their local properties, and they remain peripheral to Ouro Verde's social and political life. They do play a significant role in the county's economic activities since they employ a number of its residents, produce a large proportion of its agricultural output, and own an important percentage of its lands. If they resided on their properties in Ouro Verde, they would undoubtedly form what Wagley and Harris (1955) have termed a "traditional upper class" since their wealth and life styles are comparable to those of the upper echelons of society in the traditional sugar-growing regions of Brazil.

The rural middle class has a fairly wide range of living standards (see Table 26) which are correlated with the extent of an individual's landholdings. The owners of large amounts of land almost invariably own tractors, cars, and trucks, consume a variety of foods, including quantities of meat and canned goods (considered luxuries by the rest of the population), and have a high rate of literacy. As one descends the economic scale, as measured by the size of landholdings, tractor and car ownership is rare, meat consumption is reduced, and literacy declines slightly. However, all those in the rural middle class own radios and sewing machines, which clearly distinguishes them from the lower segments of rural society.

The houses of the rural middle class, although larger and more spacious than those of their town counterparts, are otherwise similar in all respects. An individual's wealth is rarely mirrored in the external appearance of his dwelling, but becomes evident upon entering when one sees a variety of modern appliances (refrigerators, gas stoves, and so on), colorful plastic upholstered chairs and sofas, and cabinets displaying glasses, dishes, vases filled with plastic flowers, and bric-à-brac of all sorts. But the furnishings of middle-class houses vary a good deal; large electric and gas appliances are never found in the houses of owners of 6 to 15 alqueires.

Wealthier landowners in the middle class are not as directly affected by lowered yields and falling coffee prices as are the less wealthy sitiante and chacrista. The latters' incomes from one coffee harvest pay expenses through the year until the next crop is brought in and sold. If the price of coffee rises or yields increase and these increments are not offset by higher cultivation expenses due to inflation, the sitiante may improve his standard of living slightly. He will buy more meat, perhaps add a room or two to his house, and purchase new clothes for his family. If the price of coffee falls and his production is no larger than the previous year, the differential must be made up by reducing consumption and spending less on nonessential items. The owner of more land is less affected by slight rises and falls in coffee prices. Since his crop is larger and he receives more money from its sale, he has additional leeway in covering basic cultivation expenses, so that small decreases in prices

TABLE 27. STANDARD OF LIVING: RURAL, LOWER CLASS (34 families)

	Owners of 5 alq. or less	Meieiros[a]	Percenteiros[b]	Renters[c]	Day laborers[d]
Meat consumption					
Daily					
Weekly	5	4	5	3	1
Less than weekly	2	9	2	4	8
Radio					
Present	5	10	3	4	2
Absent	2	3	4	3	7
Sewing machine					
Present	5	13	1	2	3
Absent	2		6	5	6
Wagon					
Present	5	6	3	1	
Absent	2	7	4	6	9
Tractor					
Present					
Absent	7	13	7	7	9
Jeep or car					
Present	1				
Absent	6	13	7	7	9
Literacy					
Literate	5	6	6	3	2
Illiterate	2	7	1	4	7

a. Coffee sharecroppers who receive 45 to 50 per cent of the crop.

b. Sharecroppers of cotton, beans, peanuts, rice, and so forth, who usually receive 70 per cent of the crop.

c. Those who pay a fixed rent on land and plant whatever they want.

d. Nine families in this category; designated as lower-lower class.

or yields will not automatically force him to lower his level of consumption.

There is no sharp break between the standard of living of the rural lower class (see Table 27) and that of the less wealthy middle-class landowners. The difference is one of degree rather than kind. Clearly, in most respects, the various occupational groups in the lower class form a distinctive unit when compared to the middle class. The life style of the chacrista who owns 5 alqueires of land is not easily distinguished from that of percenteiro who works alongside him harvesting crops. Not infrequently the meieiro de café who sharecrops highly productive coffee trees has an income larger than that of the marginal landowner whose small harvests barely supply him with enough money to cover basic expenses.

Virtually no member of the rural lower class can afford to eat meat on a daily basis, and even weekly consumption is possible only during the few months a year when crops are sold and there is cash on hand. Most landowners with small holdings have radios, sewing machines, and wagons, but almost none owns jeeps, trucks, or tractors. As one moves down the occupational hierarchy, these items become less common, and the rate of literacy continues to decline. There is some difference, however, between the living standards of percenteiros and renters and that of meieiros de café. The two former are less likely to own radios and sewing machines, but the literacy rate among these groups remains fairly constant.

Houses belonging to members of the rural lower class are not readily distinguishable in external appearance from those of the middle class, although the latter are usually somewhat larger. The lower-class houses, however, are furnished with rough-hewn wooden tables, chairs, and bureaus, and one rarely encounters the more expensive factory-made furniture of the middle-class home. Open-air kitchens in back of the houses are equipped with wood-burning stoves and ceramic kilns for baking bread. A single faucet near the house is the only source of water.

The rural lower-lower class, made up entirely of day laborers, is the poorest socioeconomic stratum in the community. Most of its members have resided in Ouro Verde for less than a year, and lack permanent homes since they continually move in search of work. This group is chronically unemployed and provides a large pool of cheap labor for local harvests. Its members are in even more difficult straits than their town counterparts, since they are not known personally to the permanent residents of the community and receive no charitable assistance of any kind.

Rural day laborers are on the lowest end of any scale of economic well-being (see Table 28). Their diet is almost entirely beans and manioc flour, with an occasional supplement of rice. Their possessions are little more than a single set of clothes, a few cultivation tools, some badly worn furniture, and a small number of pots, dishes, and other household utensils. Very few own radios or sewing machines, and none owns a wagon. Illiteracy is widespread among rural volantes and their children rarely attend school regularly, since they are not often in one county long enough to be enrolled.

Rural day laborers have no permanent homes in Ouro Verde and live in whatever dwelling their current patrão has available on his property. These usually are one- or two-room shacks, with a cooking area in the back, a few benches, a table, and kapok-filled mattresses placed directly on the dirt floor. A considerable portion of the volante's meager income is spent hiring a truck to move his few possessions from one property to another. But he has little choice in this matter, for he must be willing to take any job that becomes available if he and his family are to survive.

TABLE 28. Comparative Standards of Living among Rural Classes (in percentages)

	Middle	Lower	Lower-lower
Meat consumption			
Daily	25		
Weekly	56	50	11
Less than weekly	9	50	89
Radio			
Present	100	65	22
Absent		35	78
Sewing machine			
Present	100	62	33
Absent		38	67
Wagon			
Present	76	44	
Absent	24	56	100
Tractor			
Present	32		
Absent	68	100	100
Jeep or car			
Present	40		
Absent	60	100	100
Literacy			
Literate	84	59	22
Illiterate	16	41	78

Source: Based on data in Tables 26 and 27.

Class Interactions

Unlike other regions of Brazil, in Ouro Verde, socioeconomic differences are not consistently reflected in actual patterns of behavior. Strong deferential attitudes on the part of lower-class members toward the upper class have been documented at length in many of the ethnographies dealing with Brazilian communities.[10] Individuals of low socioeconomic status use the respectful *o senhor* form of the third person singular when addressing those of greater wealth and education; the latter use the more familiar *você* in conversations with those lower on the social scale. An entire series of rigid behavioral patterns is exhibited between individuals of different classes in many parts of Brazil, and failure to adhere to accepted standards is considered a breach of conduct. In many communities the wealthy patrão who socializes informally with his workers and treats them as friends, inviting them to dinner or in for a cup of coffee, would be looked at askance by other members of his social group, since he would be breaking the traditional rules of interclass etiquette. A worker who enters his patrão's house and takes a seat in the living room as though he were an invited guest would cause raised eyebrows, since he would not be acting in the deferential manner expected of his class.

Traditional patterns of behavior such as these do exist in Ouro Verde, but since class lines are not as sharply drawn as in many areas of Brazil, interclass behavior follows less rigid paths. The county's recent settlement, the absence of a resident upper class, the lack of disdain for manual labor, and the existence of a comparatively large middle sector may explain the relative flexibility of class interactions. This is not meant to imply that there are no class-specific behavioral patterns in Ouro Verde. While the sitiante and sharecropper whom he employs address one another using the informal "você," this is not the case with the fazendeiro and his workers who always maintain the respect-deference relationship reflected in the "o senhor–você" dichotomy. Similarly, although the poorer townspeople address the mayor as "o senhor," he never reciprocates with this respectful term.

A few examples illustrate how patterns of etiquette mirror the socioeconomic divisions of the community. Lower-class artisans, day laborers, and sharecroppers will never enter the waiting room of the local hospital without an invitation from the nurse. They stand outside waiting for her to appear, no matter how serious the nature of the complaint. When she asks what the problem is, they will recount their reasons for coming to the hospital in lowered voices with heads bowed and gazes fixed firmly on the ground. At no time will they look at her directly or state the reasons for the visit

10. See, for example, Harris (1956), Hutchinson (1957), and Margolis (1966).

in anything approaching normal conversational tones. Before allowing them to enter the hospital, the nurse will inquire whether they have an *ordem*[11] from their patrão guaranteeing payment of any expenses incurred. In contrast, when a prosperous landowner or storekeeper appears at the hospital, he brushes past the other patients in the waiting room and makes his way directly to the doctor to whom he gives the reasons for his visit.

Very few of the poorer residents of Ouro Verde attend the bimonthly dances sponsored by the municipal government. Most cannot afford the CrN$ 5,00 admission fee and the cost of the refreshments. In addition, many say they do not have the "proper" party clothes to wear to these dances and would be "embarrassed" to appear in their ordinary everyday clothes. The children of the poor stand outside the entrance of the building where the dance is held watching the arrivals, but they never enter. There are also a number of men and women at the doors, taking occasional glimpses to see what is going on inside. It is clear that economic rather than class segregation is operating at these dances, since anyone who can pay for a table may attend and there is little exclusiveness involved,[12] but economic factors successfully keep most members of the lower class out of these functions.

At least one social event, the birthday party given by the mayor for his son, clearly was limited in class representation. About thirty-five or forty children and thirty adults were invited. Without exception they belonged to what has been termed the town and rural middle class, and none of the poorer store employees, sharecroppers, day laborers, or chacristas was present. About halfway through the party a group of seven adolescent boys came in. They were dressed in work clothes, wore no shoes, and contrasted sharply with the other children and adults who wore suits and party dresses. No one paid any attention to these arrivals who stood off in a corner joking and talking among themselves. As the food and cake already had been served they helped themselves to the leftovers and took swigs of soda from the half-empty coke bottles around the room. These boys had not been invited to the party but wandered in off the street. Still, no one made any move to ask them to leave and they were simply ignored.

11. An ordem is a slip of paper signed by the worker's employer which states that he will cover a specified amount of medical or other expenses.

12. A few members of the lower class attend these dances from time to time and do not appear to be treated differently from anyone else.

Despite these and other similar incidents, many of the residents of Ouro Verde deny that there is discrimination of any kind against the poorer members of the population, some vehemently insisting "we are all equal here." This claim is made most frequently by people from the Northeast who are quick to note the differences between the *classes sociais* (social classes) in their home states and those in Ouro Verde. As evidence for this supposed equality, a fazenda administrator from Paraíba remarked, "I often invite my volantes in to have cachaça with me, but my father back home never would have asked his workers into the house. There are no proud people [*gente orgulhoso*] here like there are in the Nordeste. It is a fine thing when sitiantes act and dress like their workers." But then he added, "But it it true that many of the poor rural folks are ashamed to enter the houses of the rich people who live in town." A prosperous sitiante who denied that there was any inequality because of wealth or education conceded that the poor were excluded from various social functions due to lack of proper clothes and sufficient money for admission.

But many members of the lower class insisted that barriers existed. One chacrista noted that the only time the rich visit the homes of the poor is during elections when they are after votes. A sharecropper said, "There is no unity between rich and poor around here. By nature the poor man is distrustful [*desconfiado*] of the rich man. I myself feel ashamed [*fico com vergonha*] when I meet a rich man." A household servant expressed her feeling about these matters in this way: "Some people in Ouro Verde are high class [*grão fino*]. They are rich and well educated. But many of them don't help the poor. They throw dirt in our faces. I am ashamed to enter the house of a rich lady for I don't have good shoes or nice clothes. Many feel this way." Feelings of embarrassment and shame are expressed continually by members of the lower socioeconomic strata when they describe their encounters with those of higher social rank. They fear that they lack proper clothes, manners, and education and are disdained by those who appear to have an abundance of these items.

Deferential behavior invariably increases when there is a wide gulf in status between two individuals, but is less pronounced among those closer on the social scale. Thus, interactions between a prosperous landowner and his workers are rigidly patterned. Not infrequently, the former will have no direct dealings with the latter, but will issue orders through an administrator who serves as intermediary. In such cases, deference is exhibited on the part of the workers in their behavior toward the administrator who takes on the role of patrão. In contrast, relations between sitiante and the sharecropper who works beside him in the fields are informal and egalitarian. They eat in each others homes, drink together in the local bar, and often are compadres.

Patron-client relationships of varying kinds and degrees are tied closely to socioeconomic differences among Ouro Verde's population. As elsewhere in Brazil, paternalism is a widespread and well-recognized phenomenon which links people of disparate social strata. Wagley has described it in its traditional form: "the patrão-worker relationship was, and still is in many localities, an economic relationship between employer and worker, landlord and tenant, or creditor and debtor. It was also highly exploitative, for the wages of the lower class . . . were notoriously low. Yet the traditional patrão-worker relationship was something more than an economic bond. It involved a sense of 'noblesse oblige' and paternalism on the part of the employer. . . . On the part of the worker it involved a sense of loyalty to the patrão, and, needless to say, political support, if and when the worker could vote" (1964:107).

In Ouro Verde, patron-client relationships fall into two categories; those between workers and employers and those between shopkeepers and customers; the customers are the debtors in the debtor-creditor relationship mentioned by Wagley. The relationship of worker and employer involves a series of reciprocal obligations clearly outlined. The basic duties which all patrões owe to their workers are the payment of the legal minimum wage, guaranteeing payment of bills incurred by the worker for medical expenses, and supplying the worker with adequate housing (*não dá casa ruim*). In addition, in the case of sharecroppers, "good" patrões will cosign their bank loans for cultivation expenses.

In return, the worker has two obligations to his patrão. He should remain with his employer for as long as he is needed and never leave his job at crucial times, for example, just before the harvest begins. His second duty is to cultivate the land with as much care as if it were entirely his own. In Ouro Verde the issue of political support is a minor one; in recent years political activity has been at a minimum, with only one candidate running for each local office.

A number of points concerning the obligations of worker to employer and employer to worker must be clarified. For example, the patrão does not pay his workers' medical bills outright. He simply signs a note agreeing to pay in the event the worker cannot, and he may loan the worker the sum in question, later deducting it from his salary. In effect, the only time the patrão actually pays these bills without later compensation is if the worker dies or is too ill to work so that his debts remain unpaid. Thus, the duty of a "good" patrão is simply to sign the promissory note.

It must be understood that this obligation is only related to the employment of sharecroppers, renters, and mensalistas, and does not include day laborers. A patrão rarely agrees to cover medical or other expenses incurred by volantes in his employ, since the latter are hired for relatively short periods and are highly mobile, and the patrão believes that these loans will never be repaid. It is true that day laborers are unlikely to stay on one landholding for any length of time, particularly if they secure better jobs elsewhere or if debts begin to pile up.[13] But sharecroppers and renters never leave before the harvest is completed, since their portion of it represents their entire income for the year.

In cases of emergency involving the few volantes who have worked for one employer for a considerable period of time, patrões may lay out small sums for medical expenses with the hope of eventually being reimbursed by the Vicentino's Charity Fund. But employers willing to assume responsibility for the debts of their day laborers are few, even though it is well known that the latter have no other source of aid. One sitiante remarked, "A poor man without a patrão and without money, dies. No doctor around here will treat him unless he is guaranteed payment."

Another reason the patrão more readily accepts responsibility for the debts of his sharecroppers is that he knows if he refuses to help them, they will be forced to work as part-time day laborers to earn extra money.[14] This outside employment will reduce the time they devote to caring for the coffee or cotton plants being sharecropped. The patrão fears that this will lead to neglect of the crops, will make for a smaller harvest, and therefore will diminish his portion of it. This is not the case with regard to renters who pay a fixed rental on the land no matter what the size of the harvest. Here the patrão has nothing to lose if the renter takes outside employment

13. According to Brazilian law, it is illegal to force a man to remain at his job because he has incurred debts to his employer or to shopkeepers in the area. But this law is frequently not enforced in the case of peões.

14. See Johnson and Siegel (1969) for an interesting discussion of the relationship between sharecropping and working for a daily wage.

to supplement his income, and for this reason he is less willing to guarantee payment of the renter's debts.

One continually hears the claim in Ouro Verde that *Fulano de tal* (So-and-so) has had a "hard time" either because he lacks a patrão or because he has a "poor" patrão who is unwilling or unable to help him. Remarks of this sort are particularly common with reference to day laborers. One sharecropper remarked, "I get angry when people say that volantes are poor because they are lazy and are *vagabundos*. I know volantes who are so weak from hunger that they can't put in a full day's work. Their poverty makes them take to drink and go mad. Did you ever see a crazy rich man walking in the street and babbling to himself? These so-called vagabundos once were real men. They worked and sweated to earn a decent living, but could never buy enough food to eat. What they always needed was a good patrão to help them. All they needed was a good patrão who would loan them CrN$ 200,00 so that they could have become sharecroppers. But these poor guys [*coitados*] never had the luck to find one." Another sharecropper stated, "A volante is the worst thing you can be in Brazil. He has nothing. No one is responsible for him. He has no patrão."

One young woman, the wife of a mechanic at the coffee-processing plant, explained the need for a patrão: "It is much better for a person to work for a patrão than to work for himself. The patrão can give a family security that it wouldn't have if the man were *independente*. When my children are sick and I have no money, Dr. Grigorio will treat them and give them medicine for he knows that my husband has a steady job at the maquina [processing plant], and that Seu Ramos will guarantee the bill. But suppose he worked for himself and had no patrão to turn to in case of emergency? We would be in real trouble. It is better to earn a little less and have a patrão than to earn more money and have no security. One thing is sure; poor people need a patrão!" One sharecropper, after expressing his indebtedness to his patrão, said with a good deal of emotion, "My patrão is like my father [*é como meo pae*]. There is no difference between them." A number of landowners felt that a worker's primary aim was to secure a good patrão, and that this was even more important to him than earning a reasonable wage. One fazendeiro remarked, "The only thing these workers want is a father. A patrão who will give them money when they need it. All the rest is secondary to them."

It is clear from these statements that to many local residents the primary role of a patrão is to insure his workers a minimal amount of security. Given the extremely low wage scale of the region, the worker who has no one to turn to in time of need necessarily leads a very marginal and insecure existence. The patron-client relationship must be seen as an adaptive one. Through it, employers are able to pay lower wages than if no such stop-gap measures were operating, while workers more willingly accept low-income positions with the assurance that, if they fall on hard times, there will be someone to come to their aid.

The relationship between shopkeeper and customer functions in much the same way. A worker with little cash on hand will become the client of a shopkeeper who is willing to sell on credit. The latter benefits from this arrangement; he is assured of the customer's fealty and can charge him somewhat higher prices along with interest on the items purchased, knowing that the worker, lacking cash and possibly unable to secure credit elsewhere, must buy from him. The worker, in turn, is afforded security through this relationship; he can always buy necessities for himself and his family during periods when he has no cash. This arrangement is particularly important in a highly seasonal economy such as that of Ouro Verde. Sharecroppers, renters, and farmers are often without money for months during the slack period before the harvest begins and the crops are sold. Thus, credit buying allows for their survival throughout the agricultural year. Debts are paid off as soon as cash is available from the sale of the harvest, and the cycle begins anew.

Compadresco relationships, so widespread throughout Latin America,[15] play a relatively minor role in interclass relations in Ouro Verde, but do serve to intensify existing blood ties within family groups. There are three principal types of *padrinhos* (godparents) found in the community: those of confirmation (*crisma*), those of marriage (*casamento*), and those of baptism (*batismo*). The last is the most important and is the only one with long-term duties and obligations. A married couple serves as padrinhos in the confirmation ceremony. This takes place when a child that has been previously baptized reaches the age of seven. In effect, padrinhos de crisma only serve as witnesses for the child's confirmation, donating CrN$ 5,00 or so to the church for the occasion. But they have no other obligations, either to the child or its parents, after the ceremony, nor is their relationship to them altered in any way.

15. See Wolf and Mintz (1950) for an analysis of the kinds of compadresco relationships found in Latin America.

Padrinhos de casamento also have no long-term importance; they are friends of the bridal couple who have agreed to serve as witnesses in both the religious and civil wedding ceremonies. In general, padrinhos[16] of this type have to be fairly *bem da vida* (comfortable or well off) since they are expected to assume part of the wedding expenses and always pay for the beer and cachaça consumed by the guests. Most informants agreed that padrinhos de casamento had no special duties to one another and never called each other "compadre," although a few claimed that they are expected to act as intermediaries and attempt to reconcile any differences that may arise between the newlyweds.

Ideally, padrinhos de batismo are expected to have long-term relationships with the parents of the baptized child (their compadres) as well as with the child himself (their *afilhado*). A couple who has been married by the church is said to "speak for the child" during and after the actual baptism ceremony. They are expected to donate at least CrN$ 5,00 to the church and cover the expenses of the small festa for friends and relatives after the baptism. But, unlike the other forms of compadresco, the duties of padrinhos de batismo do not end upon completion of the religious ceremony. They have the obligation of caring for their afilhado should anything happen to the child's parents, and, according to church doctrine, they are responsible for the child's "spiritual education," as well as his material well-being. A wealthy padrinho may be expected to help finance his afilhado's education or start him on a career. The child, in turn, must show as much respect for his padrinhos as for his parents, and periodically ask them for their "blessings" (*abenços*). The relationship between padrinhos and the child's parents should be a close and yet formal one. Compadres must show respect for each other and always address one another with the respectful "o senhor" form of the third person singular. This formality is demanded even if they were close friends or relatives who addressed each other in the familiar "você" before becoming compadres.

This description of the ideal role of padrinhos de batismo reflects actual behavior in only a handful of cases. In many instances, people had to stop and think when asked who their compadres were, and even then rarely knew their compadres' surnames.[17] When asked if their compadres ever aided their afilhados in any

16. *Madrinha* is the feminine form of padrinho.
17. This was only true for compadres who were not otherwise related.

way, most people seemed puzzled, often shrugging their shoulders and replying, "Oh, we hardly ever see him (or her)." One Northeasterner complained that in Ouro Verde compadres do not show sufficient respect for each other, explaining, "Sometimes they even call one another 'você.' Such a thing would never happen in the Northeast. Here compadres have an argument and stop speaking to each other. And soon they don't even remember that they are compadres!" I encountered only a single case in which the padrinhos de batismo actually assumed responsibility for their afihada after the death of her parents, although there were innumerable instances of children left to fend for themselves because of the death or illness of their parents.

An important question at this point is which individuals are chosen to serve as padrinhos de baptismo. The most important source of compadres is the family itself. Grandparents and siblings of the child's parents are the two groups of consanguineal kin most frequently asked to serve, and this holds true for all segments of the population, both rural and urban. Many informants said that compadres must be "people who you can trust" (*pessoas de confiança*), and this was the explanation for choosing them from within the family.

Other informants stated that it always was preferable to select compadres who are "a little better off" than oneself (*sempre tentar de escolher uma pessoa que tem mais recursos, quem é mais bem da vida*). One sitiante said, "You have to pick somebody with at least a little money for how else is he going to be able to pay for the festa after the baptism? But still the most important thing is to choose someone who is a friend."

A number of informants said that the ideal compadre is one's own patrão, and, in fact, many renters, sharecroppers, and mensalistas do ask their patrões to serve as godparents to their children. But there appears to be a direct correlation between an employer's wealth and social status, and whether or not he is asked and agrees to serve as his workers' compadre. Sitiantes regularly become godparents to the children of sharecroppers and renters employed on their holdings, but no cases were encountered in which absentee landowners served in this capacity. The same is true of fazenda administrators. None of them was compadre to any of the workers they supervised, and a few openly stated that they had no desire to become involved in the obligations which this relationship, in its ideal form, demands. But even owners of small holdings served as compadres only to workers who had been with them for a number of years, and in no case were they padrinhos of the children of day laborers in their employ.

A few of the prosperous crop buyers in town are compadres to the intermediaries from whom they purchase agricultural produce. Instead of charging them the usual 5 or 6 per cent monthly interest on outstanding debts, the crop buyers allow their compadres to pay only the finance costs charged by the banks. The intermediaries, in turn, are bound to sell their crops to these buyers, often at slightly lower rates, so that both parties benefit.

The mayor, town councilmen, and other *homens de responsibilidade* (men of responsibility)[18] in the community are much sought after as compadres. The mayor alone has about sixty afilhados, and he had trouble remembering all their names. Many residents, particularly those in the lower socioeconomic strata, ask local officials to serve as their compadres, in the hope that, as a result, special favors will be granted. In reality, however, only a few of the compadres of these "men of responsibility" receive assistance of any kind.[19] More commonly, the latter simply serve as padrinhos during the actual baptism ceremony, and their obligations end there.

The most important function of compadresco in Ouro Verde is to "reinforce already existing blood ties," rather than to "enlarge numerically and spatially the number of ritually related kin" (Wolf and Mintz 1950:355). Although there are instances when compadresco relationships cross class lines, the majority are not only between members of the same socioeconomic group, but between those who are already related by consanguineal ties. In that case, compadresco simply emphasizes the existing duties and obligations between kinsmen since, presumably, a child's grandparents or uncles and aunts would be responsible even if they were not "ritual kin." Likewise, siblings and parents and children would expect assistance and favors from one another even if the additional ties of co-parenthood were absent.

Ties of compadresco between sitiante and sharecropper or renter may be seen as crossing class boundaries to some extent, but in these cases the individuals involved do not occupy very different niches in the socioeconomic hierarchy. Only in the few instances

18. Owners of large general stores, crop processors, and so on.

19. In a few cases the mayor gave menial jobs (sweeping the prefeitura, digging ditches, working on a road crew) to some of his compadres who were badly in need of employment.

in which the poorer members of the community seek out men of wealth and power as compadres is ritual kinship truly "vertical" rather than "horizontal" (Wolf and Mintz 1950:364). However, ties between individuals of highly divergent social strata are weak and short lived, and are of a very different quality than those between individuals of similar economic backgrounds.

As noted, there is a slight distinction between the three-class town and rural socioeconomic systems outlined and the class divisions actually recognized by the local residents. In general, they simply distinguish between a large lower class, usually termed "os pobres" (the poor), and another, smaller sector, variously called "a classe média" (the middle class) or "os ricos" (the rich). Sometimes a further differentiation is made between the "regular poor" and the coitados, those who work as day laborers or are chronically unemployed.

There is significant agreement among nearly all socioeconomic sectors in Ouro Verde as to the membership of the local upper class.[20] When asked who belonged to this particular stratum of society, residents repeated the same names over and over. Among town residents they included the local doctor, all of the crop buyers and processors, the men who own the five largest general stores, the mayor (who owns a prosperous pharmacy and a sítio), and the wealthier landowners (those with over 20 alqueires of land) residing in town. In the rural area, the names most frequently mentioned were those of absentee landowners, the Japanese owner of a large chicken farm, and others with holdings of at least 20 alqueires. Sometimes the distinctions were even more refined; a few informants stated that, although a particular sitiante did not own an extensive piece of land, he was "rich" because his coffee trees were of excellent quality and produced unusually large harvests.

A number of those named as members of the upper class insisted that there were no truly wealthy people residing in Ouro Verde. One fazendeiro, a man most definitely included in the local upper class, stated, "There are no rich people in Ouro Verde. Sure some own land here, but where do they live? In São Paulo, Londrina, and Curitiba. Here we only have poor people [*só fica os pobres*]. The rich, what do they have to do with us? Maybe they visit their

20. For the sake of consistency, I will refer to the highest socioeconomic stratum in Ouro Verde as either "the rich" or "the upper class," although it should be remembered that these terms are relative, and the group in question more properly belongs to the national middle class.

fazendas once or twice a year." The owner of a large general store said, "There are no rich here, but there are some tubarões[21] who are always trying to consume the little guys."

But what are the criteria for classifying someone as rich or upper class? There are different opinions, but landownership is almost invariably involved. One chacrista stated, "The rich are those who own land and are not in debt. But even the sitiante who owes money to someone isn't poor, because if you have some land you must be fairly comfortable [*remediado*], but this is not enough to be rich." A sharecropper noted, "The rich are those who are *tranquilizado da vida* [lead a calm life]. But to be this way you must have a sítio of, say 25 alqueires or so." One sitiante insisted that to be "well off" it was not only necessary to own land, but also to have productive coffee trees on it.

A number of informants indicated that only those who live "on their own account" (*vivem da conta própria*), that is, those who are not in debt and who live independently on their own resources, may be considered "comfortable." Education and "manners" rarely were identified as important criteria of upper-class membership, reflecting the fact that many wealthy landowners and shopkeepers have had only one or two years of schooling and in this respect differ little from their lower-class neighbors. One woman, the wife of the owner of a large coffee-processing plant who lives part of the year in São Paulo, was an exception to this rule, and clearly used educational and social criteria in her definition of class: "Here the people are middle class or lower [*média para baixo*]. The middle class, the storeowners and fazendeiros, have money, but they still live in a very simple way. There are fazendeiros here who are well off, but they have no social life [*não tem vida social*]. They are uneducated, don't dress well, and live like pigs. Sure the people around here think that someone who has four million cruzeiros and a sítio is rich, but to me this is not rich."

In all instances informants agreed that there were many more poor then rich in Ouro Verde. As one sharecropper put it, "For the most part the people here are weak [*fraco*]. Even those that own sítios." A seamstress said, "Ouro Verde really is a land of poverty [*terra de pobreza*], although there are a number of people who are comfortable."

The poor seem to be scattered about equally throughout the

21. Tubarão literally means "shark," but the term is often used to refer to entrepreneurs who take over small farms and businesses and consolidate them.

town and rural areas, and most work in various agricultural occupations as sharecroppers, renters, and day laborers. Others are employed as shop assistants, handy men, and independent artisans. Very frequently, however, landowners with less than 5 alqueires are included among the poor. Thus, from the local point of view, landownership per se does not necessarily exclude someone from lower-class status. The extent of the holding, the quality of the land, and the size of its yields are all recognized as important determinants of economic well-being. One sitiante put it in these terms: "Most chacristas [those with 5 alqueires or less] are poor, but if they have good coffee trees they may be very comfortable. But a man with 10 alqueires of weak land planted in lavoura branca is much poorer than one with 5 alqueires planted in coffee trees that produce 150 sacks of coffee per alqueire."

A number of informants made a point of distinguishing between owners of small farms and sharecroppers and renters, stressing that the former could borrow money from the bank in their own names using their land as collateral, while the latter had to have their patrões or other landowners cosign their loans. In the words of one chacrista, "Sure there are very poor sitiantes. But even a sitiante who has no money, has a name [*tem nome*]. He can go to the bank and get a loan or buy on credit at a store for everyone knows that he owns land and isn't too much of a risk." Thus, while the landowner with a very small holding often is indistinguishable in life style and income from the sharecropper who works beside him, he is always able to buy on credit and secure bank loans in his own name.

Those without land are invariably classified as belonging to the lower class, but a further distinction is often made between sharecroppers and renters, on the one hand, and day laborers and the indigent poor, on the other. The former are said to be poor, but they have fairly steady positions and, more importantly, a patrão to turn to in times of emergency. Volantes and those who live on charity do not have even this minimal amount of security, and are, therefore, viewed as the most marginal group in the county. The following statements by different informants are typical of local attitudes toward this segment of the community:

> The real poor in Ouro Verde are the volantes who accept any job no matter how bad the pay just in order to stay alive. They work today so they can eat tomorrow.

> The real poor fellows [coitados] are the volantes. They never stay in one place for they have to move around to find work. They don't stay in any place long enough to call it home.
>
> The volantes are so poor that even when they get work in the harvest they can hardly do it for they are weak from malnutrition. To be a volante is no laughing matter.

Some of the larger landowners and storekeepers had a less sympathetic view of the volantes' plight:

> Some of the volantes here just have no luck in life, but others are in that condition because they just don't like to work.
>
> The volantes here are *caboclos*.[22] They are lazy by nature because of their Indian blood. You can't change them, but you might be able to do something with their children if you start teaching them early enough. The only thing a caboclo wants is the protection of a patrão.
>
> These people [volantes] don't want land. Giving them land would be like giving rice and beans to a woman who doesn't know how to cook.
>
> The workers around here live like animals [*bichos*]. You can't call them people.

In sum, the residents' views of socioeconomic differences within the community mirror, to a significant extent, actual differences in occupation, landownership, and other criteria. The three-part division of middle class, lower class, and lower-lower class corresponds fairly closely to the emic distinctions between "os ricos," "os pobres," and "os coitados" or volantes.

Social Mobility

Opportunities for upward mobility in Ouro Verde during the early years of settlement contrast sharply with the current situation, a direct result of changed economic conditions, specifically those in agriculture. During the first decade after the founding of the county, a large number of agricultural workers gradually amassed sufficient capital to purchase small holdings and become landown-

22. In the Northeast and Amazon regions caboclo refers to anyone of mixed Portuguese and Indian descent, but in southern Brazil the term is used to refer to rustic backwoods types, and often more specifically to agricultural laborers.

ers. Two distinct paths were followed to achieve this end. In the early 1950s, a significant number of formadores de café (men who contracted for periods up to six years to plant and care for coffee trees) were able to buy small sítios on the frontier with the money they earned from the sale of the one to three harvests they received in compensation. This system had passed into oblivion by 1960 at which time the entire county was settled and all of its lands were under cultivation. A more recent route to landownership is by sharecropping either highly productive coffee trees or cotton. During particularly large harvests, when high prices were being paid for the crop, a number of sharecroppers were able to make down payments on small farms in areas being opened for settlement.

How does a man secure a profitable sharecropping position which enables him to purchase a small holding? Very few day laborers become sharecroppers. In order to secure a sharecropping position of any kind, a man must have a small amount of savings, usually not less than CrN$ 150,00 (U.S. $48), to tide him over until the harvest is completed and the crop is sold, and day laborers earning subsistence wages cannot accumulate this amount. In some cases, however, patrões whose volantes are deeply in debt to them have arranged sharecropping positions for the workers so that they can pay their debts with earnings from their share of the harvest. But in these instances the day laborers were never able to amass any savings because of their indebtedness, so that this type of mobility never led to landownership.

In a few exceptional cases, day laborers who have been employed by the same patrão for an extended time and who are considered good workers may be offered sharecropping positions. This is very rare, however, since it is in the landowners' interest to contract only men with enough savings to support themselves and their families until the harvest. Ideally, of course, landowners seek men who can assume at least a portion of the cultivation expenses, clearly an impossibility for day laborers. The highly tenuous position of volantes who manage to secure sharecropping positions may be illustrated: a family of day laborers, after having worked on the same holding for a number of years, were rewarded with a 2-alqueire plot to sharecrop. When one of the children became ill the following year, the family's small savings from their share of the harvest was wiped out, and they were forced to resume their position as volantes.

Once a man secures a contract to sharecrop coffee or lavoura branca, his continued upward mobility, as measured by the acquisition of land, is dependent upon many variables.[23] First, and perhaps most important, is the quality of the land he is sharecropping and the size of the harvests it produces. Second, the prices paid for coffee or cotton during the years he is sharecropping are a major determinant of his income. Still another factor is the natural conditions which prevail throughout the year; if a major frost or drought occurs, harvests may be halved, resulting in a sharp decline in profits. Finally, the terms of the sharecropping contract are significant, since they set the percentage of the harvest to which the sharecropper is entitled and the amount of cultivation expenses he is expected to assume. This last factor is not of overriding importance, however, since the terms of the contract are adjusted to the quality of the land being sharecropped. For example, poor land, producing less than 30 sacks of coffee per 1,000 trees, will be sharecropped on a 50–50 basis; on highly productive land averaging 80 sacks per 1,000 trees, the sharecropper will receive only 40 or 45 per cent of the harvest and may be asked to cover a larger portion of the cultivation expenses.

Whether or not a sharecropper remains in the same position for many years or is able to save enough money from his share of two or three harvests to buy a small sítio on the frontier depends on these factors and others which can only be termed "luck" or "chance." In a number of cases, sharecroppers who had slowly amassed sufficient capital to make down payments on small holdings were forced to spend the entire amount on medical bills when wives or children fell ill. In Ouro Verde it is not uncommon to encounter men who have been sharecropping coffee or lavoura branca for seven or eight years in order to accumulate enough money to buy a sítio on the frontier. But this can also be accomplished in a relatively brief time if there are one or two unusually large harvests to sell. One sitiante noted that, despite his having worked for ten years as a colono and sharecropper in Ouro Verde and neighboring counties, he was never able to amass enough capital to purchase land, and would still be landless today had he not won a jeep in a church raffle—he sold it in order to buy a 5-alqueire sítio.

23. Most sharecroppers have always been employed as such, but if they have some capital and are hard workers, the terms of their contracts gradually improve, and, more importantly, the trees which they sharecrop become of increasingly better quality.

A few examples will illustrate the typical route from sharecropping to landownership. The Moretos, a family of Italian descent, worked for ten years in Ouro Verde, first as formadores de café and later as coffee sharecroppers. As formadores they were entitled to three harvests, the last of which was expected to be large enough to give them sufficient money to buy a small sítio on the frontier. A fairly severe frost killed this hope and the family accepted a sharecropping contract once it became clear that landownership was out of the question, at least temporarily. They sharecropped fairly unproductive land for two years, receiving one-half of the harvest in payment. After this, they moved to a holding whose coffee trees were among the most productive in the county. They stayed there for three years; they received only 40 per cent of the crop, but were compensated for their smaller share by the abundance of the harvests. The family was finally able to purchase a 5-alqueire sítio on the frontier with the money saved during the last sharecropping contract.

A few years ago a chácara owner in the community made his first land purchase, 10 forested alqueires in Cascavel, a frontier county about 300 kilometers southwest of Ouro Verde. For seven years before this, he sharecropped cotton in Paranacity, an adjacent county, accumulating capital for his intended purchase. Three years ago he sold the holding in Cascavel and bought a 2-alqueire chácara in Ouro Verde, all he could afford since local land prices are far higher than those on the frontier. He now intends to sell the chácara which is far too small to support his married sons and their families and reinvest in a larger holding on the frontier.

One man sharecropped coffee for four years in Rolandia, a thriving county settled in the late 1930s, 160 kilometers east of Ouro Verde. He bought 20 alqueires of forested land in Ouro Verde between 1958 and 1960. There were two reasons why such a large purchase was possible: land was considerably less expensive at that time, far less than at present even when inflation is taken into account; and he sharecropped highly productive trees[24] on rich terra roxa soil. Even though his share of the harvest was only 30 per cent, he amassed a considerable amount of money from the sale of only four harvests.

One factor stands out in these examples and in dozens of others

24. He sharecropped 9,000 trees and claimed that harvests ranged from 160 to 200 sacks per 1,000 trees, figures never reached by even the most productive trees in Ouro Verde.

which could be cited. In all cases the transition from formador or sharecropper to landowner was made in two or more geographically distinct communities. The reason is simple: by the time a man saves enough money to buy a small farm, land values in the area in which he had been sharecropping have risen sharply, and only the less costly frontier lands fall within his means. Thus, upward mobility, measured by the acquisition of land, rarely takes place in one community. One informant, a resident of Ouro Verde since 1952, claimed that not a single sharecropper in the county had ever been able to purchase land there. This was confirmed by a number of other long-time residents. However, there are a few former sharecroppers now in Ouro Verde who left the county after buying land on the frontier only to sell it and return to the community to invest in small sítios. But this in no way alters the basic pattern since their *initial* step upward, the original land purchase, was made in an area other than that in which they had worked as sharecroppers.

While the absence of local upward mobility holds true for sharecroppers, there are a handful of men who held formador contracts during the first years of the county's settlement and subsequently bought small holdings in the community. These purchases were all made prior to 1955, when Ouro Verde was still a frontier area with low land values and very sparse population. Still, it should be emphasized that the vast majority of formadores de café in Ouro Verde who bought land did so elsewhere.

The frontier, then, must be viewed as an important socioeconomic outlet for those in the county who are successful sharecroppers but cannot afford local farms at inflated prices. The relatively inexpensive frontier land compares favorably to that in Ouro Verde. Although the lands to the west now being opened up for settlement are of mediocre quality, covered with mixed and sandy soil similar to that in Ouro Verde, they do have the decided advantage of being virgin lands. Because they are virtually untouched, frontier soil produces high yields, at least for a few years, without the application of costly fertilizers. In addition, some areas of the frontier are less subject to frosts than Ouro Verde and neighboring counties, and the constant threat of "losing everything" is reduced. Finally, the frontier region begins within 150 kilometers of Ouro Verde and is even closer to other settled communities. It is easily accessible in the dry season over many dirt roads, and because of the proximity it is not an extremely expensive undertaking for a man simply to pick up and move his family and possessions there.

The potential for upward mobility through sharecropping has decreased steadily over the last few years, and, with one notable exception brought about by the unusually large cotton harvest of 1968, this traditional path toward landownership has nearly ceased to exist. Perhaps the most important factor in this is the continual decline in the number of sharecropping positions available, a result of the ever increasing areas given over to pasture at the expense of coffee and other cash crops. Sharecropping positions, especially desirable ones on productive land, are in short supply, and there is great competition for the few that are open. It is becoming increasingly necessary for a man who wants to secure one not only to demonstrate solvency but to assure the landowner that he will be able to assume a large portion of the cultivation expenses.

A second factor affecting opportunities for upward mobility is the continual decrease in average coffee yields throughout the county. Sharecroppers are receiving fewer sacks of coffee in return for their labor than they did ten years ago, although the percentage of the crop to which they are entitled is the same. Finally, the financial return on the sale of coffee has fallen off steadily. As indicated, the price paid per sack of unprocessed coffee has been reduced by nearly two-thirds over the last fifteen years, and the resulting difficulty in accumulating sufficient capital to buy a small farm can well be imagined.

After 1960 (a rough cut-off point), it became increasingly difficult, if not impossible, to make the transition from sharecropping to landownership through coffee cultivation in Ouro Verde. The process was a gradual one; as time passed fewer and fewer sharecropping positions were available, and in most cases those that were open were less lucrative than they had been in the past. One informant estimated that, given today's conditions, it would take a coffee sharecropper at least ten years to save enough money to buy a small frontier sítio, even without the occurrence of major frosts or droughts.

The growing importance of cotton in Ouro Verde and many of the adjacent counties has slowed down this general trend. Since 1965, cotton cultivation has greatly increased, and the 1967–68 harvest was the largest in the county's history. Because of the unusually large harvest, the result of optimal weather conditions, a number of sharecroppers in Ouro Verde were able to buy frontier land with the money received from the sale of their share of the crop. The stories of these families have become proverbial throughout the county, and men who sharecrop coffee continually rue the fact that they did not change over to cotton. Claims that some families made profits of CrN$ 2,000,00 to CrN$ 3,000,00 (about U.S. $600 to $1,000) were difficult to verify, but, given the size of the harvest, these figures are not improbable. Yields were so high in some areas of the county that a few men who sharecropped only 5 alqueires of cotton earned enough to buy 10-alqueire sítios on the frontier. This contrasts with earlier harvests when a man had to sharecrop at least 10 alqueires of cotton in order to purchase a sítio of comparable size.

Those who rented land and planted cotton on it also did remarkably well in 1968. One man took out an average of 400 arrôbas of cotton per alqueire on land which he rented for 55 arrôbas per alqueire. Three families who rented land on one large holding were all able to buy small farms near the frontier town of Umuarama.

The fertility of the land on any holding is an important factor in the size of cotton yields, and production was not uniform throughout the county. The majority of sharecroppers and renters who cultivated cotton during this period averaged 100 to 150 arrôbas per alqueire, far too little, given the expenses of cultivation, to accumulate sufficient capital to purchase land. On one large fazenda, not a single sharecropper averaged over 150 arrôbas per alqueire, and some harvested considerably less owing to the generally poor condition of the soil. Not one of the fifteen renters on another fazenda was able to buy a sítio, despite high cotton yields, because, after they paid off an exorbitant rental and debts plus interest to their intermediary, little remained of their profits from the sale of the crop. In sum, while the current boom in cotton has benefited a number of families (a rough estimate is that between 5 and 10 per cent of all sharecroppers and renters who cultivated over 4 alqueires of cotton bought land), its effects are by no means countywide.

While it is true that during the last two or three years cotton cultivation has replaced coffee sharecropping as the principal route of upward mobility, it is questionable how long this trend will last. It will probably not be very long. Unlike coffee, cotton lacks government price supports so that large price fluctuations occur from year to year, depending on the size of the harvest. In 1968 the initial price paid per arrôba of cotton was CrN$ 6,60, but, when the true size of the yield was made known a few months later, the price plummeted to CrN$ 4,50 per arrôba. Those who held off selling their crop expecting the price to rise were severely hurt. Also, under average conditions, cotton produces less profit per alqueire of land than coffee does, given the present price structure of both crops, and cotton is more sensitive to minor variations in weather than coffee is. A little too much sun or rain can halve the size of the cotton harvest, whereas coffee trees are only affected by extremes of cold and drought. The optimal weather conditions which prevailed during the 1967–68 growing season occur only once every five or six years. Finally, the current expenses of cotton cultivation are fairly low, involving, in addition to labor costs, only the purchase of seed and insecticide. But cotton has been cultivated extensively in Ouro Verde only since 1964, and, while the soils now produce well, yields will soon deteriorate if fertilizer is not applied. Fertilizer for land planted in cotton costs an average of CrN$ 200,00 per alqueire, and this added expense, when it becomes necessary, will cut into profits severely. Given the uncertainty of prices and weather conditions, it is not likely that many cultivators will be willing to risk this additional investment in the crop.

Taking all these factors into account, the current cotton boom and the opportunities for upward mobility which it affords are seen in clearer perspective. The notion that cotton will be the wave of the future in Ouro Verde and the surrounding counties must be dismissed. It should be remembered that the cultivation of cotton on many holdings is a temporary measure carried out to fulfill the stipulations of the coffee eradication contract. As soon as the contract expires, most large landowners intend to change the land now in cotton and other crops to pasture. For this reason, renters and sharecroppers will find it increasingly difficult to secure contracts, and this final route for the upwardly mobile in the rural area of Ouro Verde will vanish.

While local socioeconomic classes are not as clearly defined as they are in many other regions of Brazil, particularly those in the old plantation areas,[25] they are slowly becoming increasingly rigid. With additional land consolidation and the gradual emigration of farmers to the frontier and the cities of Paraná and São Paulo,

25. See Hutchinson (1957) and Margolis (1966) for detailed accounts of the socioeconomic hierarchy in the Recôncavo region of the Bahian sugar coast.

this previously important "buffer" group between the masses of landless workers and the few wealthy landowners has declined, both numerically and in percentage of the local population.

From the data, it should be clear that one well-vaunted characteristic of frontier society in general, and the North American frontier in particular, occurs only to a limited degree in Ouro Verde, and presumably in the other counties of the region undergoing similar changes. This is the theory made famous by the American historian Frederick Jackson Turner, that the frontier exerted a strong democratizing force in United States history, and that each new frontier provided "a gate of escape from the bondage of the past" (Turner 1920:38). Turner saw the American frontier as an outlet for the upwardly mobile, affording urban laborers in the eastern cities an opportunity to rise in wealth and status through the acquisition of free or very inexpensive frontier land. Whether or not this theory holds true for the United States,[26] it is only partially applicable in the area of Paraná under study.

A considerable amount of social mobility, as measured by the acquisition of land, existed during the first decade of Ouro Verde's settlement, and insofar as that period is concerned, it is true that the frontier offered opportunities not found in "older" regions. But in the area of sandy soils northwest of Maringá, the regime of the upwardly mobile was short lived as a result of economic and ecological conditions largely beyond the control of the local population. It is now virtually impossible for the landless worker to buy even a small holding from his earnings in coffee cultivation, and the opportunities for advancement afforded by the current "cotton boom" will undoubtedly be of brief duration.

26. See Shannon 1968 for a critique of Turner's hypothesis.

7. Coffee's Decline: Causes and Effects

OURO VERDE is a community undergoing rapid economic changes which are reflected in alterations of local land divisions, work systems, population size, class structure, and patterns of mobility. A series of interrelated factors, all concrete and subject to measurement, is responsible for the change in the county's economic base.

The variables involved in the decline of coffee in Ouro Verde have been separated into two sets (economic and ecological) for heuristic purposes, with no intention of placing greater emphasis on either. Three factors, soil depletion, frosts, and falling prices, are most responsible for the changing patterns of agriculture in the community. Coffee pests, rising cultivation costs, the government eradication program, and the existence of inexpensive frontier land are secondary factors in coffee's decline, and their impact would probably have been reduced were it not for the three primary ones.

Decreasing soil fertility, frosts (and, to a lesser extent, severe droughts), and lowered coffee prices are all phenomona whose combined effect on local agriculture is far greater than their individual impact. Soil depletion leads to greatly reduced yields which, in turn, are diminished further by frosts. Cultivators, therefore, simply have less coffee to sell, and in recent years have received a comparatively poor price for that which they do have.

Coffee yields in Ouro Verde have declined continually almost from the time of the first harvest in 1954–55, despite the fact that until 1961 more and more trees came into production. This decline is traceable directly to the rapid loss of chemical and organic elements in the county's mixed sandy soil. Likewise, frosts have played a significant role: despite the relative infrequency of major frosts (of the sort which occurred in 1955, 1963, and, most recently, 1969), they do a great deal of damage, and, if severe enough, they affect the size of two or three consecutive harvests or even kill the coffee trees. In addition, the nearly annual occurrence of geadas brancas, light frosts which "burn" only the topmost branches, sometimes reduces the size of harvests, particularly in the low-lying areas of the county. Finally, the price currently being paid for coffee by the Brazilian Coffee Institute[1] is only one-third of the amount received by farmers during the early years of the county's settlement. Thus, reduced yields combined with lower prices have significantly reduced the cultivators' margin of profits, making it impossible for many farmers to support their families and forcing them to sell their land.

Perhaps the most important of the secondary factors is the rise in cultivation expenses. This is classified as a secondary factor because it is partially the result of soil depletion. Higher cultivation costs arise largely from the increasing need for chemical fertilizer, an expensive item that never had to be purchased during the first decade of coffee cultivation in the county. While it is true that increased labor costs also have added to basic cultivation expenses, there can be no doubt that the recent need for fertilizers is the principal factor in increased capital output. But, because lower prices are received for the crop, many cultivators are reluctant to invest in fertilizer since this expense would cut further into their already meager profits. As a result, yields remain low, since in most cases little is done to revitalize the fertility of the soil.

Coffee pests, particularly broca, are a relatively minor factor in decreasing yields and increasing cultivation expenses. The insecticide used to combat this pest is fairly inexpensive and is used widely. Still, when broca-infested coffee trees first became common in the county in the early 1960s, many farmers' harvests were re-

1. The price paid to farmers by the Brazilian Coffee Institute is, of course, directly influenced by coffee prices on the world market. See Appendix 3.

duced by as much as 50 per cent until insecticides were applied the following year.

As noted, the federally financed eradication program is not the cause of coffee's decline in Ouro Verde and over a wide region of northern Paraná, but the program has accelerated a process that was already under way. Of the county's 12 million coffee trees, 6.5 million have been cut down since 1962, most of them under the auspices of the eradication program. While the aim of the program was to eliminate unproductive trees, many growers took advantage of the opportunity for cash payments and cut down even those that were moderately productive. Had the program never been instituted, the elimination of low-yield trees would have been a far more gradual process. Farmers would have received nothing for the eradication of their trees, and probably would have been reluctant to bear the entire financial burden of replanting their land in other crops and in pasture.

The final factor involved in the slow demise of coffee in Ouro Verde is the most difficult one to evaluate. The proximity of inexpensive frontier land surely has had some effect on the changes in agriculture taking place in the county, but how does one measure precisely the magnitude of the frontier's influence? Has the presence of virgin lands only 150 kilometers from Ouro Verde hastened the decline of coffee in the community? I believe it has. Why should a farmer with few resources, aside from his 5 or 10 alqueires of partially exhausted land, go into debt to pay for fertilizer and other cultivation expenses when he can profitably sell his holding and buy a larger tract of virgin land on the frontier?[2] Clearly, it is not necessary to call up the spectres of "immediatist values," "aversion" to modern agricultural technology, or "lack of feeling" for the land to understand the continued attractiveness that the frontier has for the cultivator in Ouro Verde. Purchasing land on the frontier is simply the most rational alternative, given the economic and ecological situations in the county.

Another question remains: If there were no inexpensive virgin lands within a reasonable distance of Ouro Verde, would the farmer make an additional effort to preserve the fertility of his current holding? He might go heavily into debt to finance fertilizer and other cultivation expenses and attempt to eke out a small profit from his coffee trees. But this would probably be a stop-gap meas-

2. Farmers can sell their holdings at a profit because local land values have increased continually since the county was first opened for settlement.

ure, and it is not at all certain, given the sandy soil of Ouro Verde and the adjacent counties, that an accomodation of this sort would alleviate the problem for any length of time. This is only speculation; the fact remains that the frontier does exist, thus making inexpensive virgin land readily accessible to the farmer in the community.

The effects on other aspects of local culture, resulting from the county's change from coffee to cattle, are numerous and varied. Some are directly traceable to the exigencies of the new agricultural regime; others are outgrowths of these primary changes. Among the basic modifications are the consolidation of small farms into larger holdings, unemployment, population decrease and emigration from the county, and the replacement of certain work systems associated with coffee cultivation by other systems compatible with cattle ranching. These changes, in turn, have affected the town's economy, its class structure and patterns of mobility, and the general atmosphere of the community, what has been referred to as a loss of "movimento."

The decline of coffee and increase in cattle are causally related to the consolidation of small farms into large fazendas. Minimum land and capital requirements are essential to insure an adequate income from cattle ranching, placing this new enterprise beyond the reach of most farmers who lack both sufficient land and capital. With the decrease in coffee yields resulting from soil depletion and frosts, a number of sitiantes sold their holdings to neighboring fazendeiros who were in the market for additional land to support their growing herds of cattle. This trend has proceeded farthest in the Vagalume region of the county where holdings larger than 50 alqueires predominate, and the few sítios that remain are lost in a sea of pasture. While this is the extreme case of land consolidation in Ouro Verde, the same process is occurring at a slower pace throughout the county.[3]

Growing unemployment is another direct result of the increasing importance of cattle to the county's economy and the concomitant consolidation of land. Precise figures are unattainable; a large por-

3. This trend toward land consolidation is limited to the regions of sandy soils north and west of Maringá. Emilio Willems (1969) points out that quite the opposite is true in the more easterly counties of northern Paraná, where there has been an increase in the number of small and medium-sized holdings (less than 20 hectares and from 21 to 200 hectares, respectively) over the last two decades. The explanation appears to lie in the great differences in soils and coffee yields in the two regions.

tion of the unemployed remain in Ouro Verde only for brief periods, then move to other areas of northern Paraná seeking work as day laborers. But there can be no doubt that this group of jobless migrants has increased in size within the last few years. Large numbers still arrive before the coffee harvest begins in June, but, unlike past years, today there is not sufficient work for all of them. With the eradication of millions of coffee trees in the county and the diminished yields of those still in production, a far smaller labor force is required for harvesting the crop.

The county's prolonged period of unemployment in September, following completion of the coffee harvest, has also been aggravated by the changing rural economy. Many of Ouro Verde's permanent residents who always worked in the harvests are finding it increasingly difficult to secure even seasonal employment. In addition, in response to low yields and low prices, landowners are attempting to cut down on their expenses, so that many of the nonessential cultivation tasks (such as frequent prunings), once done by resident day laborers, have been eliminated.

Another effect of the changeover and a partial result of unemployment is the decrease of local population and emigration from the county. Since 1962, Ouro Verde's population has declined by about 2,200, a conservative figure since migrant day laborers are not included in the census. Unemployment resulting in the emigration of sharecroppers and day laborers does not account for the entire loss, however, because many farmers have left the county after selling their local properties and buying land on the frontier. Despite the countywide loss of population, the town's population has increased since 1962 by some 400 people, all of whom had previously lived in the rural area. Some of these are farmers who own land in the county, but have contracted it to sharecroppers and moved to town to educate their children. But part of the increase is a result of the current state of agriculture in the rural area. Perhaps 10 per cent of the sitiantes who sold their land to fazendeiros did not invest the selling price in frontier holdings, preferring to buy a jeep or a small store and move to town.

In answer to why some chose these alternatives in light of the present state of the town's economy, one factor is that the occupation of motorista or professional driver is still a somewhat lucrative one. Farmers hire jeeps to transport their crops to the processing plants, and many families rent a jeep to go shopping in a neighboring county. While there is some evidence that the market for motoristas will soon be glutted, this has not yet occurred and many sitiantes express the desire to sell their land and enter this profession. The reasons for buying a small shop in town are more complex. A number of stores have gone out of business for lack of customers. But the town's population has expanded somewhat from the influx from the countryside, and some former landowners hope to take advantage of these new potential customers. In addition, a few sitiantes have moved to town so that their grown children could work in the bank or prefeitura and add to the family's income. But, in at least a handful of cases, this change in occupation has resulted in failure. Some farmers who sold their land and bought stores in town have since sold out for lack of business and have returned to the countryside as sharecroppers. These examples of downward mobility are few, but should more and more sitiantes move to town and become marginal proprietors, this trend probably will increase.

As expected, the rural areas suffering most from population loss are those in which the changeover from coffee to cattle has been the most extreme. The population of the Vagalume, for example, has decreased by nearly 60 per cent over the last six years; in the Santa Maria region, where coffee and lavoura branca still predominate, the loss has been about 10 per cent.

Labor arrangements in Ouro Verde have undergone significant modifications, directly traceable to changes in the county's agricultural base. As a rule, work systems associated with coffee cultivation (sharecropping, day and piecework labor, work gangs, and the colono system) have either disappeared or have declined greatly in importance. Labor arrangements compatible with lavoura branca cultivation (tenant farming, here referred to as renting) and cattle ranching (mensal labor, or workers paid a fixed monthly wage) have become increasingly common.

The colono system, never widespread in Ouro Verde, has, with one exception, met its demise. Colonos were contracted on a few of the county's large fazendas until about 1960, but they were gradually replaced by volantes, since the labor legislation protecting the latter was easier to circumvent.

Another labor system that has declined in popularity is the work gang headed by an empreiteiro or "gato." These gangs were contracted for labor-intensive tasks such as planting and harvesting coffee trees, constructing barns, building fences, and clearing land. Since very little coffee is being planted and those trees that are still in production are giving smaller yields, the labor gang is no longer employed in coffee cultivation. Today an empreiteiro and his men occasionally are contracted to eradicate coffee trees and plant pasture.

Sharecropping has always been a common labor arrangement in Ouro Verde and still is, although its importance has diminished since 1960. While there has been a reduction in the number of sharecropping positions available in the county because so many coffee trees have been replaced by pasture, even those positions that are still open no longer afford the opportunities for economic advancement that they once did. This too, is tied to the greatly reduced yields of the producing trees, and, thus, the smaller return which the sharecropper receives for his labor.

The system of renting land was introduced into Ouro Verde soon after the first contracts were signed for the eradication of coffee. Renters cultivate only lavoura branca, never coffee, so that this labor system has become prominent in those areas of the county given over to cotton, peanuts, rice, and other annual crops. In all likelihood, this will be a short-term arrangement; most renters cultivate fazenda lands which will be turned into pasture once the eradication contracts expire.

One other labor arrangement, work paid for on a monthly basis, has increased in use since the changeover from coffee to cattle got under way. All cowhands and fazenda administrators receive a fixed salary at the end of the month, and, of course, these employees are associated largely with cattle ranching. It is to be expected that as additional land is converted into pasture, the monthly wage will become a permanent and prominent fixture in the county.

Of the secondary results of the change in Ouro Verde's agricultural structure, none is more obvious or important than the impact on the town's economy. A number of general and dry goods stores have closed since 1962; others are constantly changing hands, their owners barely obtaining an adequate income from them. Other stores which still belong to the original owners have suffered a sharp decrease in volume of sales, and are no longer the profitable enterprises that they were when coffee ruled the county's economy. Population decrease in the rural area and the tightness of money, factors clearly linked to coffee's decline, account for the slackening of business activity affecting all town enterprises from the local barber shop and bars to the hotels and butcher shops.

Among the effects which the changeover has had on Ouro Verde's class structure and patterns of socioeconomic mobility, the gradual reduction in the size of the rural "middle class" is undoubtedly the most noteworthy. As more and more farmers with sítio-sized holdings sell their land and move to the frontier, a widening gap in the community's class structure is increasingly apparent. Fazenda-sized holdings have become more common, with a concomitant increase in the number of individuals owning large amounts of land. At the same time, the landless day laborers, sharecroppers, and renters, although no greater in number than a decade ago, now represent a larger percentage of the county's population. Thus, the significant group of owners of small and medium-sized farms is gradually being depleted, leaving a pyramidal class structure with a small number of wealthy fazendeiros at the apex and a large mass of landless agricultural workers at the base. While it is too soon to note any major change in interclass relations, it is not unlikely that class lines will rigidify and take on an increasingly hierarchical character with more formal patterns of interclass behavior.

Sharecropping highly productive coffee trees, once the principal avenue of social and economic advancement in Ouro Verde, no longer serves as an outlet for the upwardly mobile. Lower coffee yields and the reduction in the number of producing trees have eliminated many sharecropping positions, and those that are still available are far less lucrative than they were in the past. Cultivating cotton on rented land has partially replaced sharecropping coffee as a route to landownership, but this trend is temporary and will disappear when cultivation costs rise sharply as fertilizer becomes necessary and when land now planted in cotton gives way to pasture. Thus, the changeover from coffee to cattle has all but erased landless workers' opportunities for socioeconomic mobility. The gradual change in the community's agricultural base is widening the gap between rich and poor, and all evidence indicates that, as more and more of the county's land is planted in pasture, socioeconomic divisions will become even more pronounced as opportunities for upward mobility disappear entirely.

There is a widespread myth concerning the nearly unlimited opportunities said to characterize frontier areas. Two variables affecting a settler's potential for upward mobility emerge from the data. First is the time of arrival in the community. Those who came to Ouro Verde during the early years of settlement found rich virgin lands that could be purchased at a fraction of today's prices and which, in addition, produced large coffee yields, whose selling price assured a handsome return. Not uncommonly, formadores and sharecroppers bought small sítios on the frontier with the profits derived from the sale of three or four harvests. Today, coffee prices are considerably lower, yields have diminished greatly, and land values, at least in Ouro Verde and the surrounding counties, have skyrocketed, all of which make it virtually impossible for new arrivals in Ouro Verde to save enough money to purchase frontier land, to say nothing of land in the community.

The second variable which must be taken into account when considering a settler's potential for upward mobility is the size of his savings upon arrival in the county. Lucrative sharecropping positions were awarded only to those who had savings for cultivation expenses and family expenses until the harvest was sold. This provision clearly excluded day laborers and others earning subsistence wages from securing sharecropping positions which might have enabled them to buy a frontier sítio. The point is, that to move upward on the social and economic scale it was necessary to start out with *something*. The settler with as little as U.S. $75 in savings might, with luck, enter into a sharecropping contract, but the day laborer who lacked even sufficient money to feed and clothe his family could never hope to obtain such a position. Thus, one's initial financial position and time of arrival in the community were important determinants of future economic success. Although the frontier, at least in this instance, certainly offered opportunities not found in the older, more settled regions of Brazil, it was hardly a panacea for the majority of the poor and downtrodden.

A final consequence of coffee's decline in Ouro Verde may be described as a profound loss of confidence in the community's future. As economic conditions worsened, pessimism and despair came to dominate the local mood. The county's residents say that the region lost its former spirit or "movimento." In Brazil, no matter how small or inaccessible a community is, it is considered a "good" place to live as long as it emulates larger towns and cities by having an air of liveliness and activity, precisely the quality which Ouro Verde now lacks. Long-time residents fondly recall the excitement and hopes of the early years of settlement. Conditions were difficult, but there was a feeling that this was a community of the future, where a farmer could live comfortably, without worry, on his few alqueires planted in coffee. Some fazendeiros hoped to make quick fortunes on this lucrative crop, then sell their holdings for large profits. But, perhaps more importantly, the county was viewed as a source of new opportunities for the sitiante, formador, and sharecropper, men of small means who for once would be able to make ends meet and, if all went well, buy small farms or a few more alqueires of land. Today, these hopes and ambitions are no longer voiced, for the people of Ouro Verde know that they no longer are realizable.

The Role of the Frontier in Brazil and the United States

The process of agricultural change in Ouro Verde is based on identifiable economic and ecologic factors, not on a distinctly Brazilian ideology or cultural tradition. In the southern United States, parallel developments took place under broadly similar conditions, although within the context of a very different cultural tradition. The common element in both cases is the exploitation of vast areas of unsettled and semisettled virgin frontier land on which lucrative cash crops were cultivated.[4]

In the southern United States, cotton spread westward from the coastal plain to the Piedmont area of the Atlantic seaboard, to the bottom lands of the Gulf States, and finally to southwest Arkansas and northeast Texas. This pattern has striking parallels with the southwestern expansion of coffee in Brazil. In each instance, the availability of inexpensive frontier land, the rapid depletion of soil, and the failure to conserve land under cultivation were common factors which led to the constant movement of the frontier.

The historian Clement Eaton has documented and analyzed the expansion of the cotton frontier in the American South and Southwest (1949, 1961). He cites the lack of soil conservation as the principal reason for cotton's decline and the subsequent migration westward: "The method of cultivating cotton in the ante-bellum South tended to exhaust the soil, especially on account of the failure to practice an intelligent rotation of crops and to check soil erosion. Consequently, the cotton planters began a steady march westward to acquire virgin soil leaving in their wake a desolate and abandoned countryside" (1949:229). At times, the parallels between the American South and the Brazilian coffee regions are striking. One only need substitute coffee for cotton, the Paraíba Valley for

4. Two other examples of similar developmental sequences, in the Paraíba Valley of Rio de Janeiro and the coffee-growing regions of São Paulo, also strengthen the case for these factors and demonstrate that where certain conditions prevail, that is, the availability of inexpensive frontier lands and a market for a lucrative crop, similar effects will result. See Stein (1957) on the Paraíba Valley and Milliet (1938) on São Paulo.

Alabama, São Paulo for Mississippi, and Paraná for the Southwest: "The cotton planters who emigrated to the virgin lands of the Southwest carried on the same wasteful type of agriculture that had exhausted their old plantations. As a consequence, in the 1840's and 1850's farms in Alabama and Mississippi were being abandoned for fresher lands in Texas and Arkansas . . . lands in Mississippi were being eroded because the farmers 'skinned' the soil, or scratched the surface only two inches deep with their plows. Many of the farmers in that state were not fixed, but ready to sell out and move to Texas" (1961:42).

The fertility of virgin frontier soil far surpassed that of the older cotton-producing regions, a fact that explains much of the attractiveness of the hinterland. During the 1850s, in newly settled areas of Texas, yields of three bales of cotton per acre were not unusual. At the same time the badly depleted land of the Upper South produced only one bale per acre (Eaton 1961:45).

In 1800, three-quarters of the nation's cotton production was in Virginia and the Carolinas, but because of the rapid depletion of soils in these states, by 1860, Georgia, Alabama, Mississippi, and Louisiana produced two-thirds of the output (Davis 1939:16). Finally, only thirty years later, Texas surpassed all of the other regions in cotton production. Westward expansion of the crop did not stop there, but proceeded into Indian territory (Vance 1929:22).

Profits made from cotton grown on virgin soil were at first extremely high. In 1801, the cultivator received 44 cents per pound, and one planter's yield from 600 acres of frontier land was valued at $90,000. But prices dropped rapidly as a result of overproduction and fluctuated throughout the century. During most of the period, cotton was the nation's chief export, and, on the eve of the Civil War, it accounted for 60 per cent of the total value of United States exports (Eaton 1949:230–31).

Why were measures not taken to preserve the fertility of the lands under cultivation? Weaver, writing about Mississippi in the 1850s, notes, "It was difficult for farmers and planters on newly cleared productive land to understand the importance of soil conservation, especially when they knew that many more thousand acres of virgin soil fully as fertile were yet available. The preachments . . . on diversification or crop rotation . . . [and] artificial fertilizers fell on deaf ears in Mississippi as long as abundant crops of cotton could be produced without any effort being made to preserve the natural fertility of the land" (1945:85). Another writer describes Alabama during the same period: "The average planter scarcely considered his land anything more than a current expense. He used neither fertilizer nor a system of crop rotation, for his one great aim was to produce cotton, planted year after year in the same fields until the ground refused to bring forth a remunerative crop. The science of deep plowing was little employed, and when shallow cultivation ceased to be profitable the planter usually moved to new lands" (Davis 1939:171).

Contemporary critics deplored the wastefulness of this type of exploitation. Senator Clement C. Clay of Alabama remarked, "Our small farmers, after taking the cream off their lands, unable to restore them by rest, manures, or otherwise, are going farther west and south, in search of other virgin lands which they may and will despoil and impoverish in like manner. Our wealthy planters with greater means and no more skill, are buying out their poor neighbors, extending their plantations, and adding to their slave force" (quoted in Eaton 1971:41).

It is clear from these statements that the seemingly "wasteful" use of southern cotton land may be explained by the high yields initially produced on virgin soils and the promise of an ever present frontier to which the farmer could migrate once his land was depleted. To the question of whether it would not have been simpler to conserve the soil from the beginning, rather than to pull up stakes and start all over again in another area, in most cases the answer is no. In Davis' words, "Generally speaking, soil conservation was a luxury far beyond the planters' means" (1939:173). With the uncertainty of the cotton market, the prior indebtedness of the planters, and their desire to buy still more land rather than preserve the old, there was little capital to invest in soil conservation. The wish to acquire additional land is not surprising: "The desire of the planter for the adjoining land of his neighbor was an urge which was seldom, if ever, resisted. The immense yield capable of being produced on a small acreage of thoroughly tilled land could scarcely be imagined" (Davis 1939:178–79).

While it is true that certain techniques, such as crop rotation, required little additional expenditure and were employed widely after a time, others, such as chemical fertilizer and improved drainage ditches, were very costly and not used extensively. The lack of soil conservation techniques on the part of farmers and planters alike was not the result of some instinctual "wanderlust" or "lack of feeling" for the land, but a rational choice, given the circumstances of price fluctuations, expensive conservation techniques, and the availability of rich, virgin frontier lands.

The data on the expansion of cotton in the southern and southeastern United States demonstrate that there are broadly similar parallels between the history of this crop and that of coffee in Brazil.[5] The common developments are grounded in the existence of unsettled, fertile frontier lands on which a lucrative cash crop could be cultivated. At different periods in their histories, both the United States and Brazil have had vast frontier areas which lured farmers and planters living in the older, more settled regions, but the attraction of the frontier would have been reduced markedly if the markets for cotton and coffee had not existed. It is the combination of available frontier lands and an important market for cash crops which accounts for the developmental parallels.

These parallel developments are not simply fortuitous coincidences, nor can they be accounted for by similarities of cultural tradition. Few ideologues would admit that the "Protestant ethic" which is said to pervade the United States has very much in common with the Brazilian "strike-it-rich" mentality. This kind of explanation leads nowhere for one reason: it is impossible to explain constants (the similar developmental sequences in Brazil and the United States) in terms of variables (the two distinct cultural traditions in question). What is clear from the discussion is that techno-environmental and economic conditions operating in both countries at the time of the expansion of cotton and coffee provide a more than adequate explanation of the parallel changes which took place in each case.

Ideological versus Material Explanations of Culture Change

At the beginning of this monograph, strong criticisms were made of mentalistic interpretations of the cyclical nature of Brazil's agricultural economy. Leeds claims that "technological stagnation" of the nation's agriculture is traceable to a peculiar set of values said to be "uniquely" Brazilian in character. Referring specifically to the coffee region, Leeds writes, "The misdirected commercialism of unilateral efforts of control, instead of concentration on the technological foundations for an inexpensive and aggressively competi-

5. One important difference in the moving frontiers in the two countries is that while cattle is replacing coffee in many areas of northern Paraná, in the United States no single crop or enterprise replaced cotton. In various localities different agricultural products were introduced after cotton: rice on the Carolina coast, vegetables and fruit in a number of former cotton-growing areas.

tive production, has grown out of the coffee region value system" (1957:576). More generally, he traces Brazil's inability to compete on the world market, the reluctance to adopt modern farming technology, and an "exploitative" productive system resulting in a deterioration of natural resources, to the nature of Brazilian social structure and its attendant "class value system" (1957:28).

A common fault in explanations of this sort is their failure to indicate why this set of values is unique to Brazil. The notion held by many anthropologists that the particular culture they are studying is not comparable to any other obfuscates the goal of the discipline, the explanation of cross-cultural similarities and differences. The reasons for the existence of a "strike-it-rich" mentality among Brazilian cultivators is seen as an odd cultural quirk and is, therefore, left unexplained. Had Leeds and others offering comparable interpretations delved more deeply into the particular set of economic and ecologic conditions under which these values were operating, they might have been better able to account for them.

The fact is that, given a vast area of fertile frontier land and a high market price for a cash crop, it is probable that a similar series of phenomena will result. Prior to 1960, the price paid for coffee in Brazil was high and the profits derived from its cultivation could not be matched by any other agricultural product. In the case of Ouro Verde, a few planters bought land with the intention of taking out five or six harvests, spending as little as possible on conservation techniques, and using the profits from the sale of coffee to invest in other enterprises. While this behavior might be termed "immediatist" since it is not concerned with the long-range effects of such practices, nevertheless, it is not uniquely Brazilian. There are few who would not attempt to take advantage of the opportunities afforded by such a situation. We have seen that a similar phenomenon occurred in the southern and southeastern United States, a fact strengthening the contention that it is the availability of fertile frontier land and the demand for a valuable cash crop, rather than a given set of cultural values, that determines this variety of exploitation.

Lest it be thought that the particular events currently taking place in Ouro Verde are limited to that community, a remarkably similar phenomenon in a more recently settled county in northern Paraná is described by Monteiro-Teixeira: "The fertility of the soil, which in certain instances is extraordinary, impedes the landowner from seeing conservation as an immediate problem. The possibility of large profits and rapid enrichment, verified so many times in the past, but also, the inherent uncertainties and risks of cultivation, the economic destiny of which depends upon factors not under the cultivator's control, as, for example, the frosts and the international politics of prices, is highly favorable to the development of this immediatist spirit" (1961:54; translation mine). He might have been talking about Ouro Verde a mere fourteen years ago.

These views bring up another factor that was undoubtedly operative in the county during its first decade of settlement. Since Ouro Verde lies in a zone of periodic frosts, the cultivator is uncertain from year to year whether his coffee trees will freeze and the harvest will be destroyed. For this reason he is most reluctant to go into debt to purchase expensive fertilizers. The risk of such an investment can well be imagined: a single frost may wipe out not only the harvest, but also the money spent on fertilizer, and the cultivator still must pay his debt to the bank or intermediary. Thus, the failure to employ modern soil preservation techniques is seen in a clearer perspective. It is related to the ecologic and economic conditions under which coffee is grown in northern Paraná, and not the ideology or traditions of its cultivators.

It may be strongly argued that the major problem with Leeds' interpretation of Brazilian agricultural cycles is that he sees the causal process operating in reverse. He insists that the social structure and the class-linked values in the regions where "boom-bust" crops are cultivated determine the "exploitative" character of the agricultural enterprise. We have seen that, insofar as Ouro Verde and the southern United States are concerned, quite the opposite is true. In these cases, the ecologic and economic conditions which prevailed during the expansion of coffee and cotton were responsible for the nature of the regimes under which these crops were cultivated and the changes that took place in the wake of their spread. While it is certainly arguable that a particular exploitative mentality developed as an outgrowth of these conditions, this mentality is a result and not a cause of the character of the enterprises in question. Thus we must conclude, after the fashion of Marvin Harris, that Leeds found assorted anthropologists "standing on their heads, and he joined them" (Harris 1968:513).

Ouro Verde and Northern Paraná—The Future?

What will be the future of Ouro Verde and the larger region of northern Paraná covered with similar types of sandy soil? It is more than likely that the changes which the community is currently undergoing will continue, and may even increase in momentum. Today, slightly less than half of the county's land is planted in coffee and indications are that there will be further reductions. Another major frost of the intensity of those of 1955 and 1963 would undoubtedly be the death knell for coffee in Ouro Verde. At this point, however, the light frosts which occur almost annually will not affect the coffee trees still in production, since they are on higher ground, and those in the low-lying areas most subject to minor freezes have already been eradicated. Thus, barring a major frost, the extant coffee trees in the county will continue to produce yields for a few more years.

Another determinant of the future of coffee in Ouro Verde is the continued availability of credit for cultivation expenses. Given the depleted state of the county's soils, the application of chemical fertilizer is rapidly becoming necessary if yields are to be even minimal. Without bank financing it is virtually impossible for cultivators to cover all of their expenses, particularly at a time when costs are rising. Even if bank loans continue to be available, substantial increases in interest rates will effectively cut off this source of financing for the owners of small landholdings. Even if massive amounts of fertilizer were applied, the costs involved in such a procedure would cut severely into farmers' profits. At some point in time, coffee cultivation in this region of northern Paraná may simply become an unprofitable enterprise.

For similar reasons, the current cotton boom will be short lived. As fertilizer becomes increasingly necessary for this crop, profits will decline, even in the unlikely event that prices remain the same. In addition, since cotton has no federal price supports and overproduction is already taking place, wild fluctuations in price are almost sure to occur. Much of the land presently planted in cotton and other annuals will be converted to pasture upon the expiration of the eradication contracts, so that the percentage of land given over to lavoura branca will decrease substantially.

While these changes will probably take place, another event, the continued expansion of cattle and pasture in the county, is inevitable. As coffee and cotton yields decline, more and more sitiantes will be forced to sell their holdings because they will no longer be able to support their families on the meager revenue derived from their land. Men who already own extensive properties in the county will simply expand their holdings by buying adjacent sítios and converting them to pasture. One local agronomist employed by the company predicts that up to 90 per cent of the area of sandy soil north and west of Maringá, which includes Ouro Verde and all of the surrounding counties, will be covered with pasture in the next ten years.

With the continued advance of the fazenda at the expense of the sítio, and the displacement of coffee and cotton by cattle, hundreds of sharecroppers, renters, and day laborers will be out of work and it will become increasingly difficult for them to find employment in Ouro Verde. Sharecroppers and renters who now cultivate coffee and cotton may be forced to accept low-paying jobs as volantes and mensalistas on local cattle ranches, or, more likely, will leave the county entirely. The labor demands of cattle ranching are minimal compared to those of coffee cultivation, and for this reason the new enterprise simply cannot support the present population of Ouro Verde. One would expect continued emigration from the county, the rate of which is likely to increase in the years to come. In addition, the economy of the town will no longer provide a convenient escape route for the rural cultivator; new town businesses, such as small bars and general stores, will become more and more unprofitable as the size of the population continues to decline.

All of these events will radically alter the make-up of the community. Instead of being characterized by a large middle group of sharecroppers and owners of small and medium-sized farms, a small segment with extensive holdings will predominate and control a large class of improverished workers. The local social structure will increasingly come to resemble a rigid, caste-like system in which the opportunities for upward mobility are nonexistent.

As local revenues from coffee and cotton continue to decrease, still another effect will become evident. Since the amount of money a county receives from the state government is dependent upon its contribution to the ICM tax, and this, in turn, is based on the volume of agricultural products exported from the county, the changeover from coffee to cattle will greatly reduce the amount of state funds Ouro Verde receives. Coffee simply has more monetary value than cattle and, therefore, produces higher revenues. The profligate expenditures on such "vital" community works as a large new bus station, improvement of the town square, and an expensive imported mimeograph machine will gradually cease as the county's funds grow smaller. But the reduction in local revenues also will adversely affect the construction of new schools and clinics, and social services in general. It is in these areas that decreasing expenditures will hurt the county, particularly the town, and the drawing power which the town has in educational terms for rural residents will be diminished.

Might not other enterprises, perhaps small industries, be developed to offset partially the decline in agriculture? The answer is a firm negative. Unlike Maringá, which has grown and flourished by attracting commerce and industry and has become progressively less dependent upon the fortunes of the surrounding countryside, Ouro Verde is totally reliant on agriculture. The prosperity of the largest enterprises in Ouro Verde, the plants which process coffee and lavoura branca, is directly linked to agricultural production in the rural area, such that as production has declined, so have these industries. Moreover, it is highly unlikely that the county will be able to attract new enterprises since it has little in the way of land, labor, or capital to offer.

The final question is whether the future of northern Paraná as a whole will follow the same course as Ouro Verde. It is probable that a similar fate awaits the regions of sandy soil north of Maringá to the São Paulo border and west to Paraguay. There are already scattered indications that coffee production is on the decline near the edge of the western frontier. In Cianorte, a county founded in 1953, many farmers participated in the federal eradication program after the 1963 frost severely damaged their coffee trees; they sold their holdings and moved to Umuarama which was then being opened for settlement. Reports of semi-abandoned towns in the Cianorte region are common and, closer to Ouro Verde, there are at least two communities which have been nearly deserted by their inhabitants and are now entirely given over to cattle ranches.

The future of the older terra roxa regions east of Ouro Verde appears less bleak. Despite damaging frosts, the rich soils of the area continue to produce high coffee yields, and cultivation is still a profitable enterprise there, although less so than in the past. In areas of terra roxa the problem is not one of soil depletion, since the land remains fertile for many years even without the application of fertilizer, but of frosts. It is simply a question of how frequent and severe they must become before coffee cultivation on terra roxa ceases to be a viable undertaking.

A possibly decisive factor in northern Paraná's future is a program of the Brazilian Coffee Institute, now in the planning stage, which will finance farmers who wish to replant coffee in areas where it has been eradicated. The plan will be limited to regions of terra roxa soils that are entirely frost free. The goal of the program is to encourage farmers in locations suited to coffee cultivation to replant coffee on up to 30 per cent of their land. An effort will be made to avoid recreating a monocrop economy with all the pitfalls it entails. The plan would limit the amount of land planted in coffee, but at the same time keep production at a high level.

Unfortunately, nearly all regions of northern Paraná lack the minimum requirements of excellent soils in frost-free zones. Since even the terra roxa lands east of Ouro Verde are subject to intermittent frosts, the institute's plan can have no beneficial effect on coffee cultivation in the state. In all likelihood, the program will give impetus to the revival of coffee cultivation in certain regions of São Paulo state. There the problem of frosts is confined to a narrower zone and there are areas of rich terra roxa soil where temperatures rarely fall below 0°C. The program could well have the effect of increasing São Paulo's coffee production to such a point that it would surpass Paraná's, and once again it would become the largest producing region in Brazil, and, therefore, in the world.

8. Postscript

The governor of Brazil's major coffee-growing state said yesterday that a frost had ruined almost 80 per cent of next year's harvest.

Governor Paulo Pimental, of the southern state of Paraná, said that the harvest probably would not exceed 3 million bags. A 14-million bag harvest had been expected.

Temperatures fell to the low 20s Thursday. The damage was estimated to total $150 million.

New York Times, *July 12, 1969*

On July 10, 1969, a major frost struck a wide area of northern Paraná, comparable in severity to those of 1955 and 1963. In Ouro Verde approximately 40 per cent of the extant coffee trees were affected.[1] The 1970 harvest was all but eliminated and it was not until the following year that the trees produced a crop. What was the effect on the county? Were the social and economic changes already under way in the community hastened by this event? The implications of the results of the frost will be considered here, and the general changes which have taken place since the time of the initial study in 1967–68.

1. This percentage may appear low in comparison to the damage done by the frosts of 1955 and 1963, but it should be remembered that by 1969 the lowest areas in the county were planted in pasture. This figure, then, represents damage to trees in elevated regions affected only by severe frosts.

Perhaps the most striking change in the community is its rapid population loss. According to the 1970 census, the total population of the county was 8,159, with 6,749 residing in the rural area and 1,410 in town.[2] This represents a countywide decline of 22 per cent, a rural decline of 27 per cent, and an urban gain of 13 per cent since 1967. The loss was not uniform throughout the rural area, and it was again the low-lying regions most affected by the frost that suffered the greatest population decline. For example, in Santa Cruz, at the southern tip of the county, approximately half of the population departed after the frost, and nearly 60 per cent of the land now is planted in pasture, compared to about 20 per cent in 1967.

The great exodus from the county occurred immediately after the July 1969 frost. Workers were discharged en masse, since the harvest was lost, and landowners lacked the money to pay them their wages. Residents tell of large trucks filled with dozens of workers leaving Ouro Verde for Paraguay and other points west. The other factor involved in the county's population loss was the continued conversion of coffee lands to pasture which proceeded apace even before the frost hastened the process. Numerous sharecropping families were dismissed from their jobs during the three-year interim as the land which they tilled was given over to cattle raising. For example, on Fazenda Cruzeiro, a 100-alqueire holding which employed fifteen sharecropping families in 1968, there were only two day laborers caring for the fazenda's herds in 1971.

Where are these people heading? The movement to the western frontier appears to be still in full swing, with the added dimension of migration into Paraguay. Two groups are leaving Ouro Verde: owners of small farms who invested their profits from the cotton harvest in larger tracts of land in Paraguay and sold their local holdings, and sharecroppers and day laborers who found themselves without work after the frost and moved to the frontier in search of employment.

Each group had different reasons for the migration westward. Sitiantes desirous of increasing the size of their holdings simply cannot do so in Ouro Verde. There is virtually no land for sale in the county, and what little is available is planted in pasture.[3] Furthermore, purchasing small holdings on the frontier seems

2. The 1967 population figures were 10,529, 9,300, and 1,229, respectively.

3. Holders of small acreages are no longer selling land planted in coffee because of the new availability of financing from the Brazilian Coffee Institute.

eminently reasonable from an economic point of view. Those who are doing so owned local sítios of 5 or 10 alqueires, usually planted in coffee and cotton. Particularly if these lands were in areas subject to frost, the wisest course was to use the profits earned in the unusually large cotton harvest of 1968 to buy land on the frontier. There was unlikely to be a repetition of that harvest, and in another year or two fertilizer and plowing operations would be required for planting cotton, expenses which would cut greatly into any potential savings. Purchasing larger frontier holdings was an especially important alternative for large families whose local sítios were of insufficient size to support them.

The motivations involved in the exodus of many sharecroppers and day laborers from the county were far less complex. There was simply no work to be had following the 1969 frost and the resultant 1970 crop failure. It was not until 1971, the first coffee harvest in two years, that the unemployment problem was alleviated and there was work for most of those who sought it.

Paraguay is gradually replacing extreme western Paraná as the final destination of many migrants. One resident estimated that roughly three hundred families from Ouro Verde and five other nearby counties have left for Paraguay since 1969 with the intention of buying land there. Probably the most important factor drawing settlers is the relatively inexpensive coffee land in that country. A sitiante selling 5 alqueires in Ouro Verde can purchase about 20 alqueires of land in Paraguay with the money from the sale. In addition, the Paraguayan government offers the settlers reasonable terms, often up to eight years to pay for the land. One drawback is the requirement that all migrants become Paraguayan citizens after two years, and some potential settlers are reluctant to buy land there because of this stipulation. Although the soils of the region in which land is being purchased are of the rich terra roxa variety, they are subject to frosts and present definite risks for the planting of coffee. For this reason, some insisted that the area was better suited to lavoura branca than coffee, although most settlers are planting the latter.

It should be noted that it is only owners of small sítios who are crossing the international frontier.[4] So far, neither sharecroppers nor day laborers are seeking work in the newly opened coffee lands of Paraguay, and the reasons for this are clear. There are few share-

4. At least a few fazendeiros in Ouro Verde have purchased Paraguayan land for investment purposes, but none has actually moved there.

cropping positions available there since most of the new holdings are small and are worked by their owners who employ extra hands only for the harvest. In addition, wages in Paraguay are low by Brazilian standards and there appears to be no shortage of local laborers to carry out the basic tasks of clearing the forest and harvesting the first crops.

Directly linked to Ouro Verde's population loss is the continued consolidation of land noted in the initial study. The areas hardest hit by frost are those in which the greatest consolidation of small sítios into large fazendas occurred. Holdings of 5 and 10 alqueires have virtually disappeared in the Vagalume region, and have greatly diminished in a number of other areas in the county. Some of the largest cattle ranches have increased in size since 1968, a few acquiring as much as 100 additional alqueires comprised of small holdings. A number of fazendeiros complained that there was little land left for sale and that they were having difficulty purchasing sufficient acreage to accomodate their growing herds.

The actual amount of land consolidation which has occurred since 1968 is difficult to estimate since the accuracy of the only records available, those compiled by the Brazilian Institute of Agrarian Reform, is questionable. In some cases, in order to avoid paying taxes, individuals buying additional land do not transfer the titles to their own names. Thus, many of the 5- and 10-alqueire sítios which the IBRA lists as being individually owned actually form parts of far larger holdings.

Labor systems in Ouro Verde have changed considerably since 1968 in type and frequency of those employed. The renting of land has all but disappeared. Sharecropping coffee and cotton is far less common. The payment of a fixed monthly wage (mensal labor) is more widespread. A new system, *bóia fria,* is replacing a number of the older labor arrangements.[5]

According to the 1970 census, there were only fourteen renters in the county. There are two reasons for the swift decline of this system: acreages planted in cotton, peanuts, and other crops traditionally associated with renting have been markedly reduced, and a new federal labor law states that all workers who plant lavoura branca, either under renting or sharecropping contracts, are entitled to 70 per cent of the harvest, the remaining 30 per cent

5. The term boia fria, slang for "cold lunch," is so called because the workers bring their lunch with them in the morning, and by the time they eat it in the fields at noon, it is cold.

going to the landowner. For example, if 1 alqueire produces 200 arrôbas of cotton,[6] 60 arrôbas or their equivalent value, a fixed amount, must be paid to the landowner. Sixty arrôbas, at an average selling price of CrN$ 12,00[7] per arrôba, entitles the landowner to CrN$ 720,00 per alqueire of rented land. This is an extremely high rental considering the fact that it is paid in advance. Even if the harvest is small, and this amount reflects more than the value of the entire crop, the rental fee is not refunded. Also, it should be recalled, under this system it is the renter who bears the entire burden of cultivation expenses.

Sharecropping lavoura branca has declined for much the same reasons, although not to the same extent as renting. There are simply fewer sharecropping positions available as more and more land is planted in pasture at the expense of cotton and peanuts. Here, too, the landowner has the right to 30 per cent of the crop, but if the harvests are relatively small, as they were in 1970 and 1971, the sharecropper and landowner are affected equally since the latter only receives 30 per cent of what is actually produced. Under conditions of declining yields, as is the case in Ouro Verde, it is hardly surprising that sharecropping has persisted and renting has not.

The number of coffee sharecroppers has also diminished. One resident estimated that there were some 40 per cent fewer meieiros de café in the county in 1970 than there had been three years earlier. This decline is also a result of the fact that there is simply less land planted in coffee than there was. Virtually no landowner with more than 15 alqueires currently contracts coffee sharecroppers, and what meieiros remain in the county are found on small farms not cultivated by the owners and their families.

A final reason why sharecropping of both lavoura branca and coffee has lost popularity is that, in 1970, sharecroppers were given the right to make bank loans in their own names, and are no longer required to have their patrões or another landowner cosign. It should be recalled that landowners often used the low-interest loans obtained in the names of their sharecroppers for personal expenses, but since this practice is no longer possible, contracting sharecroppers has lost one of its former advantages.

Day laborers are gradually being replaced by bóia fria, although the two labor systems have much in common. One important dif-

6. This is the average yield at present in the county.
7. The official exchange rate in July 1971 was CrN$ 5,25 to U.S. $1.00.

ference exists which accounts for the increased use of the latter. In 1970, indemnification laws applying to day laborers were passed. These give all workers employed on a single holding for more than ninety days accident and medical benefits from the Instituto Nacional de Providência Social. Under the law, both the day laborer and his employer are required to contribute to this fund, and all workers are supposed to receive a monthly minimum wage of CrN$ 184,00. While these provisions cover both day laborers and men employed as bóia fria, the laws are more easily circumvented in the case of the latter.

Bóia fria is essentially a system which employs day laborers as a group rather than on an individual basis. On most mornings, announcements are made on the loudspeaker advertising jobs available on a number of fazendas in the county. At the same time, trucks pass through town picking up men who are in need of employment for the day, and bring them to local fazendas at the landowners' expense. Those employed as bóia fria usually work on one holding for only a few days, and are then hired in the same manner by another landowner who is short of hands.

The primary difference between those who work in a bóia fria crew and day laborers is that the former do not live on the sítios or fazendas on which they are employed, and rarely remain on any one job for more than a few days. It should be apparent that this arrangement allows landowners great latitude in ignoring labor laws. They are not eligible for INPS benefits unless they are employed on one holding for more than ninety days, which is never the case, and they are paid on a daily basis so that their numerous employers can disclaim any responsibility if they do not receive the monthly minimum wage. In fact, the prevailing rate for bóia fria labor is CrN$ 6,00 per day, making it virtually impossible for these workers to earn the monthly legal minimum.

Thus, the increasing popularity of bóia fria is related to the way this system can be utilized to bypass labor legislation, which is far more strictly enforced in the employment of permanent and semipermanent workers, i.e., sharecroppers and day laborers. The system offers other advantages. Landowners can get low-interest loans to pay the wages of their bóia fria crews, although the loans often actually are used to meet personal expenses. Furthermore, the system allows a maximum amount of flexibility in adjusting the size of the work force to the tasks at hand. Crews of any size can be hired for as many days as necessary, and the landowner is not saddled with a resident labor force which becomes superfluous if the harvests are small or if there is a general crop failure.

Bóia fria crews are usually employed to cultivate and harvest coffee and lavoura branca on large holdings, and rarely are found on sítios of less than 15 alqueires which are worked by the owners themselves. Occasionally, they are hired on cattle fazendas to perform labor-intensive tasks such as fence building or barn construction, but ranchers still are heavily reliant on a small number of mensal laborers for the day-to-day operation of their enterprises.

One may well ask who these men are who make up the bóia fria crews. Most are transients in the county, some recent arrivals from the Northeast, and they rarely remain in Ouro Verde for more than three or four weeks. A few are permanent town residents who join the crews during the slack season when there is little other work available. In all cases, men currently employed on bóia fria teams would have worked as independent day laborers in the past.

All the evidence indicates that the county is witnessing a gradual simplification of its once highly diverse system of agricultural labor. This trend reflects the fact that the number of landholdings has decreased while their average size has increased. In addition, fewer landowners are planting cotton, peanuts, and other cereal crops, cultigens associated with a wide variety of labor arrangements.

The agricultural picture in Ouro Verde has changed a good deal since 1967. One startling event, the planting of new coffee trees, is found in the middle of an otherwise predictable situation. These figures on current land usage from the 1970 census give a synopsis of recent trends: lavoura branca, 1,533 alqueires,[8] 17.5 per cent; coffee, 2,266 alqueires, 25.5 per cent; pasture, 5,089 alqueires, 57 per cent. The conversion of coffee land to pasture has continued during the three-year interim, with the total area planted in coffee down 12 per cent since 1967 and that in pasture up by 13 per cent. There are no reliable figures available for 1971, but this trend appears to have persisted even though there are approximately 800,000 new coffee trees in the county.[9] The total cultivated area in coffee has decreased since 1967 despite the new plantings because of the severe damage inflicted by the 1969 frost. Far more old trees were cut down as a result of frost damage than new ones were planted,

8. This figure is highly questionable since all informants agreed that there was less lavoura branca planted in 1970 than in 1967, when the figure was 1,467 alqueires, or 16.5 per cent.

9. New coffee trees are all of those which have not yet produced their first harvest, that is, all trees under four years of age.

thus diminishing the net acreage. In July 1971, there were about 4.5 million coffee trees in Ouro Verde, approximately 3.7 million of them in production. This represents a decline of 1.2 million from the 1967–68 total of 5.7 million producing trees.

The consequences of the frost and the resulting eradication of additional coffee trees are reflected in greatly decreased yields for the county as a whole. The entire 1970 harvest was eliminated due to frost damage, although it was not severe enough to actually kill the trees. Estimates for the 1971 harvest varied considerably depending upon the optimism of the informant, but most fell within the range of 313,000 to 360,000 arrôbas of cleaned coffee. The 1968–69 harvest, it may be recalled, produced 530,000 arrôbas.

Soon after the 1969 frost, officials of the IBC made a major policy decision: to finance the planting of new coffee trees in certain limited areas under carefully controlled conditions. This was in keeping with IBC's previously mentioned plan of maintaining production at a high level by circumscribing coffee cultivation to regions ideally suited to it, while at the same time encouraging its demise in areas with poor soil and those subject to frosts. What is surprising is that this financing is being made available to a number of landowners in Ouro Verde and the surrounding counties, a region which hardly seems to meet the criteria outlined in the program. I received no adequate explanation for this possible breach of policy, aside from the insistence of IBC officials that the planting of new trees was being carefully monitored and that they would not be financed in locales which had a history of low coffee yields.

Thus far, approximately 700,000 coffee trees have been planted in Ouro Verde under the auspices of the IBC program. They are limited largely to the higher areas in the western half of the county, and none has been planted in the low-lying Vagalume region. In every case the young seedlings either have replaced older frost-damaged trees or lavoura branca, but none has supplanted pasture.

For the most part, it is the owners of smaller holdings in the county who are taking advantage of the replanting program. The typical cultivator requesting IBC financing owns 5 to 20 alqueires of terra mista land located in areas which are affected by only the most severe frosts. His holding had been previously planted either in lavoura branca, from which he received an inadequate income, or coffee trees, which were heavily damaged by the 1969 frost. This is not to imply that there are no fazendeiros involved in the program, since at least one has planted 100,000 seedlings and a few

Newly planted coffee trees

A local vaqueiro

others have begun replanting on the most elevated portions of their properties.

In order to be eligible for the IBC's CrN$ 2,20 for each new tree, the farmer must follow certain procedures. New trees must be started from seedlings rather than from seeds which has been the usual practice. While this involves a greater initial expense, the cultivator eventually is compensated since these trees will produce a harvest about one year earlier than those planted from seeds. In addition, the farmer is required to plant the new trees on a contour (*curva de nível*), to prevent erosion, and at certain specified distances, depending on the quality of the soil. All seedlings must be planted in the highest areas of the holding, and finally, both chemical and organic fertilizers must be applied in particular amounts at prescribed intervals. Before financing is approved, an agronomist from the Bank of Brazil must oversee all of these operations to insure that they are carried out properly.[10]

One interesting consequence of the replanting program is that the average coffee yields of individual cultivators have risen by about 10 sacks per 1,000 trees, even though countywide yields have declined. The explanation for this is that most coffee groves which did not produce an average of 50 sacks per 1,000 trees were cut down after the 1969 frost and either were replanted in seedlings or converted to pasture. Since these low-yield trees have been eliminated, the overall average number of sacks per 1,000 trees has risen. Thus, in 1971, average production in Ouro Verde was 60 sacks per 1,000 trees, or 120 sacks per alqueire.

There is a new threat facing coffee cultivators. Coffee rust (*Hemiteia vastatrix*), a fungus which attacks the leaves of the trees and inhibits the development of the beans, first appeared in Brazil in 1970 in the northeastern state of Bahia. Presumably, it came from somewhere in West Africa. Since then, rust has destroyed coffee trees in Minas Gerais and Espiríto Santo, and it has recently appeared in the state of São Paulo. Its spread is extremely difficult to control since the spores of the fungus are transported by the wind, on the skins of animals, or by human carriers. Although the importation of coffee seedlings into Paraná from other states has been prohibited in an attempt to control the disease, it is doubtful that this will be effective. Thus far, no coffee rust has been located in Paraná, and an IBC team found absolutely no

10. IBC's replanting program is administered through local branches of the Bank of Brazil.

evidence of it on the 170 properties visited in Ouro Verde.

Cattle ranching has continued to make inroads in the county's agricultural makeup. According to the 1970 census, there were 22,914 head of cattle in Ouro Verde, and their number had increased to approximately 25,000 by 1971. This is a growth of 20 per cent over the 1968 figure of 20,000. As mentioned, the area devoted to pasture has increased by about 13 per cent since the time of the initial study. This would seem to indicate that the average number of head per alqueire has risen, and this is the case, in fact. In 1968, there were a number of fairly extensive holdings with relatively few heads of cattle. Since that time fazendeiros have been enlarging the size of their herds, so that on a countywide basis the average number of head per alqueire has increased.

The cotton boom brought about by the unusually large harvest of 1968 has failed to recur in Ouro Verde. During 1969 and 1970, a great deal of additional land was planted in cotton by local farmers who hoped the substantial profits made by many cultivators in 1968 would again be realized, but the harvests of those years were small as a result of too much rain. In 1971, yields rose somewhat, to an average of 200 arrôbas per alqueire, but profits were disappointing due to a sizeable increase in cultivation expenses. The need for fertilizer accounted for most of the rising costs, and there was the added expense of tractor rental for harrowing the soil on land previously planted in cotton.[11] Since the prices received for the crop just kept up with inflation, most landowners and sharecroppers were reluctant to invest in fertilizer, without which yields remained low. The current situation was summed up by the manager of the agricultural post: "You can't get ahead with cotton any more. You don't use fertilizer for the crop because it isn't worth it. The expense is great and you are not assured of a return on your money."

The present outlook for cereal crops is even less promising than it is for cotton, although they are encountering similar problems. Since much of the lavoura branca grown in the county is cultivated by sharecroppers, increasing costs resulting from the need for fertilizer constitute a particularly heavy burden. Landowners are reluctant to finance the new cultivation expenses since they are only entitled to 30 per cent of the harvest, making such an investment hardly worthwhile. This dilemma is reflected clearly in the rapid

11. These two items increase the cost of cotton cultivation by about CrN$ 400,000 per alqueire.

decline of peanut yields in Ouro Verde. In the 1967–68 harvest, 2.4 million kilos of peanuts were produced in the county; in the 1970–71 harvest, the yield had fallen to 1.2 million kilos.

Since 1968, changes have occurred in the agricultural technology employed in the county, particularly in coffee cultivation. As a result of IBC's replanting program and the stipulations attached to it, contour planting and the use of seedlings have become more common, and fertilizer is being applied to seedlings at the time of planting. This is a considerable change from the past, when fertilizer, if it were used at all, was applied only after the trees produced their first harvest. The application of fertilizer has become more widespread in the county, with about 90 per cent of all coffee cultivators using chemical or organic fertilizers. Use of this costly item is no longer a matter of choice, since, in the words of one local agronomist, "Today, coffee that is not fertilized produces almost nothing at all."

Virtually no one in the county, however, is employing fertilizer in cotton cultivation. It is expensive, and since there are no price supports for the crop, there is a general reluctance to lay out a large sum without a guaranteed return. For the same reason, fertilizer is not being used in the cultivation of other lavoura branca crops.

Since the initial study, there have been a number of important changes in the policies of the lending institutions available to county residents. Immediately after the 1969 frost, the IBC began financing the replanting of coffee through the local offices of the Bank of Brazil. Action was swift, for it was widely feared that there would be a massive spontaneous eradication of coffee trees by cultivators hard hit by the frost. IBC made low-interest loans to cover the agricultural expenses incurred for the ruined 1969–70 coffee crop and, according to one reliable informant, between 70 and 80 per cent of the local landowners borrowed from this source. In addition, IBC made interest-free loans for one year to those coffee cultivators who agreed to use the funds for chemical fertilizer. This was an incentive for those who had never used fertilizer, and, in any case, farmers were forced to buy fertilizer for their coffee trees or they could not borrow money from the bank for other cultivation expenses. All contracts for cultivation expenses between the IBC and local landowners were made for two years, since, as a result of the frost, there was no coffee harvest in 1970 and cultivators could not be expected to repay their debts until the following year. As another means of discouraging widescale eradication of damaged coffee trees, officials of the Bank of Brazil lowered interest rates for loans covering cultivation costs. The annual rates in effect in 1971 were 9 per cent on loans up to CrN$ 9,000,000, 12 per cent on loans up to CrN$ 15,000,000, and 17 per cent on loans of more than CrN$ 15,000,000. These progressive rates were designed to keep interest down for those who could least afford it, that is, poorer cultivators who were unlikely to borrow very large sums. Moreover, given the rate of inflation in Brazil, the real interest rates on all of these loans were negative.

In late 1968, a new branch of the Bank of Brazil opened in Paranacity, just three kilometers from Ouro Verde. This proved to be a minor boon for local residents; before this, the closest branch was in Nova Esperança, some 22 kilometers away. One bank assessor noted that, aside from this added convenience, the complicated paper work involved in a loan application had been simplified. Many illiterate sitiantes who had been reluctant to apply for loans at the Bank of Brazil now found the process less painful.

What has happened to the town's economy in this three-year interval? The consensus is that the movimento in town has not declined as much as might have been expected, given the 1969 frost and the current agricultural situation. The explanation lies in the continued migration from the rural areas to the town; this accounts for the 13 per cent population increase in the town since 1968. Following the 1969 frost, this movement gained momentum; there were no jobs in the rural sector for sharecroppers or day laborers, and many sitiantes sold their holdings in despair and came to town in search of work.

The only new town enterprise is a small dairy which processes milk and cheese. It is owned by two men from São Paulo who have other dairies in that state. Up to 12,000 liters of milk a day are sold to the dairy by county residents, all of whom seem pleased with the arrangement since it offers them an additional small but steady income. The dairy has only twelve full-time employees, so it hardly provides a solution to local unemployment problems.

Virtually all proprietors of the small stores in town agree that business fell off drastically following the 1969 frost and remained poor through the spring and summer of 1970 because of the lack of a coffee harvest that year. All businesses, however, were not equally affected by the frost. Food stores (armazens) generally were less hard hit by the crop failure since, as one informant put it, "people still had to eat." Variety stores and those selling fabrics saw huge declines in sales, probably because their wares were considered luxuries during a time of economic hardship. The owner of one fabric store, for example, estimated that his business fell off by over 50 per cent in the months following the frost, and the proprietress of a variety store offered a similar figure.

Business activity has recovered to some extent since late 1970, largely as the result of the minor population influx from the countryside and a partially renewed optimism concerning coffee's future in the county. Still, there have been a number of business failures since the period of the initial study. One of the town's two pharmacies and three town and two rural armazens have closed for lack of customers.

There has been an important change since 1968 in seasonal variations in local sales. Business activity was brisk during the cotton boom of that year and, in fact, surpassed the movimento created by the coffee harvest. Quite the reverse was true in 1971. Since the amount of land planted in cotton is greatly reduced and average yields have declined considerably, far fewer local residents benefit from whatever profits are still made from this crop. The coffee harvest, on the other hand, can still produce heightened business activity and stimulates other enterprises.

Ouro Verde's two coffee-processing plants are still in operation. The larger continued to function after the 1969 frost by processing its stored coffee, but this small supply gave out, and the plant was forced to close during the 1970 season since there was simply no coffee available for purchase. The owner of the plant was fairly optimistic about the prospects for the 1971 harvest, pointing to the fact that average yields in the county were up slightly as a result of the replanting program.

The changes which Ouro Verde's social structure and patterns of social mobility were undergoing in 1967–68 have continued to some extent. One trend observed at that time has gained momentum—the increase in absentee ownership in the county. While the vast majority of owners of large holdings always lived outside the community, this pattern has become even more pronounced as additional land has been planted in pasture and holdings have grown in size. Since cattle ranching, even on vast acreages of land, requires an extremely small labor force, the fazendeiro's presence as overseer is unnecessary. As a result, even the few landowners who lived on their holdings or visited them frequently no longer do so.

A number have moved to Maringá, and the owner of the second largest fazenda in the county has returned to his native Germany. By mid–1971, there were only two landowners with more than 75 alqueires residing on their properties permanently.

Due to the unreliability of available statistics, it is difficult to determine with any degree of certainty if there has been any relative or absolute change in the number of holders of small acreages in Ouro Verde. There has been a reduction in the number of sítios of 10 alqueires or less in certain areas of the county and, looking at the figures for land consolidation and emigration, it appears likely that there are fewer sítiantes than there were in 1968.

What is more certain is that there has been an important decline in the number of sharecroppers in the county, although, again, precise figures are not available. With additional land planted in pasture, sharecropping positions are even more difficult to come by than they were three years earlier, and landowners have become even more selective about awarding sharecropping contracts. Families with a number of small children and little or no savings are the last to be chosen for such positions, and they are usually forced to leave Ouro Verde and seek work elsewhere.

With the increasing importance of bóia fria as a labor system, there has been a concomitant rise in the number of landless workers in the county. Since most men employed in bóia fria crews are transients, usually remaining in the community for only three or four weeks, the true size of this segment of the population is difficult to determine. It was particularly large, however, at the time of the re-study since this coincided with the coffee harvest during which the demand for bóia fria labor is greatest.

The opportunities for upward mobility in Ouro Verde, as measured by the acquisition of land, have virtually ceased to exist in the three years since the initial study. All informants agreed that sharecropping cotton is no longer a path to landownership, because increased cultivation expenses and smaller yields have cut profits severely. Even those sharecroppers who have sufficient savings to cover their living and cultivation expenses until the harvest is in, and do not require financing from the bank or their patrões, no longer can save the sum required for the purchase of a small sítio on the frontier. The last sharecroppers in Ouro Verde who were able to make the transition to landownership did so in 1968.

The prospects of coffee sharecropping leading to socioeconomic mobility are even less bright. One only need recall that the coffee harvests of 1969 and 1970 were eliminated by the frost to realize the impossibility of accumulating enough money from the proceeds of coffee to buy land. What the impact of the replanting program will be on upward mobility through coffee sharecropping is unclear, but the program is on so small a scale that it will not create many new sharecropping positions. This fact, along with the continued uncertainty of climatic factors, makes it unlikely that sharecropping coffee will ever again be an important road to landownership.

Downward mobility, that is, the movement from landowner to sharecropper or sharecropper to day laborer, continues to be rare in Ouro Verde. The only cases encountered in the community were those attributable to personal misfortune. For example, one sitiante was forced to sell his 2-alqueire holding to pay off debts incurred during an illness, and he is now a salaried employee at the gas station in town.

It is impossible to be certain that downward mobility does not exist; we know only that it does not take place in the county itself. It is a fact that sharecroppers no longer able to secure contracts in Ouro Verde are moving farther west. If they cannot get sharecropping positions there, they may find it necessary to work as day laborers or on bóia fria crews. While this is all highly problematical, it should be recalled that the only cases of upward mobility among local residents have taken place outside of the county.

In order to make this postscript complete, it is necessary to review briefly local attitudes towards the county's future. It is not surprising that these attitudes are inextricably linked to the inhabitants' perceptions of coffee's future. There has been a general reawakening of optimism in Ouro Verde, sometimes to a degree that appears unwarranted to the outside observer, and it is almost entirely due to the replanting program. A common view is that coffee yields will increase as a result of the wider use of modern agricultural techniques encouraged by the Brazilian Coffee Institute's financial assistance. Related to this is the belief that the spread of pasture will come to a halt. The manager of the Posto Rural, for example, thinks that the areas devoted to pasture eventually will become stabilized at about 40 per cent of all cultivated land in the county. This estimate is very low in view of the fact that the current figure is 57 per cent, and it is extremely unlikely that any pasture will be reconverted to coffee or other crops.

A number of local residents have adopted an attitude of cautious optimism concerning Ouro Verde's future. The owner of the coffee-processing plant had no illusions that the local economy would ever return to what it was in the mid– and late 1950s, when coffee was at its peak. He remarked that the incursion of pasture and the loss of population simply made a full recovery impossible. On the other hand, he believes the population exodus will cease, and that people will become anchored to the community by the replanting program.

Perhaps the most realistic explanation of the minor wave of euphoria now sweeping the county was offered by an assessor for the Bank of Brazil: "Sure everything looks rosy now, but you must remember that this is only in comparison to 1970 when we had no coffee harvest at all. People look back to last year when no one earned anything from coffee, so now they are bound to be happy and think that all of their problems are solved. This is nothing new around here. The whole history of this region is, 'If it doesn't freeze, the harvest will be good next year, *se Deus quiser*.' "

Appendixes

1. Sample Questionnaire

I. *General Information*

1. name of household head
2. location of house
3. house owned rented from whom
4. household head married single widowed sep.
5. religious civil both common law
6. origin of household head
7. ethnic origin generation naturalized
8. origin of wife
9. ethnic origin generation naturalized
10. total no. of children living in household
11. other relatives in household
12. other relatives in Ouro Verde
13. no. of years in Ouro Verde
14. other places of residence aside from birth and Ouro Verde
    a. yrs. job
    b. yrs. job
    c. yrs. job
15. occupation of household head's father

II. *Employment*

1. primary employment of household head
2. secondary employment of household head
3. wife's occupation

4. other family members who work
   a. relation job earnings
   b. relation job earnings
   c. relation job earnings
5. other employment in Ouro Verde before present one

III. *Agriculturalists* (including landowners, renters, and sharecroppers)
1. is land owned rented sharecropped
2. number of alqueires
3. does landowner live on property
4. is he a farmer or administrator
5. if absentee, is there a resident administrator
6. number of family members who work on farm
7. their relationship to household head
8. are there hired hands
   a. volantes how many
   b. colonos how many
   c. sharecroppers how many
   d. renters how many
9. how are they paid average monthly pay
10. how are family members paid average monthly pay
11. are hired hands given subsistence plots
    a. where
    b. how large
    c. what crops can they plant
12. are hired hands' houses free rent
13. other benefits they receive
14. when are hired hands employed
    a. average no. during harvest
    b. average no. rest of year
15. are hired hands used in coffee cultivation other crops
16. if household head owns land, does he ever work for wages
    a. when
    b. where
    c. earnings
17. was the land bought from CMNP 2nd hand
    a. year
    b. price paid per alqueire
18. additional land bought since initial purchase
    a. how many alqueires
    b. year
    c. from whom
19. has any land been sold since initial purchase
    a. how many alqueires
    b. year
    c. to whom
20. is mutirão ever used
    a. when
    b. with whom
21. is the landowner compadre to any of his workers
    a. who
    b. how many
22. no. of alqueires worked by volantes % of total
23. no. of alqueires sharecropped % of total

24. no. of alqueires rented % of total
25. other land owned outside Ouro Verde
    a. where no. of alqueires
    b. where no. of alqueires

IV. *Agriculture*

1. no. of alqueires in coffee % of total
2. no. of alqueires in pasture % of total
3. no. of alqueires in forest % of total
4. no. of alqueires in lavoura branca % of total
    a. in corn
    b. in cotton
    c. in peanuts
    d. in rice
    e. in beans
    f. in manioc
    g. in other crops
5. total number of coffee trees
    a. at present
    b. five years ago ten years ago
6. are trees young old average age
7. was any coffee eradicated under the government's program
    a. how many trees
    b. percentage of total
    c. what is now planted on the eradicated land
    d. will pasture be planted after contract expires
    e. will coffee be replanted after contract expires
8. was any coffee eradicated outside of government's program
    a. when
    b. how many trees
    c. percentage of total
9. was coffee destroyed in the frosts of:
    a. 1955 how many trees % of total
    b. 1963 how many trees % of total
    c. other years how many trees % of total
10. were trees killed no. of harvests lost
11. has drought adversely affected the trees
    a. when
    b. percentage of total
12. has broca been a problem
    a. when
    b. percentage of trees affected
13. have yields varied greatly from year to year
    a. by how much
    b. high yields low yields
14. is insecticide used against broca
15. is fertilizer used on coffee
    a. what kind
    b. how much per tree
    c. costs
16. are trees planted on a contour
17. are selected seeds used
18. is fertilizer, insecticide used for lavoura branca
    a. for which crops

b. how much
c. costs
19. total number of cattle selected breeding
20. if cattle in, coffee out difference in size of work force
21. when were cattle first bought
22. type of cattle
23. is a tractor owned
a. is it ever rented out
b. how many owned
24. is credit ever used to finance crops
a. Banco de Brasil
b. private bank
c. general stores
d. other
25. which crops are financed
26. how much is borrowed
27. what interest rate is paid
28. where is coffee processed rice peanuts
29. is coffee sold to IBC or processor
30. where are other crops sold
31. does family ever catar café for processor
32. are pigs raised
a. how many
b. home use or for sale
33. are chickens raised
a. how many
b. home use or for sale
34. other animals raised
a. what ones
b. home use or for sale
35. does farmer grow any of his own food
a. what crops
b. percentage of lavoura branca for home use
c. percentage bought in store

V. *Sharecroppers*
1. what % of crop is given to landowner
2. what crops are used as payment
3. what crops belong entirely to sharecropper
4. who pays for cultivation expenses
a. % paid by landowner
b. % paid by sharecropper
5. does landowner finance sharecropper

VI. *Renters*
1. is rent paid in cash or with part of the crop
2. what crops are used to pay rent
3. how much per alqueire is paid for rent
4. who pays cultivation expenses
a. % paid by landowner
b. % paid by renter
5. does landowner finance renter

VII. *Day Laborers*
1. how long has family been on present holding
2. has day laborer worked on others in Ouro Verde
   a. which ones
   b. for how long
3. has day laborer worked on holdings in other parts of northern Paraná
   a. where
   b. for how long
4. has day laborer ever returned to holding where he worked previously
5. when moving to new holding does day laborer move only with wife and children or also with friends and relatives
6. who pays for moving expenses costs

VIII. *Nonagriculturalists*
1. type of business, employment
2. is business owned salaried employee
3. if owner, is there hired help how many
4. do family members work in business
   a. how many
   b. how are they related to owner
5. how long in present job business owned
6. previous employment in Ouro Verde
7. if skilled, where was training received
8. was land ever owned
   a. how many alqueires
   b. where
   c. why and when was it sold
9. are datas owned in town how many
10. did family live on sítio before moving to town
11. does family cultivate public land

IX. *Possessions and Standard of Living*
1. type of house wood material other
2. inside kitchen type of stove
3. radio owned
4. sewing machine owned
5. refrigerator owned
6. car truck wagon
7. no. of times a week meat eaten
8. is fruit eaten regularly times per week
9. are vegetables eaten regularly times per week
10. are eggs eaten regularly times per week
11. how often do children drink milk
12. usual daily diet
13. are there household servants how many

X. *Education*
1. is household head literate only sign name
2. is wife literate only sign name
3. level of education of household head
   a. no. of years of school
   b. primary ginásio colégio other
   c. do children between 7–14 attend school
   d. do children miss school during harvest

XI. *Religion*
1. religion of household head
2. religion of wife
3. if Protestant, when and where did conversion take place
4. membership in religious associations

2. *Coffee Production in Brazil*

Coffee exported from Brazil—1,000 bags of 60 kilos

Average harvests	Rio de Janeiro	São Paulo	Minas Gerais	Espiríto Santo	Paraná	Others	Total Brazil
1881–90	3,626	1,853					5,479
1891–1900	3,114	4,116					7,230
1901–10	1,094	9,252	2,772	511		202	13,831
1911–20	812	9,305	2,446	670		158	13,391
1921–30	945	11,131	3,445	1,249	175	309	17,254
1931–40	921	15,252	3,868	1,586	610	534	22,771
1941–50	469	7,874	2,638	1,655	1,062	364	14,062
1951–60	242	8,618	3,261	1,923	5,867	527	20,438
Selected harvests							
1880–81	4,402	1,204					5,606
1933–34	905	21,850	4,062	1,859	600	358	29,634
1959–60	362	15,601	4,494	1,907	20,410	947	43,721

Source: IBC 1965.

3. *New York Market Average Annual Spot Prices of Brazilian Coffee, 1954–64* (Type: Santos 4)

Year	U.S. cents per pound
1954	78.71
1955	57.09
1956	58.10
1957	56.92
1958	48.41
1959	36.97
1960	36.60
1961	36.01
1962	33.96
1963	34.11
1964	46.66
1965	44.71
1966	40.83
1967	37.82

SOURCE: adapted from Pan-American Coffee Bureau 1967.

Glossary

afilhado, godchild.
algodão, cotton.
alqueire, land measurement in São Paulo and Paraná, 2.42 hectares, about 6 acres.
altofalante, loudspeaker.
armazem, general store.
armazenista, owner of an armazem.
arrendatário, renter, one who pays a fixed rent for use of the land.
arrôba, a unit of weight, about 15 kilograms or 33 pounds.
bandeirantes, "flag bearers"; groups of adventurers who penetrated the Brazilian interior in the seventeenth and eighteenth centuries in search of gold and slaves.
bazar, shop.
bebida, drink.
benção, blessing.
beneficiar café, to sort and hull coffee beans.
bicho, animal.
boca de sertão, "mouth of the backlands"; town at the edge of the frontier.
bóia fria, "cold lunch"; a work system in which groups of men are hired to do specific agricultural tasks for which they are paid on a daily or piecework basis.
broca do café (*Hypothenemus hampei Ferrari*), a coffee pest which burrows into the beans.
caboclo, anyone of part Indian descent, rustic backwoodsman.
café, coffee.
café em côco, unprocessed coffee beans.
café limpo, "clean coffee," processed coffee beans.
campeiro, cowhand.

campo cerrado, grassland with bushes or trees.
capanga, hired gunman.
capataz, foreman.
carne sêca, sun-dried meat.
carroça, wagon.
cartório, civil registry.
casa de saúde, public health clinic.
casa de tecidos, fabric store.
casamento, marriage.
catar café, to separate coffee beans by hand according to their quality.
chácara, small landholding, usually 5 alqueires or less, located close to a town.
chacrista, owner of a chácara.
chuva de pedras, hailstorm.
cidade municipal, county seat.
classe média, middle class.
coitado, poor thing.
colono, worker paid on a monthly basis to care for a given number of coffee trees.
comadre, godmother in relation to godchild's parents.
comarca, judicial district.
compadre, godfather in relation to godchild's parents.
compadresco, of or concerning the relationship between a godfather and the child's parents.
cova, small hole in which coffee seedlings are planted.
crente, "believer," Protestant.
criar gado, to raise cattle.
crisma, confirmation.
cristão, Christian.
Cristão do Brasil, Protestant sect.
cruzeiro, Brazilian monetary unit.
cruzeiro novo, "new cruzeiro," about U.S. $.28 in 1968.
curandeiro, curer.
curso normal, teacher training program.
curva de nível, contour planting.
data, urban lot.
desquite, legal separation.
distrito de paz, municipal subdivision.
doces, sweets.
doutor, "doctor," title used for college graduates in Brazil.
empreiteiro, head of a labor gang or labor contractor.
engordar gado, to fatten cattle.
estrada, road.
farinha de mandioca, manioc flour.
fazenda, large landholding, usually over 30 alqueires in Paraná.
fazendeiro, owner of a fazenda.
fazendinha, small fazenda.
febre aftosa, hoof and mouth disease.
feijão, beans.
feira, market.
ferrugem de café (*Hemiteia vastatrix*), coffee rust, a fungus which attacks the leaves of the tree and inhibits the development of coffee beans.
festa, party.
fiado, on credit.
fiscal, assessor.

formador de café, a worker contracted to plant and care for coffee trees for a specified number of years.
frigorífico, slaughterhouse.
fubá, maize flour.
gato, "cat"; slang for labor gang foreman.
geada, frost.
geada branca, "white frost"; light frost.
geada negra, "black frost"; severe frost.
geada sapecar, singeing frost.
ginásio, similar to junior high school.
grileiro, squatter.
grupo escolar, primary school.
imposto, tax.
intercalado, intertilled.
intermedíario, middleman.
jardim de infância, kindergarten.
lavoura branca, refers to annual crops, that is, rice, corn, beans, cotton, peanuts, and so on.
leilão, auction.
madrinha, godmother in relation to godchild.
mamona, castor beans.
máquina de arroz, rice-processing machine.
máquina de café, coffee-processing machine.
maquinista, owner or operator of a coffee- or rice-processing machine.
materneiro, worker who cares for cows during pregnancy and birth.
meeiro, "halfer"; coffee sharecropper who receives at least 50 per cent of the crop.
mensalista, worker paid a fixed monthly salary.
milho, corn.
mineiro, native of the state of Minas Gerais.
mínifundio, small landholding, usually under 5 alqueires.
motorista, professional driver.
movimento, activity, liveliness.
muda de café, coffee seedling.
município, county.
mutirão, cooperative labor party.
ordem, "order"; paper guaranteeing payment of a worker's debt.
o senhor, you, formal third person singular.
padrinho, godfather in relation to godchild.
palha de café, dried outer shells of coffee beans, sometimes used as fertilizer.
parteira, midwife.
patrão (patrões), employer, boss, patron.
pau-de-arara, "parrot's perch"; crowded open-air trucks used to transport laborers from the Northeast to the South.
paulista, native of the state of São Paulo.
peão (peões), peon, member of a work gang.
peneira, round sieve used to separate debris from the coffee beans.
pensão (pensões), boarding house, pension.
percenteiro, "percenter"; sharecroppers of coffee or lavoura branca who receive less than 50 per cent of the crop.
peroba, a hardwood tree common in northern Paraná.
pinga, synonym for cachaça, an alcoholic drink made from sugarcane.
pobre, poor.
por dia, per diem.

por empreita, piecework.
posto de agricultura, agricultural station.
povoado, hamlet.
praça, town square.
praga mineira (*Leucoptera coffeella*), a coffee pest.
prefeito, mayor.
prefeitura, town hall.
promotor público, labor investigator.
redução, mission.
rezador, one who prays.
rico, rich.
roça, subsistence plot.
safra, harvest.
sede da comarca, seat of a judicial district.
sede do município, county seat.
segunda mão, second hand.
semeadeira, seeding machine.
sertão, backlands; often refers specifically to the arid interior of northeastern Brazil.
servente, general handy man.
sitiante, owner of a sítio.
sítio, small farm, usually 6 to 30 alqueires.
terra arenosa, sandy soil.
terra mista, a mixture of terra roxa and sandy soil.
terra roxa, a dark red porous soil particularly well suited to coffee cultivation.
terra solta, plot of land on which only one crop is grown.
terreiro, coffee drying terrace.
tubarão, "shark"; slang to describe a wheeler-dealer or big-time operator.
vales, scrip.
varzeões, low-lying lands bordering streams, often planted in rice.
vereador, town councilman.
você, you, familiar third person singular.
volante, day laborer.

Bibliography

Bernardes, Lysia Maria Cavalcanti.
1953. O problema das frentes pioneiras no estado do Paraná. *Revista Brasileria de Geografia* 3:335–84.

Candido, Antonio.
1964. *Os parceiros do Rio Bonito.* Rio de Janeiro: José Olympio.

Carlson, Reynold E.
1951. The basis of Brazil's economy. In *Brazil: portrait of a half continent,* eds. T. L. Smith and A. L. Marchant. New York: Dryden Press.

Companhia Melhoramentos Norte do Paraná.
n.d. *Suas realizações em mais de 30 anos de trabalho.* Maringá.

Davis, Charles S.
1939. *The cotton kingdom in Alabama.* Montgomery: Alabama State Department of Archives and History.

Dozier, Craig L.
1954. Northern Paraná, Brazil: settlement and development of a recent frontier zone. Ph.D. diss., Johns Hopkins University.
1956. Northern Paraná, Brazil: an example of organized regional development. *Geographical Review* 46:318–33.

Eaton, Clement.
1949. *A history of the old south.* New York: Macmillan.
1961. *The growth of southern civilization.* New York: Harper and Row.

Edel, Matthew.
1969. The Brazilian sugar cycle of the seventeenth century and the rise of West Indian competition. *Caribbean Studies* 9:24–44.

Freyre, Gilberto.
1964. *The masters and the slaves: a study in the development of Brazilian civilization.* Translated from the 4th ed. of the Portuguese, *Casa grande e senzala,* by Samuel Putnam. New York: Alfred A. Knopf.

Fundação Getúlio Vargas.
1967. *Conjuntura econômica international.* No. 11. Rio de Janeiro.
Furtado, Celso.
1965. *The economic growth of Brazil.* Berkeley: University of California Press.
Galeano, Eduardo.
1968. Brazil and Paraguay: colony and sub-colony. *Monthly Review* 20:19–29.
Harris, Marvin.
1956. *Town and country in Brazil.* New York: Columbia University Press.
1968. *The rise of anthropological theory.* New York: Thomas Y. Crowell.
Hutchinson, Harry W.
1957. *Village and plantation life in northeastern Brazil.* Seattle: University of Washington Press.
Instituto Brasileiro de Café.
1964. *Cafecultura no Paraná.* Rio de Janeiro.
1965. *Cultura e adubação de cafeeira.* Rio de Janeiro.
Instituto Brasileiro de Geografia e Estatística.
1967. *Dados sobre o município de Cruzeiro do Sul.* Paranacity.
Instituto Brasileiro de Reforma Agraria.
1966. *Manual de 4 grau.* Curitiba.
James, Preston E.
1933. The coffee lands of southeastern Brazil. *Geographical Review* 22:225–44.
1959. *Latin America.* New York: Odyssey Press.
Johnson, Allen, and Siegel, Bernard.
1969. Wages and income in Ceará, Brazil. *Southwestern Journal of Anthropology* 25:1–13.
Knight, Rolf.
1969. Why don't you work the way other men do? Seasonal and short-term employment in Zafria and non-Zafria sugar cane regions. Ph.D. diss., Columbia University.
Leeds, Anthony.
1957. Economic cycles in Brazil: the persistence of a total culture pattern; cacao and other cases. Ph.D. diss., Columbia University.
Margolis, Maxine L.
1966. Usina Dom João: the social structure of a Brazilian sugar plantation. Columbia-Cornell-Harvard-Illinois Summer Field Studies Program. Mimeo.
Martins, Araguaia Feitosa.
1962. *Mutirão cafeeiro.* São Paulo: Editora Brasiliense.
Milliet, Sergio.
1938. O roteiro de café: análise historico-demográfico da expansão cafeeira no estado de São Paulo. *Estudos Paulistas,* no. 1. São Paulo.
Monbeig, Pierre.
1952. *Pionniers et planteurs de São Paulo.* Paris: Librairies Armand Colin.
Monteiro-Teixeira, Duglas.
1961. Estructura social e vida econômica em uma area de pequena propriedades e de monocultura. *Revista Brasileira de Estudos Politicos* 12:47–63.
Morse, Richard.
1958. *From community to metropolis: a biography of São Paulo, Brazil.* Gainesville: University of Florida Press.

Morse, Richard, ed.
1967. *The bandeirantes: the historical role of the Brazilian pathfinders.* New York: Alfred A. Knopf.

Müller, N. L.
1956. Contribuição ao estudo do norte do Paraná. *Boletim Paulista de Geografia* 22. São Paulo.

Nicholls, William H.
1969. The agricultural frontier in modern Brazilian history: the state of Paraná, 1920–65. In *Cultural change in Brazil. Papers from the Mid-west Association for Latin American Studies.* Muncie: Ball State University Press.

Normano, J. F.
1935. *Brazil: a study in economic types.* Chapel Hill: University of North Carolina Press.

Pan-American Coffee Bureau.
1964. *Annual coffee statistics,* no. 28. New York.
1967. *Annual coffee statistics,* no. 31. New York.

Pelto, Pertti J.
1970. *Anthropological research: the structure of inquiry.* New York: Harper and Row.

Rowe, J. W. F.
1963. *The world's coffee.* London: Her Majesty's Stationery Office.

Schurz, William Lytle.
1961. *Brazil: the infinite country.* New York: Dutton.

Shannon, Fred A.
1968. A post-mortem on the safety valve theory. In *Turner and the sociology of the frontier,* eds. Richard Hofstadter and Seymour Martin Lipset. New York: Basic Books, Inc.

Smith, T. Lynn.
1963. *Brazil: people and institutions.* Baton Rouge: Louisiana State University Press.

Spiegel, Henry W.
1949. *The Brazilian economy: chronic inflation and sporadic industrialization.* Philadelphia: University of Pennsylvania Press.

Stein, Stanley.
1951. The passing of a Paraíba coffee plantation. *Hispanic-American Historical Review* 3:331–64.
1957. *Vassouras: a Brazilian coffee county, 1859–1900.* Cambridge: Harvard University Press.

Turner, Frederick Jackson.
1920. *The frontier in American history.* New York: Henry Holt and Company.

Vance, Rupert B.
1929. *Human factors in cotton culture.* Chapel Hill: University of North Carolina Press.

Vianna Moog, C.
1964. *Bandeirantes and pioneers.* Translated from the Portuguese by L. L. Barrett. New York: George Braziller Inc.

Wagley, Charles.
1963. *An introduction to Brazil.* New York: Columbia University Press.
1964. *Amazon town: a study of man in the tropics.* New York: Alfred A. Knopf.

Wagley, Charles, and Harris, Marvin.
1955. A typology of Latin American subcultures. *American Anthropologist* 57:428–51.

Weaver, Herbert.
1945. *Mississippi farmers, 1850–1860.* Nashville: Vanderbilt University Press.

Willems, Emilio.
1969. The rise of a rural middle class in a frontier society. Paper read at the Midwest Association for Latin American Studies Conference, Ball State University.

Wolf, Eric R.
1966. San José: subcultures of a "traditional" coffee municipality. In *People of Puerto Rico,* ed. Julian Steward. Urbana: University of Illinois Press.

Wolf, Eric R., and Mintz, Sidney W.
1950. An analysis of ritual co-parenthood (compadrazgo). *Southwestern Journal of Anthropology* 6:341–68.

Index

Absentee landowners, 61, 167–70; increase after 1969, 247–48; residents' views of, 202; social class of, 180–81, 188–89
Adventists, 29, 105, 108
Agricultural cycles, 2–4, 227–28
Agricultural post, 29, 95–96, 173
Agricultural supplies, purchase of: on credit, 97–98, 100; expenses in subrenting, 142–43; in Ouro Verde, 29, 96; by renters, 100, 137; by sharecroppers, 100–101, 136, 137; by subsharecroppers, 144–45. *See also* Agricultural technology
Agricultural technology, 154–55, 170–76; coffee drying terraces, 174–75; coffee seedlings, 245; coffee trees, varieties, 174; contour planting, 174, 245; correlation of technology and size of landholding, 175; in cotton in the United States, 225–26; hoes, 175; plows, 175; rising cultivation costs as cause of coffee decline, 217; tractors, 175, 177. *See also* Fertilizer; Insecticide
Alagoas, 41
Alliance for Progress, 106, 185
Alqueire, 37
Altofalante, 27
Amazon Valley, 3–4
Apucarana, Paraná, 22
Araraquarense region, São Paulo, 40
Arrendatários. *See* Renters
Assembly of God, 105–9 passim
Associação de Crédito e Assistência Rural do Paraná (ACARPA), 53, 169, 173

Bahia, 3, 4, 243
Banco Brasileiro de Descontos, 39
Banco do Brazil, 96, 104, 178; bribery of officials, 98; coffee eradication program payments, 54; and IBC replanting program, 243, 245–46; interest rates for agricultural loans, 97; loans for specific agricultural products, 100; source of loans, 97–99
Banco Commercial Norte do Paraná (BANCIAL), 27, 96–97
Bandeirantes, 18, 19
Banking, 96–104, 237, 245–46
Baptism, 199–200

Baptists, 29, 105
Beans, 56, 91, 101, 115, 125, 155, 157–58; as credit payment, 104; in day laborers' diet, 152; in eradication program, 52; labor requirements, 70; as lavoura branca, 55; prices 54, 59
Birth control, 115
Boa Vista, Paraná, 19
Bóia fria, 237, 238–39, 240, 248, 249
Boll weevil, 173
Botucatú soil, 26
Brasilia, 48
Broca (*Hypothenemus hampei* Ferrari), 10, 173; a cause of coffee's decline, 216–17; effects on coffee in Ouro Verde, 46, 49, 87; use of insecticide to prevent, 216–17
Buddhists, 105
Businesses and stores, 26–27, 86–87, 90, 121–22; dairy, 246; effects of coffee's decline, 81, 83, 221; relation of sales to agricultural cycle, 91, 93, 94–95; sales after 1969, 246–47; social class of owners, 181, 183

Caboclo, 206
Cacao, 4
Cachaça, 46, 94
Café em côco, 46
Café limpo, 46
Cambará, Paraná, 21
Campinas, São Paulo, 14
Carlson, Reynold E., 4–5, 6
Cascavel, Paraná, 209
Castelo Branco, 87, 89
Castor beans, 60, 136, 155, 158; as fertilizer, 173; and eradication program, 52; labor requirements, 70; price, 61
Catholicism, 4
Catholics, 29; aid to unemployed, 75; Marianas (religious organization), 106; priest, 105–6, 107, 119; Vicentinos (religious organization), 107
Cattle ranching, 68–69, 79; advantages over coffee cultivation, 67; after coffee eradication, 62–63; consolidation of landholdings, 70–73, 218; costs and profits, 66, 67, 96; effects on social structure, 7–8; increase of cattle in 1956, 62; increase of cattle after 1969, 244; labor requirements, 67, 70, 159, 164, 167–68; land requirements, 7, 66–67; number of head in Ouro Verde, 62; pasture, 65, 157; ranching in western Paraná, nineteenth century, 19; slaughterhouses, 65; suitable soils, 66; work systems, 81, 154. *See also* Coffee-cattle cycle
Ceará, 3
Chácaras, 22, 31; crop yields, 177; eradication program, 51–52; labor usage, 161–63; land usage, 155, 157; loans for cultivation expenses, 98; prices, 37; sales, 22; sales contract stipulations, 37–38; size, 124; social class of owners, 180, 183, 184, 189–91; social mobility of owners, 209
Cianorte, Paraná, 22, 23, 232
Clay, Senator Clement C., 226
Coffee: and collapse of Vargas regime, 17–18; cycles, 5–6, 12–14, 18–23 passim; demand for slaves, 12; demand for virgin land, 12; depression, effects on production, 21; early plantations, 22; eradication program in northern Paraná, 51; explanations for decline, 13; export quotas, 18; frosts, 15, 17; growth of plantations, 12; harvest dates, 74; history of production in Brazil, 11–12; indebtedness of planters, 13; intertilling, 55; in Mato Grosso, 84; in Minas Gerais, 14; in northern Paraná, 4, 19–23 passim, 232; overproduction, 6, 15, 17; in Paraíba Valley, 4, 12–13; in Paraguay, 4, 236; pests, 10, 12, 49, 173, 243–44; prices, 17–19, 21–23, 46–48, 89, 174, 215–16; profits, 13; regulation of production, 101; and rented land, 8; in Rio de Janeiro, 12; in São Paulo, 13, 14–18, 51, 233; settlement of coffee regions, 12; world market, 6–7; yields, 15, 17, 49–51. *See also* Coffee-cattle cycle; Coffee in Ouro Verde; Fertilizer; Insecticide; Valorization programs
Coffee-cattle cycle, 123, 154; businesses and stores, effects on, 9, 121–22; coffee eradication program, effects on, 51–53; consequences in Ouro Verde, 70–85, 218–24; and

decline in labor needs on sítios, 166; explanations, 9–10; future, 230; land consolidation as result, 218–19; and movimento, 9, 122; nonagriculturalists, effects on, 81–83; in northern Paraná, 7; in Paraíba Valley, 11; population size, effects on, 119; reactions of Ouro Verde residents to, 83–85, 223–24; reduction in middle class as result, 222; reduction in social mobility as result, 222; in São Paulo, 14–15; since 1969, 244; unemployment in Ouro Verde, effects on, 73, 79, 120, 219; work systems, effects on, 219. *See also* Coffee; Coffee in Ouro Verde

Coffee in Ouro Verde: acreages, 42–43, 240; amounts processed, 87; costs of cultivation, 47–48, 67, 215–16; credit, effects on, 230–31; drying terraces, 161, 174–75; eradication program, 10, 51–52, 167, 215, 217, 241; effects of frosts, 10, 42, 44–46, 70–71, 184, 215, 230, 234; harvest, 153; IBC role in future of, 232–33; inavailability of loans for new plantings, 100; intertilling, 56; labor requirements, 67, 70, 159–70 passim; new trees, 240–41, 243; processing, 86, 87, 89, 247; profits, 67; regional competition, 49, 51; replacement by cattle, 10; spacing of trees, 174; wages for cultivation, 150–51; yields, 44, 47, 177–79, 211, 243. *See also* Coffee; Coffee-cattle cycle; Frosts

—decline of: consolidation of land holdings as result of, 70–73; frontier as factor, 10, 54; effects on renters, 81, 141; effects on sharecroppers, 80, 238; effects on social mobility, 208, 211; reasons for, 42–44, 48–49, 215–18, 229–32; soil depletion as factor, 215

Colônia Mineira, Paraná, 19

Colonos, 79, 80, 81, 127, 136; and coffee-cattle cycle, 8; contract arrangements, 133; in Ouro Verde, 133–34, 220; in São Paulo, 131, 133

Compadresco, 199–203

Companhia Melhoramentos Norte do Paraná (CMNP), 26, 31, 71, 73; classification of Paraná land divisions, 23, 124; current holdings in northern Paraná, 23; current holdings in Ouro Verde, 39; founding of, 23; land sales in Ouro Verde, 37–38; settlement of Ouro Verde, 33, 35

Companhia de Terras Norte do Paraná, 21–23

Contour planting. *See* Agricultural technology

Corn, 56, 57, 101, 125, 157–58; as a credit payment, 104; labor requirements, 70; as lavoura branca, 55; prices, 54, 59; processing for flour, 90; purchase of seed, 173; and soil depletion 155; and subrenting, 142

Cornélio Procopio, Paraná, 19

Cotton cultivation, 3, 8, 55, 57, 58, 78, 134, 138, 154, 155, 157, 169, 237; effects of boll weevil, 173; effects of coffee eradication, 52, 59; effect on movimento, 91, 93; fertilizer, 60, 173, 213, 254; future, 230; harvest, 74, 87, 140, 150–51; harvests' effects on business, 93–94; labor requirements, 70, 135–36, 159, 162–63; as loan collateral, 101; prices, 59–60; profits, 211–12; purchase of seed, 139, 142, 173; by renters, 80–81, 221; replacing coffee, 15; school absenteeism during harvest, 151; social mobility and profits, 212–13; on sítios, 166; in southern U.S., 224–27; by subrenters, 142; in Vagalume, 65; yields, 60, 142, 143, 179, 211–12, 244

Cristão do Brasil, 29, 105, 107, 108

Cultural change, 227–29

Curitiba, Paraná, 9, 33, 120, 203

Datas, 39, 75

Davis, Charles S., 227

Day laborers, 6, 8, 26, 76, 78, 79–81, 86, 120, 129, 154, 161, 163, 164, 167, 249; advantages/disadvantages in hiring, 152–53; affected by spread of cattle ranching, 77; church attendance of, 106, 107; compared to colonos, 133–34; as consumers, 94; credit buying, 152; daily work, 150; diet, 115–16, 152, 191–92; employment by coffee processors, 89; employment by sharecroppers, 135–36, 145; enrollment in adult literacy classes, 111; food costs, 152; health care, 114; illit-

eracy, 112, 119; labor laws, 152; lack of patrões, 197; living conditions, 151–52; malnutrition, 115–16; piecework, 50; replacement by bóia fria, 238–39; school attendance of children, 112, 151; seasonality of work, 147, 149; social class, 181, 185, 186, 188, 193–94; social life, 105; social mobility, 207; wages, 148–52; working conditions, 151
Diamonds in Brazil, 3
Disease, 116
Divorce, 186
Dozier, Craig L., 21

Eaton, Clement, 224
Education, 106, 110–13, 119, 151, 183–84
Eradication program, 7, 157–58. *See also* Coffee; Coffee-cattle cycle; Coffee in Ouro Verde
Espírito Santo, 243
Estrada de Ferro São Paulo-Paraná, 21
Estrada Funda, 72–73, 78, 79, 159

Family members in agricultural labor, 161, 163, 164–65
Fazendas: absentee ownership, 167, 168–70: administrators, 167, 169; cattle, 167–68; coffee cultivation, 157–58, 167; coffee eradication program, 52, 53, 157–58, 167; consolidation of small holdings, 218; crop yields, 177; a factor in unemployment, 77–78; increase in number, 231; labor usage, 154, 166–70 passim; land usage, 157–58; owned by CMNP, 23; sale, 22; size, 124, 237; in Vagalume, 72; working conditions, 151–52
Fazendeiros, 12
Fertilizer: cost by type, 216; for coffee, 170–72; for cotton, 173, 213; for cotton in U.S., 225–26; effects on coffee yields, 178; for peanuts, 173; requirements for different coffee types, 174; use after 1969, 245; use on fazendas, 177
Formadores de café, 35, 127, 131–33, 137; advantages, 132; contract arrangements, 131–32; found in frontier areas, 128; a means of social mobility, 207, 210; role in settlement of Ouro Verde, 127; social class, 181, 183
Freyre, Gilberto, 181
Frontier: and agricultural cycles, 5, 228; appeal of, 7, 10; as a cause of coffee's decline, 10, 215, 217–18; clearing of, in Ouro Verde, 35; coffee lands in Paraná, 21; destruction of forests in northern Paraná, 25; effects on coffee production in Ouro Verde, 11; effects on population migration, 7, 11; effects on sharecroppers, 11; Goías, 7; land purchase, 54; Mato Grosso, 7; migration from Ouro Verde, 120, 235; Paraguay, 236; parallels between U.S. and Brazil, 224–27; Paraná, 7; reasons for migration to, 235–37; role in social mobility, 11, 210–11, 222–23; in southern U.S., 224–27; Turner's thesis, 11, 214; work systems, 128
Frosts: a cause of coffee's decline, 215, 216; correlation of frost-prone regions and eradication program, 52; effects on business in Ouro Verde, 81–82; effects on cattle increase, 61; effects on coffee, 10, 15, 17; effects on coffee in Ouro Verde, 44–46, 84, 234–35; effects on migration, 9; fear of, affecting fertilizer usage, 171–72; IBC aid to frost-free areas, 233; months of occurrence in Ouro Verde, 95; of 1955, 42; of 1969, 234–37; in Paraná, 25
Fruit trees, eradication of, 52, 59
Furtado, Celso, 14–15

Germans, 40
Goías, 3, 7, 19
Gold, 3
Goulart, João, 89
Government in Ouro Verde, 116–19
Guarani Indians, 18, 19
Guarapuava plateau, 24
Guayra, 18

Harris, Marvin, 113, 181, 184, 193, 229
Health services, 113–16, 198
Hutchinson, Harry W., 181, 193, 213

Iguacú River, 19
Insecticide, costs of, 173

Instituto Brasileiro de Café (IBC), 47–48, 63, 65, 89, 101, 216, 235–37, 249; eradication program, 51–54, financing new coffee plantings, 241–43, 245; loan rates, 245–46; price supports, 6
Instituto Brasileiro de Reforma Agraria (IBRA), 125, 237
Instituto Getulio Vargas, 48
Instituto Nacional de Providência Social (INPS), 48, 239
Inter-American Coffee Agreement, 18
Italians, 31, 40, 107, 108, 117, 209
Ivaí River, 23, 25

Jacarézinho, Paraná, 19
James, Preston, 14, 21
Japanese, 31, 35, 40, 72, 90–91, 94, 105, 113, 117, 165, 203
Jaquariaiva, Paraná, 19
Jesuits, 18, 19
Johnson, Allen W., 197

Knight, Ralph, 152

Labor gangs: advantages over day laborers, 129; attitudes toward, 130; contracting, 128; decline in Ouro Verde, 131; disadvantages for coffee cultivation, 129; disappearance due to coffee-cattle change, 220–21; empreiteiro system, 81, 127–31, 148; "gatos," 33, 35, 81, 128; living conditions, 130–31; peões, 33, 35, 127–30, 132; recruitment of unemployed for, 129
Labor laws, 77, 81; and bóia fria, 239; and day laborers, 152–53, 238–39; minimum wage, 148; and renters, 142; and sharecroppers, 142
Labor systems. *See* Bóia fria; Colonos; Day laborers; Formadores de café; Labor gangs; Mensalistas; Renters; Sharecroppers; Work systems
Labor unions, 153
Land usage, 155–59
Lavoura branca, 55, 82, 98, 137–38, 157, 207–8; acreage, 240; on chácaras, 155, costs and profits, 67; effects of eradication program, 58–59; effects of frosts, 155; fertilizer, 173; increase due to coffee's decline, 56–57; intertilled with coffee, 56; labor requirements, 69; land requirements, 58; laws concerning planting, 237–38; in Paraguay, 236; prices, 57; and renting, 80, 138–39, 221; risks of planting, 57–58; securing credit for, 100; and sharecropping, 80, 238; on sítios, 165; in Vagalume, 65; work systems, 79; yields after 1969, 244–45
Leeds, Anthony, 4, 6, 227–28, 229
Limeira, São Paulo, 14
Lobato, Paraná, 26, 33
Londrina, Paraná, 22, 23, 33, 49, 83, 203
Lord Lovat, 21, 23

Madrinhos. *See* Compadresco
Malnutrition, 115–16
Mamona. *See* Castor beans
Mandaquacú, Paraná, 33, 35, 37
Manioc, 101; as lavoura branca, 55; effects of eradication program on planting, 52; farinha in Ouro Verde, 56; in day laborers' diet, 152
Manual labor, related to social class, 181, 183
Maquinistas. *See* Coffee
Maranhão, 3
Margolis, Maxine L., 193, 213
Maringá, Paraná, 23, 33, 37, 49, 76, 83, 102, 104, 120, 122, 128, 149, 169, 172, 214, 218, 231, 232, 248; Adventists in, 108; founding by CMNP, 22; migration from Ouro Verde, 75; pasture land, 7; soils, 24
Marriage, padrinhos of, 199–200
Martins, Araguaia Feitosa, 168
Mato Grosso, 7, 25, 66, 84, 131
Meeiros. *See* Sharecroppers
Mensalistas, 76, 78, 81, 134; as cowhands, 154; increase in due to coffee-cattle change, 154, 220–21; patron-client relationships, 197; wages, 154
Methodists, 105, 109, 119
Milliet, Sergio, 23, 224
Minas Gerais, 23, 108, 129–30, 168; coffee rust, 243; diamond rush, 3; gold rush, 3, 19; population movement to coffee region, 12, 75; ranchers from, in Paraíba Valley, 14; rice exported to Ouro Verde, 90
Minas Velhas, Bahia, 181
Mintz, Sidney, 199

Mogiana, São Paulo, 15, 40
Mogi-Mirim, São Paulo, 14
Monbeig, Pierre, 15
Monocrop systems. *See* Agricultural cycles; Coffee; Coffee-cattle cycle
Monteiro-Teixeira, Duglas, 229-30
Motoristas, 87
Movimento, 105, 121, 122; defined, 9; effects of coffee-cattle cycle, 9, 218; effects of cotton harvest, 91, 93; in Ouro Verde, 9, 83, 246
Municípios, average size in Brazil, 116
Mutirão, 168

Noroeste region, São Paulo, 40
Northeast, Brazil, 4, 9, 33, 35, 40–41, 108, 129, 168, 195, 201, 206, 240
Nova Esperança, Paraná, 27, 33, 72, 77, 96–97, 107, 116, 117, 128, 130, 143, 246

Ourinhos, São Paulo, 19, 21
Ouro Verde: absentee landowners, 168–70; agricultural mechanization, 76; agricultural structure and importance of loans, 101; attitudes of residents to coffee-cattle cycle, 83–85, attitudes of residents toward future, 249–50; banking, 96–104; church attendance, 107; civil registry, 95, 122; colonization companies, 40; credit buying, 93; description, 26–27, 29, 31, 33, 37; disease, 116; education, 106, 110–13, 115, 119, 183–84; employment, 86, 87, 120, 121; future, 229–33; government, 116–19; health services, 113–16; holidays, 109; house furnishings, 29, 31, 75, 184, 189, 191; immigration to, 40–41; as independent county, 116; land consolidation, 71–73, 237; land distribution, 125, 127; land prices, 37–40; land purchase, 39–40, 73; location, 26; loan intermediaries, 101; loss of confidence by residents, 223–24; market, 91; marriages, 95; meat prices, 93; movimento, 9, 83, 246; occupations of inhabitants, 26; police role in securing laborers, 128–29; population, 26, 78, 86; prices of household items, 146; relation of town to agricultural enterprises, 86–87; religious life, 105–9; road and rail system, 33, 37; rural properties, 154–55; rural-urban migration, 119, 120, 219–20, 235, 246, 247; sanitary facilities, 116; settlement, 26, 33, 35; social life, 105–10; soils, 26; "suburban zone," 31; town population increase, 78–79, 246; unemployment, 73–79, 218–19, 235; white collar workers, 87. *See also* Businesses and stores; Cattle ranching; Coffee in Ouro Verde; Day laborers; Lavoura branca; Mensalistas; Population; Renters; Sharecroppers; Social class; Social mobility

Padrinhos. *See* Compadresco
Palha de café. *See* Fertilizer
Papaya, 59
Paraguay, 23, 25, 131, 232, 235; frontier, 7, 236; land prices, 236; movement of coffee into, 4
Paraíba (state), 195
Paraíba Valley, Rio de Janeiro, 1, 4, 12–14, 224
Paraná (state), 2; attraction of frontier to residents, 10; cattle ranching, 19; climate, 24; coffee cycle, 5–6, 18–23; Commodity Transfer Tax, 110; frontier land, 7; future, 229–33; geology, 24; Guarani Indians, 18; Jesuits, 18; known as Guayra, 18; nineteenth-century exploration, 19; pasture, 7; railroads, 19, 21, 23; settlement, 18, 19, 21; soils, 24; spread of coffee, 4, 6; topography, 25; vegetation, 25. *See also* Coffee; Coffee-cattle cycle; Frontier; Population
Paranacity, Paraná, 106, 108; agriculture, 118; attempts to combine with Ouro Verde, 117–18; Banco do Brasil, 246; coffee processing plants, 89; market, 91
Paranaguá, Paraná, 122
Paranapanema River, 19, 24–25, 33
Paraná Plantations Limited, 21–23
Paraná River, 24
Paranavaí, Paraná, 33, 108
Pasture. *See* Cattle ranching; Coffee-cattle cycle
Patron-client relationship, 196–99
Peanut cultivation, 54, 57, 78, 86, 134, 138, 149, 155, 157, 158, 163,

164, 237; acreage, 56, 240; effects of eradication program on, 52; fertilizer, 173; harvest, 74, 87, 153; insecticide, 173; labor requirements, 159; as lavoura branca, 55; as loan collateral, 101–2; prices, 60; processing, 87; purchase of seed, 173; and renters, 80–81, 221; yields, 179, 244–45
Percenteiros. *See* Sharecroppers
Peroba, 29
Pimental, Paulo, 234
Pirapó River, 26
Political parties, 116, 118
Population: decrease, due to coffee-cattle cycle, 8, 9, 78–79, 119–20, 218, 219, 235; effects of decrease on Ouro Verde businesses, 71, 81, 83, 221; emigration from Ouro Verde, 120, 219–20; European emigrants to coffee regions, 19; government-subsidized migration to northern Paraná, 19; migration from Northeast to Amazon, 4; migration of unemployed to Ouro Verde, 75–76; of Ouro Verde, 26; origins of Ouro Verde residents, 40; rural-urban migration in Ouro Verde, 119, 120, 219–20, 235, 246, 247
Portuguese, 2, 18, 117
Praga mineira (*Leucoptera coffeella*), 173
Presbyterians, 29
Protestants, 105, 107

Ramie, 52
Reducciones (Spanish missions), 18
Renter-intermediaries, as credit system, 104
Renters, 6, 8, 26, 78, 120, 134, 167; church attendance, 108; compadresco relationships, 202–3; contracts, 80, 138–39; disappearance after 1969, 237; increase, due to coffee-cattle change, 220–21; and intermediaries 101–3, 104; labor laws, 147; lavoura branca cultivation, 80, 138–39, 141; loans, 100; patron-client relationships, 103, 197; and purchase of agricultural supplies, 139; sales of crop, 140, 141; securing credit, 103; selection of land, 140; size of rental plots, 140–41; social class, 181
Revolution: of 1930, 17–18; of 1964, 89, 116, 118
Riberão Preto, São Paulo, 19
Rice cultivation, 56, 57, 58, 86, 91, 101, 115, 125, 133, 134, 135, 138, 155, 157; as credit payment, 104; effects of eradication program on, 52; labor requirements, 70; as lavoura branca, 55; prices, 54, 59; processing, 90; by renters, 221; in South Carolina, 227; in varzeões, 31
Rio Bonito, São Paulo, 163
Rio de Janeiro (city), 12
Rio de Janeiro (state), 4. *See also* Paraíba Valley
Rio Grande do Sul, 19
Roças (subsistence plots), 158
Rolândia, Paraná, 209
Rubber, 3–4
Russians, 40

Santa Cruz, Ouro Verde, 235
Santa Maria, Ouro Verde, 73, 78, 82, 170
Santa Maria, Paraná, 65, 87
Santo Antonio da Platina, Paraná, 19
Santos, São Paulo, 19, 22
São Paulo (city), 9, 19, 33, 40, 120, 203, 214–15
São Paulo (state), 7, 22, 108, 118, 120, 123, 129–30, 144, 168, 174, 232; coffee-cattle cycle, 14–15; coffee cultivation, 51; coffee cycle, 14–18; coffee rust, 243; colono system, 21; European immigrants, 19; fazendas, 21; frosts, 45; migration of residents to Ouro Verde, 75; soil depletion, 14–15
Schurz, William L., 6–7
Serventes, 87, 90
Sharecroppers, 6, 8, 26, 78, 79–82, 86, 120, 154, 158, 163, 164, 165; availability of positions, 137; church attendance, 108–9; and coffee cultivation, 134–36, 238; compadresco relationships, 202–3; contract arrangements, 134–35, 136, 137, 138; crop sales, 136; decline, 24, 220–21, 222, 237, 248; diet, 91, 137; disadvantages, 135; emigration from Ouro Verde, 236; families used as laborers, 135, 136; health care, 114, 137; illiteracy, 119; influence of frontier, 11; and intertilling, 136;

labor laws, 147, 237–38; labor requirements, 135; lavoura branca cultivation, 80, 238; loans, 100–101, 102; meeiros, 134; patron-client relationships of, 197; percentage of crop given to landowner, 237–38; percenteiros, 134, 138; purchase of agricultural supplies by, 137; rates of land rental, 140; school attendance of children, 112–13; securing credit, 103–4; securing a position, 207; social class, 180, 181, 185; social life, 105; social mobility, 207–14. *See also* Subsharecropping
Siegel, Bernard, 197
Sitiantes: as consumers, 94; church attendance, 107; diet of, 91; migration to frontier, 235–36; reduction in number, 248
Sítios, 21, 31, 35, 77; adaptation to coffee eradication, 58–59; bank loans secured by owners, 97–100; corn cultivation, 59; crops sold to intermediaries, 103; eradication program, 53; family of owners used as laborers, 164; labor usage, 163–66; land usage, 157; plow use, 175; prices of, 37; reduction in size of labor force, 166; sale of, 22, 37–38; school attendance of children of owners, 112–13; size, 124; social class of owners, 189–90; in Vagalume, 72; working conditions, 151–52
Slavery, 13
Slavs, 40
Social class, 180–214 passim; and compadresco, 202–3; and diet, 183, 187, 191; and discrimination, 195; education, 183–84; forms of address, 192–93; future changes, 231; increasing rigidness, 213–14; indigent poor, 185–86, 187; interaction, 192–202; lower class, 181, 184–85, 190–91; lower-lower class, 181, 185–87, 191–92; and manual labor, 181, 183; middle class, 8, 181, 183–84, 189–90; occupation, 181; ownership of land, 180, 187–88; residence, 184, 185, 191; residents' view on, 183, 195, 203–6; reduction in middle class due to coffee's decline, 213–14, 221–22; in rural areas, 180, 181, 187–92; standards of living, 183, 189; in town, 180, 187; upper class, 188–89. *See also* Social mobility
Social mobility: and coffee-cattle cycle, 11; and cotton cultivation, 212–13; decrease in, due to changeover to cattle ranching, 211, 222, 248–49; downward, 249; and formadores de café, 207, 210; and frontier, 11, 210–11; and geographical movement, 11, 209–10; and sharecropping, 207–14; and size of savings, 223; and time of arrival in community, 222–23. *See also* Social class
Social structure: changes due to cattle ranching, 7–8; effects of frontier, 10–11; in Paraná, 6
Soil: conservation, lack of in southern U.S., 225, 227; depletion, a cause of coffee decline, 215; depletion in Paraíba Valley, 13–14; distribution in northern Paraná, 24; erosion, 12; nutrients used in intertilling, 155; in Ouro Verde, 26, 43–44; in Paraguay, 236; suitability for coffee cultivation, 44; suitability for pasture, 66; in Vagalume, 158; yields in Ouro Verde, 44. *See also* Terra arenosa; Terra mista; Terra roxa
Sorocaba, São Paulo, 19
Sorocabana, São Paulo, 4
Spanish, 18, 31, 40, 105–6, 107, 108, 117. *See also* Jesuits
Spiegel, Henry W., 5
Spiritualists, 105
Standard of living. *See* Social class
Stein, Stanley, 5, 12, 13, 224
Stores. *See* Businesses and stores
Subrenters, 141–43
Subsharecroppers, 141–43; advantages for landowners, 147; contract arrangements, 144; cultivation expenses, 145; employment of day laborers by, 145; household expenses, 145–46; purchase of agricultural supplies, 144–45
Subsistence plots, 158
Sugar cultivation, 3, 59, 91

Taxation: and coffee prices, 48; and coffee processing, 89; Commodity Transfer Tax, 110, 117–18, 122–23,

231–32; lack of, on agricultural post supplies, 96. *See also* Valorization programs
Terra arenosa, 24, 44, 174, 178
Terra mista, 24, 26, 43–44, 174, 178
Terra roxa, 14, 24, 43–44, 49, 51, 172, 174, 177, 233, 236
Texas, 224, 225
Tibagí River, 22
Turner, Frederick Jackson, 11, 214

Uberaba, Minas Gerais, 14
Umuarama, Paraná, 22, 232
Unemployment, 9, 235; resulting from coffee to cattle changeover, 73–79, 219; social class of unemployed, 181
Uniflor, Paraná, 106
Utilities, 27

Vagalume, Ouro Verde, 31, 33, 65, 237; altitude, 158; businesses, 82–83; coffee-cattle cycle, 158–59; consolidation of landholdings, 71–72, 218; distribution of land, 72; eradication program effects, 52; frosts, 44; population loss, 79, 220; renters, 81; soils, 158; unemployment, 76–77
Valorization programs, 17–18
Vargas, Getulio, 17
Viana Moog, C., 4
Vila Franki, Ouro Verde, 31, 81
Vila Rica, Paraná, 18
Volantes. *See* Day laborers

Wagley, Charles W., 113, 181, 184, 196
Willems, Emilio, 218
Wolf, Eric, 199
Work systems: changes in due to coffee-cattle changeover, 70, 79, 218–21; changes in, after 1969, 237; future of, 231; in Ouro Verde, 79–81; related to altitude and soils, 159; related to size of holding, 159; renter-intermediaries, 104. *See also* Bóia fria; Colonos; Day laborers; Formadores de café; Labor gangs; Mensalistas; Renters; Sharecroppers

Latin American Monographs—Second Series

Number 1 (1965): *Fidel Castro's Political Programs from Reformism to "Marxism-Leninism"*
by Loree Wilkinson

Number 2 (1966): *Highways into the Upper Amazon Basin*
by Edmund Eduard Hegen

Number 3 (1967): *The Government Executive of Modern Peru*
by Jack W. Hopkins

Number 4 (1967): *Eduardo Santos and the Good Neighbor, 1938–1942*
by David Bushnell

Number 5 (1968): *Dictatorship and Development: The Methods of Control in Trujillo's Dominican Republic*
by Howard J. Wiarda

Number 6 (1969): *New Lands and Old Traditions: Kekchi Cultivators in the Guatemalan Lowlands*
by William E. Carter

Number 7 (1969): *The Mechanization of Agriculture in Brazil: A Sociological Study of Minas Gerais*
by Harold M. Clements, Sr.

Number 8 (1971): *Liberación Nacional of Costa Rica: The Development of a Political Party in a Transitional Society*
by Burt H. English

Number 9 (1971): *Colombia's Foreign Trade*
by J. Kamal Dow

Number 10 (1972): *The Feitosas and the* Sertão *dos Inhamuns: The History of a Family and a Community in Northeast Brazil, 1700–1930*
by Billy Jaynes Chandler

Number 11 (1973): *The Moving Frontier: Social and Economic Change in a Southern Brazilian Community*
by Maxine L. Margolis